KT-428-943

THE ULTIMATE GUIDE TO SPORT EVENT MANAGEMENT AND MARKETING

Stedman Graham
Joe Jeff Goldblatt, C.S.E.P.
Lisa Delpy, Ph.D.

McGraw-Hill
New York   San Francisco   Washington, D.C.   Auckland   Bogotá
Caracas   Lisbon   London   Madrid   Mexico City   Milan
Montreal   New Delhi   San Juan   Singapore
Sydney   Tokyo   Toronto

McGraw-Hill

A Division of The McGraw·Hill Companies

Library of Congress Cataloging-in-Publication Data

Graham, Stedman.
    The ultimate guide to sport event management and marketing /
Stedman Graham, Joe Jeff Goldblatt, and Lisa Delpy.
        p. cm.
    Includes bibliographical references and index.
    ISBN 0-7863-0244-5
        1. Sports administration. 2. Sports—Marketing. I. Goldblatt,
    Joe Jeff. II. Delpy, Lisa. III. Title.
GV713.G62 1995   94–33952
796'.06'9—dc20

Printed in the United States of America
        5 6 7 8 9 0 DO 1 0

Dedication

This book is dedicated to you. The sport and special event professionals, the managers and marketers, students, athletes, fans, spectators, and others who join us in the further development of this exciting profession.

Stedman Graham
Joe Jeff Goldblatt, C.S.E.P.
Lisa Delpy, Ph.D.

"Let the games begin!"
Traditional proclamation at the opening of the world's largest sport event, the Olympic Games.

Foreword

The sport event management and marketing field is *big business* and has grown enormously during the last two decades. From small participatory events to the mega hallmark events seen by millions, this industry had mirrored the explosive growth of media, entertainment, and tourism.

This worthy volume has arrived at a critical time in the development of this growing profession. I am certain that this text will provide useful information for a wide range of sport event management and marketing enthusiasts: from those considering entering the profession to those with extensive professional experience. The broad information covered in the text will prove invaluable to those with a variety of professional experiences who are rapidly ascending to organize and produce effective sport events.

There are very few books of this kind in the marketplace because the profession is so new. My experience in television and in the "big event" business has reinforced my appreciation for well-executed events. Trial and error produce costly mistakes, so having a blueprint and reference materials are essential. The numerous checklists and the extensive appendix contained in this volume will make this a resource book for your entire career. For those who are learning about this exciting profession, this book is a must.

Dick Ebersol, President
NBC Sports

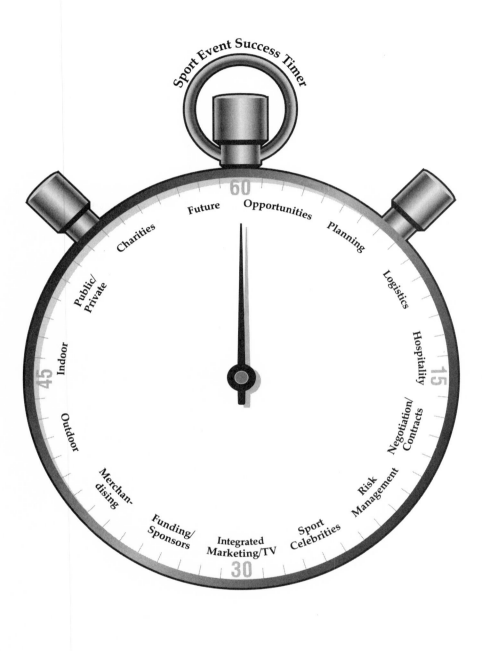

Preface

In my early years of high school, I was determined to live my life beyond the basketball court. Fortunately, I had mentors to assist me in my journey. My mother and father; my high school coach, John Roberson; and my third-grade Sunday school teacher, Inez Edmonds; all encouraged me to be my best on the court and off. Throughout these pages, Joe, Lisa, and I will provide you with a similar guide to becoming the best professional you can be in the exciting field of sport event management and marketing.

Stedman Graham

Opening Ceremonies

In the darkened hush of Barcelona's opening ceremony stadium, 65,000 spectators along with 19,000 athletes, dancers, and actors held their breath in anticipation of an unprecedented special event. Collectively their focus was upon a lone individual dressed in simple white clothing.

Despite a pronounced limp resulting from childhood polio, 37-year-old archer Antonio Rebollo from Madrid walked confidently to his designated mark, drew a single arrow, and dipped its tip into the blazing flame of the Olympic torch.

Then, as the tension nearly rose to the breaking point, Rebollo grasped the bow and arrow. As hundreds of millions of people watched over television, the muscles in Rebollo's right arm strained from the forceful pulling and his eyes were riveted on the giant cauldron over 70 meters away.

As the archer released his fiery arrow, the spectators in the stadium, the television audience, and indeed the world seemed to pause in awe as they focused their collective hopes on this single event. The flaming arrow soared in a perfect arc over the heads of the assembled crowd, whose eyes traced its golden path.

Next, a huge sound—like a pilot light igniting a giant furnace—
roared. The archer had hit his mark and the spectators were
instantly on their feet applauding, shaking hands, and embracing
total strangers in tribute to the first spectacular athletic accomplishment of the Barcelona Olympic Games. This unique and
highly symbolic special event marked the beginning of the magic
of the XXV Olympiad.

Background

The event described above is illustrative of the many sport special
events produced annually. As the sport and entertainment fields
grow closer together and event marketing continues to receive a
greater percentage of corporate marketing budgets, the need for a
book focused entirely on sport event management and marketing
is substantiated. Statistics throughout the text about the number
of job opportunities, economic impacts, and trends in sport event
marketing and management provide further evidence of the need
for this first-of-its-kind book.

As a reader of *The Ultimate Guide to Sport Event Management and
Marketing*, you will become acquainted with the history and evol-
ution of this dynamic field and learn the skills necessary to succeed
in it. The three authors view this book as a guide for anyone interested in the field, regardless of race or sex. The sport event management and marketing field is wide open, but applicants must
nonetheless be qualified. Use this book and the information it
presents as the key to opening doors and breaking through glass
ceilings.

Defining Sport Event Management and Marketing

The term *sport event management and marketing* includes the administration, coordination, and evaluation of any type of event related
to sport. Examples are from local school and community sport
events, not-for-profit and corporate events, intercollegiate sport
programs, and amateur and professional league activities such as
the Olympic Games and Super Bowl.

Who Should Read this Book?

The Ultimate Guide to Sport Event Management and Marketing is for anyone interested in breaking into the sport event profession or for those who have incidently found themselves challenged with the task of producing a sport event for any organization, profit or nonprofit. In others words, whether you are a corporate event planner, the local charity fund-raiser, a volunteer, the director of a high school sport championship game and award banquet, a league official, or someone looking for a new and exciting career, this book is for you.

Why You Should Read this Book

The materials provided on the subject, the professional vocabulary and background, the pertinent checklists, and the creative ideas in this book are certain to assist you in achieving the professionalism, excitement, exposure, profit, and other critical objectives necessary for success.

To better understand the professional field of sport event management and marketing, we will take you behind the scenes —from the back office to the front office, from the locker room to the television control room—to understand how special events in sport can be effective and profitable. You will meet dozens of successful professionals who have helped establish and shape this growing field. Their experiences will help you avoid many of the pitfalls and failures that have befallen them.

Use the coach–player metaphor as a guide to develop your own ideas for effective sport event programs. A winning coach often serves as a mentor to his or her players. World-renowned coaches such as Vincent Lombardi, Lou Holtz, Eddie Robinson, "Big House" Gaines, and John Wooden understand that in order to win with people, coaches must capitalize on the assets of each player and blend them to build a consistently successful organization.

We encourage you to evaluate the assets you bring to this profession (e.g., creativity, persistence, detail orientation) and to look for mentors who can help you further develop your talents. The examples that are provided in this volume will certainly

enhance, and perhaps accelerate, your achievement. Your rate of accomplishment, however, will largely depend on your ability to identify mentors and adopt and adapt their advice to your own needs.

If you are using this book to develop sport events for the organization you represent, remember that each event is a distinctly personal representation of the culture of the individual sponsor or presenter. Do not use the examples we have given as a final plan but as a catalyst to your thinking process.

If you are using *The Ultimate Guide to Sport Event Management and Marketing* as a springboard to a new or expanded career in this field—good for you! Sport special events is a proven growth area; the opportunities are ripe for finding a meaningful and lucrative career path. Once again, however, the role of a good mentor cannot be overemphasized. After reading this book through thoroughly, continue your research by interviewing successful individuals in the field and developing an apprenticeship relationship with an organization or professional that you respect and admire. This experience will bring an even greater meaning to your reading and the practical experience will greatly enhance your chances of finding a position in this highly competitive field.

A formal education in sport event management and marketing can also assist you in your professional development and career search. See Appendix II-A for more information on potential careers opportunities.

How to Obtain the Most Benefit from this Book

We recommend that you read this book in sequential order to gain the maximum benefit. To assist you with retention and understanding, we have used several techniques to serve as anchors for your thinking processes.

First, each chapter begins with a thought-provoking question. Pause and contemplate this question before reading the chapter. Often, more can be learned from a well-constructed question than from the answer that follows. We try to provide our own answers for each question, but ask yourself whether other answers might be more relevant to your own interests. Also ask yourself where you can find more information to help you better understand the answers to the questions.

As you proceed with your reading, study the Sport Event Timing Model at the beginning of each chapter to maintain your perspective and measure your progress in covering the material presented.

Next, each chapter concludes with a checklist of key points presented under the headings of "Game Highlights" and "Play Book."

"Game Highlights" will remind you of the key points from the chapter. The "Play Book" provides brief definitions of important terms used in the chapter. Be sure you review these key points and definitions before continuing. The text also has two sections tiitled "Photo Finish" that have photographs of successful sport events that relate directly to both parts of the text. You may wish to flip to an appropriate photo as you read in order to understand the breadth and scope of the event described. Overall, we have organized the book in a skill-building style; you should master one set of skills before venturing to the next chapter.

The Ultimate Guide to Sport Event Management and Marketing is divided into three major parts. Part 1 (Chapters 1–8) provides an overview of the emerging sport event profession and general strategies to succeed. Part 2 (Chapters 9–15) offers more concrete guidelines on how to produce sport events successfully and economically. Part 3 is the reference section that includes sample contracts, invitations, contact lists, and a bibliography.

Beginning with Chapter 1, you will learn about the many opportunities and history of the sport event profession. Chapter 2 describes an organizational framework to help in planning your event by measuring strengths, weaknesses, opportunities, and threats. Chapters 3 and 4 use organizational charts, checklists, and examples to illustrate the numerous details involved—and the creativity and flexibility required—in producing sport events.

In Chapters 5 and 6, you will learn how to protect against possible litigation and loss of investments. Chapters 7 and 8 follow appropriately, focusing on methods to maximize your investments through the use of celebrities and integrated marketing.

Chapters 9 and 10 show the various ways to raise capital for sport events, including corporate sponsorships and merchandising.

Chapters 11 and 12 take you onto the field, enabling you to learn how to produce all types of outdoor and indoor events. The purpose of these chapters is not to provide details of a specific sport event, but to illustrate the special considerations and features of different sports and how to adapt entertainment and sponsorship ideas to them.

Chapters 13 and 14 narrow the focus to sport events that benefit both private and public properties and non-profit charities.

Chapter 15 provides final advice for entering the emerging sport event management and marketing profession.

The authors recognize the difficulty of capturing the entire body of sport event management and marketing knowledge in this first volume. Therefore, we have endeavored to give priority to those aspects of the field that are currently most critical. This process is subjective; therefore, we apologize to sport event managers, officials, coaches, athletes, sponsors, and fans whose sport is not represented. However, many of the suggestions are universal in nature and may be applied in a cross-disciplinary manner. In addition, the appendix lists many resources that are sport-specific.

It is our desire that you will not only read the chapters but continue to return to them for further study. This book is meant to be equal parts of inspiration, motivation, and education.

The word *education* is derived from a Latin word meaning "to extract." If this book is to fulfill its mission of serving as an educational tool for you, your level of accomplishment will be determined directly by your desire to extract information. We can only open the door for you to this new profession. Your desire and hunger to succeed, coupled with experience and mentoring, will ultimately draw you through this entrance and determine the height to which you rise.

Legendary Super Bowl halftime producer, Robert Jani, often challenged his staff to "dream big dreams" and "aim high." Unfortunately, Jani died before our industry developed into maturity. However, his inspiring productions are a great legacy that have established the trend for spectacular and dramatic sport events. Often describing himself as a teacher, Jani said before his death that he had planned to write a book. The book was never written, but perhaps you will accept Bob Jani's challenge and not only dream big dreams and aim high, but through your efforts write a new chapter in this dynamic profession.

This volume is a memorial to those who pioneered in sport special events. It also is a challenge to you to surpass their accomplishments through your own imagination and vision.

The successful event manager and marketer share the same discipline, instinctive talent, and tenacity of the best athletes. So take your turn. Like Rebollo, select your arrow and focus your vision. Grasp this book as though it were the archer's mighty bow. The distance you reach will be determined by the effort you expend. Take aim, fire, and let the games begin!

Stedman Graham, Joe Jeff Goldblatt, and Lisa Delpy

Acknowledgments

The metaphor of a successful team describes many effective organizations. Indeed, excellent teamwork is the most efficient and productive process for achieving goals and objectives.

The authors of this first book focused entirely on sport events certainly understand this. Without this committed, generous, and talented team of sport and special event professionals, we could not have amassed so much valuable information.

Therefore, we must acknowledge those teammates who believe as we do that successful sport programs are special events. These individuals and organizations comprise the most successful team of all. They are responsible for the remarkable achievement of helping sport find a mass audience through reinventing itself as a special event medium. Pioneers all, their early and long labors have given the audiences of today and tomorrow the opportunity to enjoy special events in sports.

We would be remiss if we did not first acknowledge the assistance received from our MVP, Dylan Aramian. Her critical eye is evident in every page of this book. She has been the writers' best friend and a rare professional whose unique and unwavering vision and extraordinary technical skill improved our performance.

The authors also gratefully acknowledge the following individuals. We apologize for any oversight or omission on this list.

All-Stars

Liane Adduci
Alan Alper
Maya Angelou
Craig Aramian
Gail Augle
Bobby Austin
Bobbi Avancena

Carl Bach
Monica Barrett
Ron Bergin
Alexander Berlonghi
Jim Birrell
Dewey Blanton
John Boulter

Andrew Brandt   Tanisha Howard
Charles Brotman   Ed Hula
Bob Brown   Klaus Inkamp, CSEP
Bob Brubaker   Clyde Jacobs
Michael Buczkowski   Jeff Jacobs
Daniel Burrus   Mamie Jacobs
Don Campbell   Chris Janson
Hill Carrow   Jennifer C. Jordan
Tolbert Chism   Guy Kawasaki
Renata Circeo   Tom Kayser
Terry Cooksey   Jack Kelly
Brian Curtain   James Kemper
Jim Dalrymple   Frank W. King
Mary Ann Davies   Phil Knight
Linda Deckard   Mira Koplovsky
Frank Deford   Jill Kriser
Mark Donovan   Andre Lanier
Sue Ann Drobbin   Mady Lesnik
Dick Ebersol   Steve Lesnik
David Falk   Barnett Lipton
Lee Fentress   Yvonne Lumsden-Dill
Dr. Virginia Floyd   Ian MacDonald
Jim Foster   Gianni Merlo
Douglas C. Frechtling, Ph.D.   Mark McCullers
Jeff Fried   Franklin Moore
Dennis Gann   LeConte Moore
Susan Gersten   Teri Morris
Barry Glassman   John Naisbitt
Mark Goldman   Suzanne O'Connor
Anita Graham   Molly O'Dea
Wendy Graham   Susan O'Malley
Bill Gray   Donna Paulino
Chris Green   Donald C. Paup, Ph.D.
Frank Grenard   Richard B. Perelman
Shmuel Ben-Gad Gudowitz   Barbara Perry
Bill Hall   Tom Peters
Dennis Harp   Gerald M. Plessner, CFRE
Donald E. Hawkins, Ed.D   Paul Porwoll
Jean Lou Hess   Dick Pound
Tom Hilton   Karen Pritzer
Denise Hitchcock, APR   Tom Reagan

Robert Rinehart
Susan Roane
Carol Rogala
Mary Ann Rose
Jeff Ruday
Beth Ruggiero
Steve Schanwald
Jean-Claude Schupp
Josephine Sherfy
Barry Silberman
Susan Silverman
Alicia Slaughter
Michael Smith
Peter Smith, Ed.D.
Dr. Valene Smith
Don Smith
Dave Steinberg
David Stotlar
Howard Stupp
Frank Supovitz
Tom Swanson
Michael Thomas

Ron Thomas
Stephen Joel Trachtenberg
Andre Treadman
Anthony Triglione
Mark Trudi
Jim Tunney
Peter Ueberroth
Osmund Ueland
Lesa Ukman
Hugh Wakeham
Tommy Walker
Mitchell Ware
James Wasson
Bob Waterman
Armstrong Williams
Ron Willis
Oprah Winfrey
Dan Witkowski
Virginia Wolf
William "Woody" Woodruff
Cynthia A. Zigmund

and the sport and event management and marketing students at The George Washington University.

We hope that you, the reader, will come to share our appreciation for these team players as you explore this field. Perhaps one day you will have the opportunity to meet some of these outstanding sport all-stars in person and thank them for their contributions that enabled us to provide you with their secret plays.

Contents

THE ULTIMATE GUIDE TO SPORT EVENT MANAGEMENT AND MARKETING

I

THE ROLE AND SCOPE OF SPORT EVENTS

"The oldest standing building in Rome is the Colosseum."

Red Smith, announcer, on the role of sports in society.

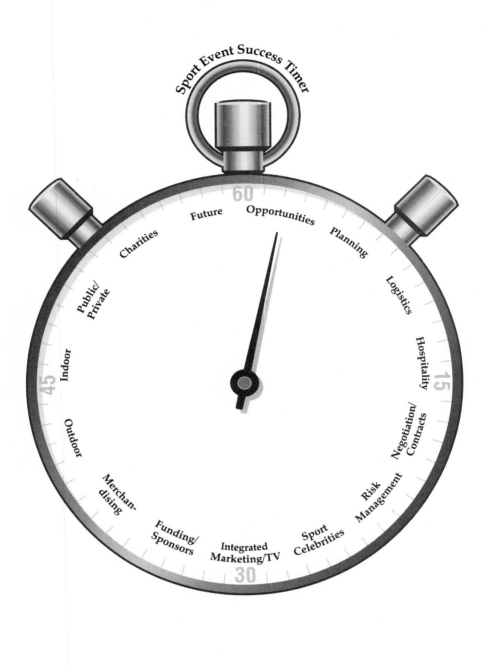

Chapter One

Emerging Opportunities:
The Benefits of Sport Event Management and Marketing

"It comes down to a very simple saying: There is a right way and a wrong way to do things. You can practice shooting eight hours a day, but if your technique is wrong, then all you become is very good at shooting the wrong way.

Get the fundamentals down and the level of everything you do will rise."

Michael Jordan

W hy is sport event management and marketing a growing industry and how can you increase your chances for rapid success?

The International Events Group (IEG) of Chicago, Illinois, estimated that spending on sponsorship of sports, music, and arts events and causes reached a record $2.3 billion in 1992. The largest percentage was spent on sport special events.

In 1987, *Working Woman* magazine reported that "corporate special events marketing was one of the hottest careers" and claimed that "more than 3,000 companies will spend more than a billion dollars to pin their names on dozens of sporting and cultural events."

A 1990 study by Sports Marketing Group of Dallas, Texas, reported that corporate America spent a total of $23.52 billion on sports marketing. Nye Lavalle, managing director of the study, claims this figure is comprehensive and includes every type of marketing activity

5

conducted by a company that embraces sport. Although the largest share went to traditional advertising, $6.2 billion went to corporate entertainment at or in connection with sport events. The expansion and interest in the job market parallels the influx of dollars to sport event management and marketing.

It's no secret that this rapidly expanding field is popular. Lee Fentress, a partner with Advantage International, headquartered in Washington, D.C., one of the largest sport marketing firms, says that his organization receives over 5,000 resumes annually. Jim Foster, former commissioner of the Arena Football League, received 250 applications in one week when he advertised for one media relations director. Nike, the shoe company, receives approximately 35,000 unsolicited résumés for everything from secretarial to sales to administrative jobs.

Although challenging to break into, sport job opportunities continue to grow in number, thanks to the seemingly insatiable appetite for sport entertainment. More than 24,000 companies and organizations are currently listed in the Sport Market Place, a national sport register. Not all sport jobs are glamorous, however. Many have tasks that are similar to other industries (sales, accounting, clerical) and the pay may be low. Nonetheless, the demand for these positions remains high because applicants want to work in an exciting and challenging profession. Many have remarked, "I get paid for doing what is essentially my hobby!"

As reported in *USA Today*, sport executive career recruiter Mark Trudi estimates that there are 4.5 million sport-related jobs today covering five major areas:

- Marketing (1.5 million)
- Entrepreneurship (1.15 million)
- Administration (500,000)
- Representation (370,000)
- Media (300,000)

In addition, Trudi identified about 720,000 other sports-related jobs that do not fit into these categories.

Basketball legend Julius "Dr. J." Erving is an example of a retired professional ball player who became a successful businessman while maintaining a dynamic link to sport. Among other businesses, Dr. J. owns a sport management firm, The Erving Group.

LINKAGES BETWEEN SPORT AND SPECIAL EVENT MANAGEMENT AND MARKETING

Sport and special events parallel one another in numerous ways. Many people consider sport events to be a subset of special events and therefore share a number of things in common (see Figure 1–1).

Professional and amateur sport requires rules to operate orderly and successfully. These rules may take the form of customs, traditions, protocol, or established player/team safety regulations. Rituals such as the singing of national anthems or the procession of athletes have become traditions; as such, their occurance has become an unwritten rule in most sport special events.

The outcomes in both sport and special events are unpredictable. However, success is more likely with training, planning, and practice. Large corporate sponsors such as Coca-Cola and M&M Mars invest heavily in research to attain the greatest return on their investment. Coca-Cola's marketing strategy typically includes painting the town red and white with ads, billboards, unbrellas, and chairs while M&M Mars lights up the surrounding landscape with its product colors of orange, green, yellow, and brown. The planning takes years, not days, of careful preparation on signage placement; media buys; local, national, and international retail promotions; sales incentive contests; on-site hospitality; travel; accommodations; and ticketing to ensure success.

In addition to a close relationship, a variety of similarities exist between sport and special events (see Figure 1-2).

Winning coaches coordinate players on the field while winning sport special event managers coach their teams on an even wider field. Special event managers may assemble as few as 20 or as many as hundreds of vendors, suppliers, and professionals. All must work together to form a winning team.

There will be no second chance. Championships are won one game at a time. The sociologist William Graham Summer once

FIGURE 1–1

The Relationship between *Sport* and *Special Event*
Management and Marketing

- Common language and symbols that lead to bonding among participants, spectators, or both.
- Rules, customs, and traditions that influence activities.
- Training, planning, and practice that reduce risk and ensure success even though outcomes are unpredictable.

FIGURE 1–2

Similarities between Sport and Special Events

- Sport events, like all entertainment programs, require several levels of professional management, including a director, an operations manager, a ticket sales/box office manager, a marketing manager, a personnel manager, a concessions manager, engineers, clerical support staff, a media/public relations coordinator, and suppliers and vendors who must work together as a team.
- Sport drama is likely to be part of a repeated pattern such as the Olympic Games or World Series. Like certain celebrations (e.g., Memorial Day, Christmas, or Hanukkah) that occur annually, recurring sport events such as the Super Bowl become an annual experience in person, or through television.
- Sport and special event industries are service-driven.

wrote,"The sport establishment is a system of antagonistic cooperation." Each vendor or player may have a private and personal agenda that must be suppressed for the sake of team victory. The only goal, shared by all, is to triumph with each sport special event.

At the 1992 conference of the National Association for Sport Sociology, Professor Robert Rinehart declared that the Super Bowl is "a modern ritual of pilgrimage in which people attend to reunite with their friends and experience the event in concert with others of similar interest." In fact, Rinehart's study of the 1992 Super Bowl in Minneapolis, Minnesota, found that individuals attended the game "to be seen, to enjoy the hoopla, to support the team, and to continue a ritual." For many, this sport special event experience is a recurring life-shaping experience.

From a strict business point of view, both the sport and special event industries are service-driven with customer satisfaction as the key to success. Sport teams constantly survey spectators to identify not only their demographics, but also their psychographics to meet their customers' needs most effectively and ultimately to retain or increase their patronage. These challenges are being met through special events in sports, especially with the expansion of the family entertainment concept and corporate hospitality programs.

Sport event producers, in conjunction with their corporate sponsors, are beginning to create all-day interactive programming for consumers. The ATP Tour Fan-Fest, for example, is an all-day side show that consumers participate in before, during, and after the main event. Each activity is designed to highlight a sponsor's product or service in a playful environment. Kodak, therefore, hosted the Kodak Korner where fans got pictures taken with cut-outs of tour players and Saga premiered its "Electronic Tennis" video game. As planning proceeds for these events, the organizer must segment each market to meet consumer and sponsor needs and to achieve specific outcomes. This process requires research and knowledge about the lifestyles of the guests and potential trends that may be incorporated to encourage participation.

One purpose of special events in sport is therefore to attract more and more people to the stadium, health facilities, and tourist destinations. Golf, tennis, and ski resorts all produce special events to attract and keep customers. David Stotlar, professor of sport management at the University of Northern Colorado, explains, "Putting people in the seats, events on the floor, and dollars in the stockholders pockets is the name of the game."

HISTORICAL PERSPECTIVE AS THE FOUNDATION FOR SUCCESS

We know that sport and special events have historical and structural connections. Now you will learn why this relationship has been solidified in the modern era and how you can benefit.

Although historical accounts credit alternatively the Greeks, Chinese, or Egyptians as originators of sport, we know from the first written account of sport, Homer's *Iliad*, that athletic competition from the beginning was part of a larger festival—in this case, the funeral games for Patroclus. Drawings found on the walls of prehistoric caves show that men and women have always enjoyed leisure, recreation, and sport, and that these activities were often coupled with celebratory or special event activities. The organizing committee for the 1994 Winter Olympic Games in Lillehammer, Norway, patterned the Game's logo, sport pictograms, and merchandising line after 4,000-year-old Norwegian rock carvings and elements of ancient Norwegian culture (see Figure 1–3).

Scholarly research also supports the marriage of sport and special events in order to enhance the sport experience through a myriad of affective activities (pregame, halftime, postgame shows; corporate hospitality tents and suites; game day promotions and giveaways). Michael Buczkowski, assistant general manager for the Buffalo Bisons, a triple A baseball team, further supports the importance of special events in sports by remarking how successful the marketing and operational slogan, "Every Game's an Event," has been in attracting record crowds to the ballpark (see Figure 1–4).

No other medium touches the lives of so many people as sport. In 1991, the Associated Press estimated that sport was a $180 billion industry and ranked it among the top 25 of America's largest industries. This figure does not include the large economic impact of sport events on host cities and surrounding areas (see Chapter 13).

Simons Market Research Bureau reported that 84 percent of all men surveyed in 1992 read the sports section. An earlier study, the 1983 Miller Lite Report, concluded that 98 percent of all Americans either participate in sport, read about sport, or watch sport events on television at least once a week. *USA Today* devotes 25 percent of its coverage to sports; about 50 percent of the sports section deals with major sports.

Television also has played a huge role in the development of this industry. In the lead with audience viewing increases, ABC's Roone Arledge was determined to get the television viewer involved emotionally. He was one of the first television producers to recognize sport as a special event medium and was determined that the television audience would enjoy the event regardless of the outcome of the competition.

To achieve this goal, Arledge used cranes, blimps, and even helicopters to obtain dramatic views of the stadium, the campus, and the surrounding countryside at an event. With hand-held cameras for close-up pictures of the spectators and players, and rifle-type microphones to pick up local sounds, Arledge made the

FIGURE 1–3
Official Sport Pictograms for the 1994 Winter Olympic Games

Utfor
Downhill
Descente

Super G
Super G
Super G

Storslalåm
Giant Slalom
Slalom géant

Slalåm
Slaom
Slalom

Freestyle kulekjøring
Freestyle Moguls
Ski artistique Bosses

Langrenn
Cross-country skiing
Ski de fond

Hopp
Ski jumping
Saut

Skiskyting
Biathlon
Biathlon

Ishockey
Ice hockey
Hockey sur glace

Kunstløp
Figure skating
Patinage artistique

Hurtigløp
Speed skating
Patinage de vitesse

Kortbaneløp
Short-track speed
  skating
Patinage de vitesse
  sur piste courte

Bob
Bob
Bobsleigh

Aking
Luge
Luge

FIGURE 1–4

1993 Buffalo Bisons
Home Promotional Schedule

April 8	OMAHA	1:05 p.m.	Opening Day
April 9	OMAHA	7:05 p.m.	fridaynightbash!
April 10	OMAHA	2:05 p.m.	Hippity Hop Egg Hunt
April 11	IOWA	6:05 p.m.	Easter Parade
April 12	IOWA	7.05 p.m.	Molson Monday/Dyngus Day
April 13	IOWA	1:05 p.m.	Two for Tuesday
April 21	NEW ORLEANS	7:05 p.m.	Business Person's Day/Secretary's Day Celebration
April 22	NEW ORLEANS	7:05 p.m.	Pizza Hut Pop-up Thursday
April 23	OKLAHOMA CITY	7:05 p.m.	fridaynightbash!
April 24	OKLAHOMA CITY	2:05 p.m.	Earth Day Celebration
April 25	OKLAHOMA CITY	2:05 p.m.	TBA
May 3	LOUISVILLE	7:05 p.m.	Molson Monday
May 4	LOUISVILLE	11:05 p.m.	Two for Tuesday/Buffalo Public Schools Day
May 5	LOUISVILLE	1:05 p.m.	Business Person's Day
May 6	PITTSBURGH	4:05 p.m.	Exhibition Game, Presented by Old Vienna
May 12	NASHVILLE	7:05 p.m.	Business Person's Day
May 13	NASHVILLE	11:05 p.m.	Pizza Hut Pop-up Thursday/Catholic School Day
May 14	INDIANAPOLIS	7:05 p.m.	Carnival Weekend/fridaynightbash!
May 15	INDIANAPOLIS	2:05 p.m.	Carnival Weekend/Darien Lake Day
May 16	INDIANAPOLIS	2:05 p.m.	Carnival Weekend/100 Club Day
May 17	INDIANAPOLIS	7:05 p.m.	Molson Monday/German Festival Night
May 28	NEW ORLEANS	7:05 p.m.	fridaynightbash!
May 29	NEW ORLEANS	7:05 p.m.	Jubilee Little League Weekend/Summer Safety Day
May 30	NEW ORLEANS	7:05 p.m.	Jubilee Little League Weekend
May 31	NEW ORLEANS	7:05 p.m.	Molson Monday/Memorial Day Picnic
June 6	NASHVILLE	6:05 p.m.	TBA
June 7	NASHVILLE	7:05 p.m.	Molson Monday
June 8	NASHVILLE	7:05 p.m.	Two for Tuesday
June 9	NASHVILLE	1:05 p.m.	Business Person's Day
June 10	LOUISVILLE	7:05 p.m.	Pizza Hut Pop-Up Thursday
June 11	LOUISVILLE	7:05 p.m.	fridaynightbash!
June 12	LOUISVILLE	7:05 p.m.	TBA
June 13	LOUISVILLE	12:05 p.m.	TBA
June 14	INDIANAPOLIS	7:05 p.m.	Molson Monday
June 15	INDIANAPOLIS	7:05 p.m.	Two for Tuesday/Italian Festival night

FIGURE 1–4 concluded

June 26	NEW ORLEANS	7:05 p.m.	Donruss Baseball Card Day
June 27	NEW ORLEANS	2:05 p.m.	TBA
June 28	OKLAHOMA CITY	7:05 p.m.	Molson Monday
June 29	OKLAHOMA CITY	7:05 p.m.	Two for Tuesday
June 30	OKLAHOMA CITY	1:05 p.m.	Business Person's Day
June 25	NEW ORLEANS	7:05 p.m.	fridaynightbash!
July 4	LOUISVILLE	7:05 p.m.	Independence Day Celebration
July 5	LOUISVILLE	7:05 p.m.	Molson Monday/Polaroid Team Photo Day
July 6	INDIANAPOLIS	7:05 p.m.	Two for Tuesday/Irish Festival Night
July 7	INDIANAPOLIS	1:05 p.m.	Business Person's Day
July 8	INDIANAPOLIS	7:05 p.m.	Pizza Hut Pop-Up Thursday
July 9	OMAHA	7:05 p.m.	fridaynightbash!
July 10	OMAHA	7:05 p.m.	Wheaties Day of Champions
July 11	IOWA	6:05 p.m.	Surf & Snuggle Tee Shirt Day
July 12	IOWA	7:05 p.m.	Molson Monday featuring "The Blues Brothers Act"
July 22	NASHVILLE	7:05 p.m.	Pizza Hut Pop-Up Thursday
July 23	NASHVILLE	7:05 p.m.	fridaynightbash!
July 24	OKLAHOMA CITY	7:05 p.m.	TBA
July 25	OKLAHOMA CITY	7:05 p.m.	Turn Back the Clock Day/Buffalo Baseball Hall of Fame
July 26	OKLAHOMA CITY	7:05 p.m.	Molson Monday
August 5	LOUISVILLE	7:05 p.m.	Pizza Hut Pop-Up Thursday/Upper Deck Card Album Giveaway
August 6	LOUISVILLE	7:05 p.m.	fridaynightbash!
August 7	LOUISVILLE	7:05 p.m.	TBA
August 8	INDIANAPOLIS	6:05 p.m.	TBA
August 9	INDIANAPOLIS	7:05 p.m.	Molson Monday
August 10	INDIANAPOLIS	7:05 p.m.	Two for Tuesday
August 22	OMAHA	6:05 p.m.	TBA
August 23	OMAHA	7:05 p.m.	Molson Monday
August 24	OMAHA	7:05 p.m.	Two for Tuesday
August 25	OMAHA	1:05 p.m.	Business Person's Day
August 26	IOWA	7:05 p.m.	Pizza Hut Pop-Up Thursday/Polish Festival Night
August 27	IOWA	7:05 p.m.	fridaynightbash!
August 28	IOWA	2:05 p.m.	TBA
August 29	IOWA	2:05 p.m.	TBA
September 3	NASHVILLE	7:05 p.m.	fridaynightbash!
September 4	NASHVILLE	7:05 p.m.	Back to School Day
September 5	NASHVILLE	7:05 p.m.	TBA
September 6	NASHVILLE	7:05 p.m.	Fan Appreciation Day

fans an integral part of the sport special event. Once the fans perceived themselves as potential performers, they began to display banners, run onto the field, and engage in numerous other attention-getting and scene-stealing activities. The parachutist who landed unannounced and uninvited ringside at the 1993 Bowe-Holeyfield championship boxing bout in Las Vegas illustrates the kind of daring escapades television has inspired.

CONSUMERISM AND THE EXPLOSION OF SPORT

Although the media were and continue to be a significant player in entrenching organized sport into American life, equal credit is due to modern consumer culture. The change of the U.S. economy from one of production to one of consumption and leisure opened the door for many sport-related enterprises. Overall, the first half of the 20th century witnessed a twelvefold increase in recreation expenditures. As early as 1909, sport manufacturing pioneer A. G. Spalding produced a catalog with more than 200 pages of advertisements for sporting goods and exercise devices.

Increased awareness of self-responsibility for personal health is another important factor in the growth of the sport establishment. Beginning in the 1970s, more and more people became apostles of fitness and, subsequently, dedicated fitness consumers. The number of commercial health clubs literally exploded from 350 in 1968 to over 7,000 in 1986. Health clubs often use special events as a marketing vehicle to attract and retain members.

YOUR ROLE IN THIS HISTORIC SPORT PAGEANT

Whether sport as special event originated with the Chinese (who are credited with inventing fireworks), the Greeks (who are credited with creating the first recorded dramas), or other historic cultures is immaterial. What is important to recognize as you develop and master your skills in this profession is that celebrating through sport is as natural as the need to exercise and maintain good health.

Whether you are a spectator or participant or both, today's sport organizations recognize that to maintain and expand interest in these games, highly creative special events experts, perhaps like you, are needed. Each generation of sport marketers must produce creative geniuses such as the father of major league baseball promotions, Bill Veeck; impresario George Preston Marshall; or the "Barnum of the Bushes" of minor league fame, Joe Engel. And we cannot ignore more recent figures such as master Olympic marketer Peter Ueberroth or television maverick Roone Arledge whose contributions have made a lasting impact upon the image of sport as special event.

Gone are the days when teams simply opened their gates and hoped that spectators would enter. For some losing teams, it is important to divert attention from a poor season by developing sport as a special event so that the score becomes incidental to the overall entertainment value the fan receives. To this end, most baseball teams feature special promotions at three-fourths of their games to generate additional excitement.

The future of sport as special event will be secure as long as there are men and women who will contribute their talent, creativity, and determination to satisfy the spectator's unquenchable thirst for entertainment.

Although the cause-and-effect relationship over the driving force in the growth of sport continues to be debated—be it through increased media attention, expanded public interest, changes in consumerism or corporate marketing—we know that sport today is a genuine special event from the tailgate party to the fireworks following the final play.

For the purposes of this book, the cumbersome term, *sport special event*, will be replaced simply and accurately with *sport event* because you now understand that every sport activity, through your creativity, can and should become a special event.

WHERE ARE THE JOBS TODAY?

Author Stedman Graham, a successful sport event marketer who has employed hundreds, reports:

There are many jobs that are created because of sport events. I have found that numerous people are affected. Events create jobs for sales, media, advertisers, food vendors, public relations specialists, laborers or union help, caterers, hotels, airlines, and more.

Often, local people will be hired to run an event that is on tour in different cities, such as the Virginia Slims tennis tournament. On a national tour, management hires a local tournament director, who in turn hires local people to manage and produce the event. Although the majority of these jobs are temporary, the experience is useful in career advancement.

World Cup Soccer is another example where temporary positions are created. The National Basketball Association (NBA) All-star Game is one of the most successful touring events in bringing jobs to local venues or putting outside contractors to work, as well as supporting local business or entrepreneurs. Temporary sport event jobs not only will provide you with valuable experience and expertise but also will assist you in developing relationships that can lead to a career in sports.

You will often find that special event jobs in sport are hidden within traditional career titles or job descriptions. Fortunately, two widely recognized directories provide job contacts in this field. *The Sports Market Place Register* lists more than 24,000 sports people and organizations. The *IEG Directory of Sponsorship Marketing* features 1,500 agencies, suppliers, and services in addition to more than 4,000 sport events and sponsorship opportunities. Do not be intimidated by these large numbers. A select list of career opportunities is found in Appendix II-A and can be extremely valuable as you conduct your own search.

WHAT CAN I EARN?

As you will see, salaries are highly flexible, depending on the level of the sport organization (e.g., Double A baseball versus major leagues), and the geographic region. In a survey of sport special events managers at colleges, Brad Bower, of the George Washington University, found the average salary range was between $25,000 and $35,000 (see Figure 1–5).

Special Message to My Fellow Athletes

I have been involved in athletics most of my life, not only as a player but as a business person. My business experiences have made me realize how far a drop it is from the playing field to the real world. When I speak with athletes, I encourage them to realize the opportunity they have to play the game they love and enjoy for as long as it is possible.

In addition, it is important to prepare yourself before you quit playing, not after, to develop other skills that will allow you to make possible career changes once your playing days are over.

To repeat, the day you stop playing in athletics becomes one of the longest falls that I have seen in any profession. But when you have prepared yourself, your past profession can only enhance what you have selected as your second career.

Stedman Graham

FIGURE 1–5
Sport Event Salary Guide

Salary Level	Potential Annual Salary*
Entry level	0 to $18,000
University sport program	$30,000
Minor league management	$40,000
Major league management	$100,000
Sales and marketing managers	$50,000 and higher
Entrepreneurs (gross revenue)	$500,000 and higher

*These figures may be adjusted upward with the addition of sales commissions, bonuses, and other incentives.

Regardless of the starting salary, each of these positions can serve as a catalyst for management to notice you quickly, thus accelerating the possibility of your promotion. The successful sport event manager often possesses strategic planning and management skills that owners seek when considering employees for advancement.

The Baltimore Orioles baseball team management includes special events as a multidisciplinary activity that utilizes the skills of not only the public affairs department but also group sales and stadium operations. The title of sport events coordinator, manager, or director is relatively new. Therefore, you may need to inquire within a variety of departments which group has direct responsibility for special event planning and management and then identify the salary range for this position.

The marketing side of sport special event management is more lucrative (see Figure 1–5). Alan Raider, author of *The Mobile Stockbroker*, states that events-oriented marketing professionals can earn more than $100,000 a year and freelance planners can earn from $1,800 to $30,000 in fees for each project. These entrepreneurs may bill a flat fee for all of their services or a percentage of the overall cost (usually from 10 to 20 percent) for larger, more complex events. The sport event planner becomes a general contractor, a position similar to a home builder.

GETTING STARTED

The first step is perhaps the most difficult and challenging of any career search. Where do you begin in the search for a career in sport events or how do you expand your current opportunities?

While it is extremely difficult to enter at top-level positions, it is not impossible. The secret is to create a plan and then work your plan until the time is right for your career opportunity.

Barnett Lipton is a respected producer who has been responsible for the 1988 NFL Super Bowl halftime spectacular that featured 88 grand pianos, the opening and closing ceremonies of the 1989 U.S. Olympic Festival, and the Opening and Closing Ceremonies of the 1990 Goodwill Games, among dozens of other major special events. Lipton learned his craft from one of the true pioneers in sport event production.

> *I went to Knoxville and helped Tommy Walker with the World's Fair. He needed a helicopter for the opening and I got him one. After that I continued working for him until his firm was sold to Radio City Music Hall Productions.*

I literally showed up, helped out, and learned a great deal, which then turned into other opportunities.

Today, Lipton is president of Eventures, Inc., a special event management firm in New York City that produces events for corporations, governments, and other organizations throughout the World. In recent years, he produced the 200th anniversary of the U.S. Constitution in Philadelphia and the New York City Operation Welcome Home Ticker Tape Parade for the heroes and heroines of the Persian Gulf conflict.

Lipton's story is an excellent example of volunteering your way to the top. Experience is one way to learn a skill. The other is through formal study. Over 100 colleges offer programs in sport management. A combination of both experience and formal study is ideal.

According to Stedman Graham, "The quickest way to the top is to learn from the experts. We are not reinventing the wheel. The work that we are doing and that is being accomplished has been done before. Trial and error is the most dangerous and expensive form of learning. You should consider interning or apprenticing with an experienced professional prior to attempting to produce your own sport events independently. A mentor can give you the advice and guidance until you have the right skills and training to go off on your own. These are essential to building a strong base that will enable you to understand the business and build a successful future for yourself and your family."

There are thousands of opportunities to volunteer your services in exchange for a priceless education. Contact not-for-profit organizations, schools, clubs, and professional event management firms. Ask them if you can volunteer to help with a forthcoming sport event. Whether your interest is golf, tennis, swimming, or some other sport, make certain you select your mentoring organization carefully.

To establish your relationship with the organization, send a letter of inquiry similar to that shown in Figure 1–6.

Make certain you do your homework prior to sending any correspondence. Find out who is directly responsible for coordinating volunteers or for organizing the overall event. Jennifer

FIGURE 1–6

Sample Query Letter

> Your Address
> City, State, ZIP
> Telephone
> Facsimile
> Date

Name
Title
Organization Name
Address
City, State, ZIP

Dear (Mr./Ms.):

Your forthcoming sport event is of great interest to me. I am writing to volunteer my services to assist you with any aspect of this activity where I might be of use.

My résumé is included for your review. I am particularly interested in [X], but am willing to help you in any area.

Good luck with this event. I will call you next Tuesday to discuss my possible involvement.

> Sincerely,
>
> Name
> Title

Jordan, venue press manager for Atlanta Committee for the Olympic Games (ACOG), suggests that you do not call the individual before you send the letter but make your follow-up call on the date that you indicated in the letter. This demonstrates your integrity and organizational skills.

Do not be disappointed if you are referred to someone else or even turned down. Be persistent and continue searching for opportunities until you establish the critical relationships necessary to succeed.

FIGURE 1–7

Common Traits of Sport Event Managers

1. Comfortable with preparing and managing a checklist of activities.
2. Projects a positive attitude.
3. Can work independently or as a member of a team.
4. Accurate and quick at details.
5. Articulate on the telephone and in written and oral communication.
6. Creative, flexible.
7. Capable of working under extreme pressure for long hours.
8. Good at working with all levels of people including volunteers.
9. Effective at balancing multiple projects simultaneously.
10. Excellent time manager.
11. Effective negotiator.
12. Finance and budget conscious.
13. Possesses good typing, word processing, and other office skills.
14. Leadership ability.
15. Quick problem solver.
16. Good motivator.
17. Desire to learn and grow.

PERSONALITY, LIFESTYLE, AND WORK STYLE CHARACTERISTICS YOU WILL NEED

With your letter, attach a résumé listing your direct or related experience to sport event projects. Sport promoter Charles Brotman says, "Send me your resume and it will be read. We never know when we might need someone with your exact skills." However, successful sport event professionals typically share several common traits (see Figure 1–7). Use this figure only as a guide. It is not applicable to every sport because each sport is different and therefore requires unique skills.

As you explore this text, you will meet dozens of sport event professionals who possess all or most of these traits.

Another important trait common to many sport event managers is that they are highly competitive. Some, though not all, were professional athletes and understand the spirit of competition and good sportsmanship. All, however, understand the importance of competition in raising the benchmark of quality with each event. The competitor they face is themselves. Each time they accept a new sport event challenge, they seek to improve their chances of success and to refine their performance.

Now that you recognize the opportunities that are rapidly emerging in sport events, you are ready to begin the critical process of planning. In Chapter 2, you will master the principles of planning to further ensure the success of your sport event.

GAME HIGHLIGHTS

- Realize that the field of sport and special events is rapidly expanding due to mass communications and greater interest in leisure.
- Seek professional employment in this field by becoming an apprentice to a mentor from whom you can learn practical approaches to this profession.
- Recognize that throughout human history people have used sport as a form of celebration; however, the exact origin of sport as special event has been disputed.
- Note that sport special events are part of tourism and are responsible for a large economic impact in the United States.
- Remember that developing special event activities in conjunction with your sport event not only enhances the overall sport experience but also can be a key element in the longevity of your event.

PLAY BOOK

common traits Seventeen attributes shared by successful professionals in the field of sport event management and marketing.

query letter The first document you send to a prospective mentor when seeking a volunteer or internship position for a specific sport event.

sport event management The planning, coordination, and evaluation of special events related to sport.

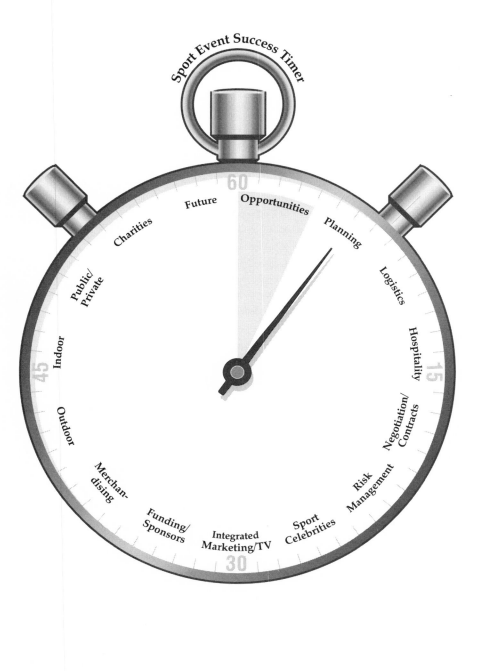

Sport Event Success Timer

60 Opportunities
Future
Charities
Public/Private
Indoor
45
Outdoor
Merchandising
Funding/Sponsors
Integrated Marketing/TV
30
Sport Celebrities
Risk Management
Negotiation/Contracts
Hospitality
15
Logistics
Planning

Chapter Two

Critical Planning to Master the Game

"Beware of the big play: The 80-yard drive is better than the 80-yard pass."

Fran Tarkenton

How does the practice of developing winning plays affect the outcome of the game and how can you use this same strategy to win with sport events?

Former Secretary of Defense Donald Rumsfeld said, "Plan backwards. Set your objectives and trace back to see how to achieve them, even though you may discover there is no way to get there and you will have to adjust the objectives."

A wise business executive once advised, "Innovate or evaporate." The same is true for the emerging field of sport events. Successful innovation hinges on the ability to create solutions for strategic challenges using the best available information.

Successful coaches invest significant time scouting the competition in order to best prepare their players for the game. Furthermore, the best coaching professionals recognize the strength and weaknesses of their players and team organization in order to be able to design winning strategies.

In this section, we will present a model for analyzing an event's strengths, weaknesses, opportunities, and threats in order to design a winning game plan for your event.

SWOT: THE STRENGTHS, WEAKNESSES, OPPORTUNITIES, AND THREATS ANALYSIS

To master the game in sport events, conduct a strengths, weaknesses, opportunities, and threats (SWOT) analysis. The SWOT analysis is a detailed examination that helps you look at internal aspects of your organization and sport event, and external variables that may affect your overall success.

The strengths and weaknesses part of the analysis allows you to look at the internal resources available in planning your sport event. Opportunities and threats provide you with crucial information for assessing external situations such as political issues that may directly or indirectly affect the plans you formulate.

Prior to conducting a SWOT analysis, you must be familiar with every detail of the sport event, including personnel, volunteers, time, date, location, target audience, and population size of the community where the event takes place.

We will use a 5K road race scheduled for a Saturday morning in April on the Mall in Washington, D.C., to examine the SWOT analysis. Organized by the George Washington University Forum for Sport and Event Management and Marketing (Forum), the event expects between 500–750 runners from the metropolitan area. Proceeds will benefit the Forum scholarship fund.

Strengths

What strengths do you as a professional bring to this event? What additional strengths can you identify within your own organization? What other resources can you identify that will strengthen your position in planning this event?

Professionals often relate strengths only to formal experience or professional certification or degree programs, but most experience is gained informally in practical situations. For example, your career may be in transition, or you are reentering the job market after many years of organizing and managing your family. In addition, you are a knowledgeable sports enthusiast. This combination of skills certainly provides you with strengths that can help you to succeed in producing your sport event.

As another example, perhaps you have organized a charity golf or tennis tournament and now wish to use this volunteer experience as an opportunity to move into a professional career. You may even have extensive professional management experience and have a keen interest in sports as an active fan. Determine how these experiences are transferable and then identify them as strengths in developing your plan.

Forum Strengths

- The Forum will provide plenty of experienced sport event managers to work at the event and marketers to sell the event.
- The Federal Park Service will provide the security for a fee. They are experienced in crowd control on the Mall and have worked at various fun runs and rallies.
- Tents donated by a Forum board member will be erected to protect runners before and after the race from the sun or rain.
- Internal and external written communications are facilitated through the use of E-mail and faxes. All promotional materials are produced in-house with a university desktop publishing system.

Use Figure 2–1 to identify the practical skills and abilities that you or others in your organization may possess.

Although your interpretation of these strengths is not an empirical science, the overall SWOT analysis will help you to identify the strong traits your organization possesses. Keep in mind that every sport event is distinct and may require a varying amount of strengths to ensure success.

Weaknesses

Courageous and professional sport event managers assess the weaknesses as well as the strengths of their organizations. These internal aspects can easily become a burden to your sport event program. Therefore, you must carefully analyze and assess these weaknesses.

The list of weaknesses can be as long as the list of strengths. Convene a brief meeting among key staff and volunteers to determine any weaknesses. Ask them to suggest internal areas

---

FIGURE 2–1
Strengths Analysis Checklist

Assess each skill by writing the term **strong**, **average**, or **weak** in the Assessment column.

Skill	*Assessment*
Financial Planning Budgeting, accounting, management	
Human Resource Management Recruiting, training, supervising, motivating staff and volunteers	
Safety, Security, Risk Management Admissions, venue grounds, spectators, players, personnel	
Hospitality Invitation design and production, amenities, coordination of logistics, hosting activities	
Food and Beverage Negotiations, quality, quantity, contract and price	
Sales and Marketing Prospecting, selling, closing, servicing	
Writing Correspondence, promotional copy, internal memoranda, newsletters, trade publication articles, media releases, follow-ups	
Leadership Ability Persuasion, motivation, listening, problem-solving skills	
Other skills or strengths:	

that are critically inadequate, that may be controlled and corrected by training, or that require elimination before their weakness erodes your entire organization. Elimination may mean that key staff or volunteers must be reassigned or even released.

Forum Weaknesses

- The Forum does not have any start-up capital, so it must rely on in-kind donations until cash is raised from sponsorships.
- Staff time is limited for this project.
- The race course is on federal land. Since no financial transactions can take place on federal land, no on-site registrations can be accepted. An alternative site must be arranged for the day of registration.
- No concessions can be sold because the event is held on federal land.

Use Figure 2–2 to identify the weaknesses that you or others in your organization may possess.

By concentrating on strengths and weaknesses, you are shoring up your organization to best handle the opportunities and threats from external variables. Getting your ship in tip-top shape at the planning stage is critical to survival on the restless seas ahead.

The external variables that may affect your sport event include both opportunities (positive) and threats (negative). Less controllable than internal variables, opportunities and threats nevertheless require careful analysis to ensure a successfully planned sport event.

Opportunities

The opportunities that present themselves may increase your revenues, generate greater positive public relations, and provide other benefits for your organization.

Forum Opportunities

- A large registration is expected at this early time of the year because athletes want to participate in this short-distance 5K race as a warm-up for longer-distance races later in the season.

FIGURE 2–2
Weaknesses Analysis Checklist

Assess each weakness by writing the term **critical, controllable** or, **eliminate** in the assessment column.

Weakness	Assessment
Disagreements among key staff and/or volunteers	
Personality conflicts among staff and/or volunteers	
Lack of trained, experienced personnel and/or volunteers	
Short planning time	
Funding problems	
Facility shortage or inadequacies	
Other weaknesses:	

- The event is held during a busy tourist weekend, so many people will be near the Mall area, creating the high visibility that sponsors find attractive.
- The president of the university has agreed to be the honorary chair for the event and run in the race.
- Students have a stake in the proceeds, so they will register and encourage their peers to run as well.

Use Figure 2–3 to identify the opportunities that you or others in your organization may possess.

Characterize these opportunities as probable if there is sufficient evidence to determine they are likely to occur. Define them as developable if an opportunity, such as proposed tourism development, is not yet firm but highly likely to occur. As you develop your plan, seek ways to integrate your activities

---

FIGURE 2–3
Opportunities Analysis Checklist

Assess each opportunity for its value by writing the term **probable**, **developable**, or **requires control** in the assessment column.

Opportunity	*Assessment*

Historical activity
Centennial, sesquicentennial, bicentennial, quincentennial
Prospective partners or volunteers
Prospective sponsors
Other major events prior to or following yours. Activities that could increase attendance
Tourism activities in the area of your event. Scenic, historical, or cultural attractions
Friendly business community
Friendly governmental agencies
Other opportunities:

---

within the macro tourism plan for the location where your sport event will be held.

Finally, determine whether an opportunity requires control. If the opportunity you have identified supports your goals and objectives, develop it. However, if it does not entirely support your end result, seek ways to control it. For example, a tourist-related activity such as a major music festival may be scheduled on the same date as your event. Control this activity to the best of your ability. Otherwise, this scheduling conflict could shift from an opportunity to a threat. A solution is to hold your event prior to the music festival so your participants also can enjoy the festival. Sponsors will get a bonus as well.

31

est to inclement weather, threats are real
ay jeopardize the overall success of your sport
ches have long preached that "a good offense
e." By recognizing as many potential threats as
possible, , ease your chances for success by identifying any
factors that may impede that success.

To determine the universe of threats that surrounds your sport
event, bring together managers from various parts of your
event-planning process. This includes risk management, volunteers, marketing, transportation, ticketing, concessions, and all
other critical departments. Ask all managers to list any potential
threats within their department and to identify any threats that
may affect the event as a whole.

Forum Threats

- Inclement weather is probable at this time of year.
- A bicycle race scheduled on the same day may attract athletes
  away from the 5K race.
- Students have threatened to rally at the event in protest of
  tuition increases.
- Local police, fire, and rescue teams may not have enough
  human resources for both your event and a competing one.

Figure 2–4 is an assessment guide to help you identify potential
threats and assess your vulnerability.

All threats that are listed in Figure 2–4 can be potentially
controlled. However, it is essential that you assess the vulnerability of your sport event within its context. For example, political
unrest may be potentially serious but requires further monitoring.
Acts of God cannot be controlled, but they can be monitored and
should be covered by insurance to reduce your financial exposure.

CREATING AND WORKING YOUR PLAN

Too many organizations spend countless hours developing plans
that are then filed away for posterity. Successful sport event
management and marketing professionals use their plans as a
critical tool to sculpt their success.

FIGURE 2–4
Threats Analysis Checklist

Assess each threat by writing the term **serious, monitor further**, or **requires coverage** in the assessment column.

Threat	Assessment
Political unrest	
Economic recession	
Negative environmental impact	
Advocacy group protest	
Violence	
Crime	
Trade union disagreements or strikes	
Acts of God	
Weather or other uncontrollable occurrences	
Other threats:	

A variety of predesigned time lines, charts, graphs, and computer programs are available to assist you; however, in most cases you will wish to create your own process. The National Hockey League's Frank Supovitz uses the following system to organize the many events for which he is responsible annually.

> Each event is completely different and therefore requires a separate strategic plan. However, for multiple events (such as the grand opening of the National Hockey Hall of Fame in Toronto, Canada, which included a parade, receptions and other events) occurring within the same period, I created individual production schedules and then incorporated them into a master planning document to create synergy between each project.

A practical approach to organization is to keep your master plan in a three-ring binder. You will see how useful this becomes when you begin to accumulate schedules, contacts, logistics, and other important information. The binder keeps them in one place where the information can be updated easily. As the event draws near and schedules become final, this binder becomes your event operations book. Copies of your plan book or portions of it should be given to everyone involved with the sport event to keep them apprised of the most current information.

Regardless of what system you use, the components in Figure 2-5 should be part of any sport event plan.

FIGURE 2–5

Sport Event Tips
Developing a Sport Event Checklist

1. Determine your projected revenues based on venue capacity and historical data. Then develop the budget and an expense plan utilizing these projections. Working realistically within this budget will cause much less stress.

2. Determine the time frame for preproduction, production, and postproduction activities. Do not be overanxious and do things that require redoing later or additional work and expense. For example, ticket sales are accompanied by advertisements and promotions. If you start your campaign too early, before the public is ready to purchase tickets, you will be expending energy unnecessarily. In addition, order brochures and promotional materials in adequate quantities. Reprinting may double the original cost.

3. Organize your time by first determining what tasks must be performed in sequential order, specifying the time and date. This is essential when licenses and permits are required. Special application deadlines and procedures may be imposed. Solicitation of corporate and foundation money is also sensitive to time considerations because of budget cycles. Do your homework and learn when companies develop their budgets, when their fiscal year ends, and when foundations consider proposals.

4. Plan backward. List each task that needs to be done and decide on deadline dates. Figure out the steps required to complete each task and the time needed. If you want people to respond to your invitation by a certain date, calculate the time for invitation design and printing, labeling, mailing, receipt, and response. Subtract this time from your deadline date and you know when to begin this task.

5. Allow for extra time (by providing sufficient padding to your schedule) to handle unforeseeable delays.

6. Confirm and verify your plans with everyone involved in the activity such as vendors, key staff, volunteer leaders, and officials. We recommend a weekly meeting with all staff and a monthly meeting with everyone involved.

continued

FIGURE 2–5 concluded

   Mailing an internal newsletter leading up to the event is not only
   informative but also keeps everyone motivated and on track.
 7. Determine what protocol is required that may affect your timing and
    sequence of events. The International Olympic Committee (IOC) requires
    that invitations to the Olympic Games be mailed exactly one year prior to the
    competition.
 8. Determine and incorporate into your planning any specific league or
    federation protocols or regulations. The National Collegiate Athletic
    Association (NCAA), for example, allows only a limited amount of alcohol-
    related advertising. Professional leagues dictate a specific time frame for
    television commercials in pregame, halftime, and postgame shows.
    Regulations on the number, size, and type of venue signage is also common.
 9. List all activities for which each department is responsible in a separate
    schedule of events. Then incorporate these individual activities into the
    master plan. Coca-Cola has developed a comprehensive project
    management computer program that lists and tracks progress on all
    activities associated with and leading to the 1996 Olympic Games in Atlanta,
    Georgia.
10. Include in your plan book a master contact form listing the names and other
    critical numbers (work, home, E-mail, fax, mobile telephone, beeper) of each
    member of your sport event management team.
11. Allow for contingency decision making in your plan. If the event is called
    because of rain, how does this affect your plan? Downhill skiing is always
    programmed on the first day of the Winter Olympics Games in case of
    weather delays.
12. Make your plan in the smallest workable increment. Use a maximum time
    window of 15 minutes. Your must plan televised sport events in second-by-
    second increments (see Chapter 8).

CONDUCTING YOUR PLANNING MEETINGS

The planning meeting sets the mood and the energy level for your
event. Figure 2–1 lists leadership as a strength. Here is your
opportunity to use this skill to empower and motivate your sport
event team members.

   To ensure a successful meeting, use Figure 2–6 as a guide to your
planning meeting.

SETTING BENCHMARKS, CELEBRATING SUCCESS, AND CONTROLLING STRESS

The Atlanta Committee for the Olympic Games (ACOG) celebrated being named the host city for the 1996 Olympic Games

FIGURE 2–6

How to Win a Gold Medal at Your Team Meeting

Step 1: Announce the meeting well in advance to allow each team member to prepare properly.

Step 2: In your meeting announcement, request that each team member submit with their attendance confirmation form any agenda items they want to cover. Circulate an agenda before the meeting.

Step 3: Post a welcome message along with a specific instruction such as "Welcome, Introduce Yourself to Everyone!" Whenever possible, provide light refreshments to offer hospitality and energize the participants.

Step 4: Tom Kayser* of Xerox Corporation suggests that the facilitator use a flip chart. Appoint a scribe to stand by the flip chart and write down the key points covered during the meeting.

Step 5: Always start the meeting on time even if all the participants have not arrived. Latecomers will probably be on time for the next meeting!

Step 6: Review the agenda and ask for any additional items. Keep the opening loose and informal, but try to follow the agenda as much as possible.

Step 7: Build consensus by calling on individual team members to ask their approval of the agenda. Ideally, when you receive comments from team members prior to the meeting, you have achieved consensus. However, use this technique throughout the meeting to draw individuals into the discussion.

Step 8: Once the agenda is approved, summarize it in terms of specific goals and objectives. Seek agreement from the rest of your event team.

Step 9: Allow each member to contribute to the discussion and encourage not only agreement but also positive dissonance.

Step 10: Keep the meeting on schedule. Ask individual team members how much time they will need to present their agenda item. Record their response and use it as a benchmark to keep the meeting on schedule.

Step 11: Alert your team members when only 15 minutes remain until the end of the scheduled meeting. Give them the option of ending on time, continuing the discussion at the next meeting, or postponing the discussion until needed.

Step 12: Always recognize and reward the participants in your meeting prior to ending. Take a moment and compliment the team members for their productivity.

Step 13: End the meeting precisely on time. Your team members will appreciate your promptness and work even harder next time to help you facilitate the meeting when they know that you respect their time.

Step 14: Analyze the positive and negative aspects of the meeting by asking your team members to list what was successful and what could be improved upon in the future.

*Xerox won the prestigious Malcolm Baldridge Award for Excellence and Kayser is the author of *Mining Group Gold* (Serif Publications, 1990) and *Building Team Power* (Irwin Professional Publishing, 1994).

with a parade and other festivities in September 1990. To continue this celebratory feeling for the employees, ACOG management plans a brown-bag lunch on the first Friday of every month up to the beginning of the Olympic Games. Guest speakers at the lunches have included many former Olympians who share their memories of Olympic participation.

Whether you are initiating or concluding your planning period, it is important to remember that you are in the celebration industry. From the smallest planning meeting to the final countdown team assembly, each step of your progress should be celebrated with ceremony and ritual.

Build into your planning cycle a series of miniature benchmark celebrations that allow you to recognize the accomplishments of your team members (e.g., the signing of the first sponsor or the groundbreaking for venue construction). Every successful plan will include many opportunities to celebrate the achievements you and your team have worked hard to attain.

These achievements may be the successful bid for a major sport event or the conclusion of your sponsorship campaign earlier than expected. Whatever the reason, take time to cheer one another. By providing much needed encouragement for your team's spirits, you accelerate the long-term success of the sport event.

Denise Hitchcock, a public relations specialist with the cable Americana Television Network, worked as a member of the management team for the 1984 Los Angeles Olympic Games. Hitchcock noted, "Peter Ueberroth was excellent at constantly rallying the troops. When our spirits started to sag, he found reasons for us to celebrate and I am certain this contributed to the success of the games."

Finally, to absolutely guarantee your success in planning your sport event, use the simple formula given below to stay on schedule and remain focused on your goal.

The Not So Secret Sport Event Formula for Success

Details + Communication + Expert input − Stress = Success

A meeting planner once remarked that more than 3,000 separate decisions are made about any meeting from the beginning of the planning cycle through the management of the event. In the sport event field, this number could easily triple because of the complexity of combining protocols, expectations of different customers (sponsors, event owner, participants, media, spectators), multiple venue sites, various ethnic cultures and populations, and your own creativity.

Indeed, both the left side and right side of the brain receive a tremendous workout as you plan your sport event. The creative as well as the logical sides are essential to your success. Therefore, details, your ability to communicate accurately and freely, and your willingness to gain access to expert advice willcertainly increase your chance for success as you plan your sport event.

It is natural to feel tension and stress when embarking on a new mission. However, allowing your natural tension to turn into stress will be extremely counterproductive to your goal. When feeling stress, try to identify what part of the planning process is causing the stress. You may find that you are not adequately prepared to handle a specialized area such as protocol or financial management.

Once you have identified the cause of your stress, you can remedy this discomfort by delegating the task to an expert on your team. Remember, stress is not productive to long-term achievement of your goal. Deal with it quickly and efficiently so you can get on with planning your successful sport event. Keeping a sense of humor is also vital.

PLANNING FOR CONTINGENCIES

Despite your most careful plan, an act of God or other catastrophic event may occur. If you have planned correctly and professionally you will be able to handle these developments with a minimum of concern on the part of your guests. The following are three examples of potential challenges to your planning program and the contingencies you might develop to deal with them. Other examples are found in Appendix I under "Sample Agreements."

Loss of Key Personnel

The loss of a senior official in your organization could be devastating to operations and staff morale. One way to plan for this contingency is to encourage your team to job share.

Request that they learn each others' jobs and set aside a specific time each week to train one another. During the 1990 Goodwill Games in Seattle, a number of key personnel left at a crucial time in the competition. Several volunteers who had demonstrated leadership potential in the early stages of the games were promoted into management positions. Their previous cross-training enabled them to finish the project successfully.

Weather Emergency

Your corporate golf tournament in Kawai is canceled because of a hurricane. A snow emergency prevents your 70,000 spectators from traveling to your championship basketball tournament. Flooding pollutes the city water system and health officials close all public venues, requiring you to cancel or postpone your gymnastics meet. Advance planning is important in handling these crises. Did you purchase cancellation insurance to protect your investment? Did you have a strategy to notify the participants of an alternative plan that is equal to or exceeds the value of the scheduled tournament? Playing the "what if?" game can help you plan contingencies and prepare for unexpected disasters.

Damage Control: Pool Cooling System Fails

According to Jack Kelly, former executive director of the 1986 U.S. Olympic Festival in Houston, Texas, and current president of the Goodwill Games, "I remember when, two hours before the swim competition in Houston was to begin, I received word that the pool cooling system was not functioning." Thinking quickly, Kelly called every ice company in the area to contribute ice blocks to cool down the pool so the meet could start on time.

SPORT EVENT PLANNING: SUMMARY

As Yogi Berra once said, "It's not over until it's over." Berra was not only a championship baseball player, but also a great strategic planner. He understood that planning has neither a beginning nor an end; it is a continuous series of events interrupted by the event itself.

As a professional sport event planner, you must constantly be planning to improve your event through a thorough evaluation process. This process begins with your first meeting and continues long after the event has concluded and you begin planning the next event.

By analyzing the strengths, weaknesses, opportunities, and threats (SWOT), you are able to take a critical look at the universe within your organization and around your event.

As you develop your plan, you will achieve success through a series of team meetings. If these meetings are organized for maximum effectiveness, you will move efficiently toward your strategic sport event goal. And if you celebrate even small successes, you will raise the self-confidence of your team and keep spirits high.

Most important, there is no challenge that cannot be overcome with proper contingency planning. Practice damage control as you develop your plan to ensure that small problems do not have overwhelming consequences. Like sport itself, practice makes perfect—or at least minimizes risks and injuries.

The famous architect Mies van der Rohe reportedly said, "God is in the details," and so it is with the first critical process of producing a successful sport event. Attend to the most minute detail, communicate freely, insist on expert input, and resist stress to achieve the sport event for which you have planned.

Planning successful sport events is equal parts art and science. In Chapter 3, you will find that designing, planning, and controlling event logistics is a not-so-precise science that will greatly influence the outcome of the artwork for your sport event.

GAME HIGHLIGHTS

- Conduct a SWOT analysis to determine the internal and external variables that may affect your event.
- Organize your meetings to reflect the success you plan to achieve with your event. After all, a good meeting is an event.
- Plan for every possible contingency and practice damage control to prevent a minor problem from becoming a major catastrophe.

PLAY BOOK

contingency plan A fundamental component of any successful planning process through which you determine how to minimize the risk of any unforeseen negative activity before, during, or following your event.

plan The continuous process through which every possible detail is communicated, using expert input while resisting stressful situations, in order to achieve your specific goals and objectives.

SWOT analysis A technique for identifying and assessing your organization's strengths, weaknesses, opportunities, and threats.

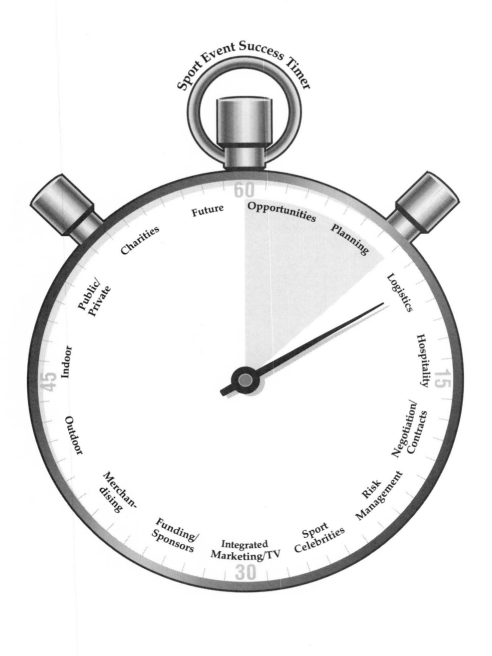

Sport Event Success Timer

Future Opportunities Planning

Charities

Public/ Private

Logistics

Indoor

Hospitality

45

15

Outdoor

Negotiation/ Contracts

Merchan-
dising

Risk
Management

Funding/
Sponsors

Sport
Celebrities

Integrated
Marketing/TV

30

Chapter Three

Designing, Planning, and Controlling Event Logistics

"You can't think and hit at the same time."

Yogi Berra

W hy is attention to the most minute detail critical to your success in planning sport events and how can you make certain that every aspect of your event is carefully designed to satisfy the needs of every constituency group?

ASKING THE RIGHT QUESTIONS

Barry Silberman, president of Centre Management, offers this important advice in producing a sport event: "Gather as much information as possible. You can never ask too many questions and if you assume that you know what your client is talking about, you may find yourself in big trouble." Silberman, for example, assumed that the soil used for bull riding and tractor pulls at the USAIR Arena would be suitable for the Spanish Riding School of Vienna. Unfortunately, he did not find out until the last minute that a different loam quality or pebble content was required for this horse event. The only solution was for staff members to scramble and pick pebbles from the soil.

Likewise, event organizers should be aware that there is a special salt-free sand used for indoor beach volleyball events. The salt in regular sand could affect the ice-making ability of the venue.

Silberman also emphasizes the need to ask the right questions. For indoor tractor pulls, it is important to find out the weight and amount of vibration that will be placed on the floor and investigate whether it will ruin any ice-making equipment under the floor. When you are asked to produce an event that you have not done before, the first thing you should do is call someone who has. You can also ask the appropriate sport governing body for recommendations (see Appendix II-E for listings).

LOGISTICS

Of the many different sport events that Barry Silberman has produced, he believes that events that attract a great many teams, extensive media, and on-site hospitality, such as the NCAA Basketball Tournament, are the most complex to host. Silberman considered the NCAA to be a "great client" because it knew what it wanted and had specific guidelines to achieve this. Throughout the event, everyone knew what they had to do and people from the NCAA monitored all activities. In all sport events, logistics are a critical consideration and a determining factor in the success of the sport event.

Often the most brilliant idea has gone sour owing to poor logistical planning. How many times have you attended a function with a magnificently displayed buffet only to stand in line for what seemed like hours because only one line was prepared rather than two? A good rule of thumb is one food or beverage line for every 75 to 100 people.

The term *logistics* is derived from the Greek *logistikos* (the science of calculating), and *logos*, which means reason. Logistics, in modern usage, also means handling the details of any operation. To combine the two, we might ask the question, can the sport event manager direct his or her creativity into a reasonable path that will produce an effective event?

The answer should be yes if you are to ensure safety, respect the public trust placed in you, and meet the goals and objectives established for the event.

In Chapter 1, we discussed the relationships between sport and special event and noted that while the outcome cannot always be predicted, practice will increase the chances for success. But when you create a logistical plan, you are certain to increase your chances for success. The level of logistical planning is directly influenced by the conditions surrounding the event (e.g., number of different sports and venues, level of competition).

In this chapter, we will examine all dimensions of logistical planning for sport events. Appendix II has samples of a production schedule and a master plan showing how logistics function within the framework of your sport event.

Figure 3–1 offers a checklist of some of the conditions that must first be determined before you can begin your logistical planning. Use this checklist as a reminder during your planning.

Once you have answered these questions, you will have a better idea of your logistical and operational requirements and can begin to develop an organizational structure. An organizational structure identifies the direct order of report so you can effectively plan and manage all the details of your event. Key positions and external contacts should also be identified to support the organizational structure (see Figures 3–2 and 3–3).

Now that you have a general idea of the organization and individuals involved in a sport event, we can provide more specific details on high-priority considerations. Keep in mind, however, the advice provided by Barry Glassman, formerly program coordinator for the Muscular Dystrophy Association: "The best way to learn how to produce a sport event is to attend and participate in as many as possible, particularly your competitors. There is no need to reinvent the wheel, just learn how to make it better."

VOLUNTEERS

Sport events typically require intensive volunteer manpower. According to Jeff Ruday, vice president, Streetball Partners of Dallas, Texas:

> A three-on-three basketball tournament with 800 to 1,000 participants will require approximately 500 volunteers. If you have 70 courts, you will need two volunteers to serve as court monitors per court per day, plus others to man refreshments, registration, score table, and so forth, not to mention setup and breakdown of equipment.

FIGURE 3–1

Sport Event Logistical Conditions Checklist

_____ What is the purpose of the event—raise money, generate media attention, product marketing, customer entertainment?

_____ How large is the event—number of participants, spectators, media, and VIPs?

_____ Will the event be held indoors, outdoors, or both?

_____ How many venues will be used and how far apart are they?

_____ What are the requirements of the facility and do they meet Americans with Disabilities Act (ADA) and health department standards?

_____ Is there a need to build or renovate the venue?

_____ How much time is required for setup and takedown of the sport event?

_____ Will food and beverages be served and, if so, what permits are required?

_____ What type of food is appropriate to serve?

_____ Will food and beverage be dispensed free, paid by prepurchased ticket, or paid with cash at the event?

_____ How many guests do you guarantee for?

_____ What type of entertainment, if any, will be provided?

_____ Are ceremonies scheduled?

_____ Will the athletes, spectators, and media arrive and depart by private automobile, private motorcoach, or public transportation (type of transportation, itinerary, and special needs)?

_____ How will staff and volunteers arrive and depart from their assigned locations?

_____ What housing requirements are needed for athletes, media, VIPs, and spectators?

_____ Is enough housing available to accommodate all contingencies?

_____ What are the sanitation needs (portable toilets guideline: 1 per 100–200 people)?

_____ Will the audience include a large segment requiring special accommodation (e.g., disabled, senior citizens, multilingual speakers)?

_____ Will the spectators pay to attend, receive free admission, or have a combination of admissions?

_____ What is the appropriate entrance fee?

_____ How will tickets be sold and distributed?

_____ What is the seating configuration—stadium, thrust (3/4 round wherein the audience sits on 3 sides of the stage), auditorium, or a combination of seating designs?

_____ Is general, reserved, or festival seating ordered for the event?

_____ How many staff and/or volunteers does your event require? (*Warning*: Experienced event managers say that 20 percent of volunteers typically do not appear the day of the event.)

_____ What additional training will be required for staff and volunteers?

_____ Should special outfitting be ordered for event staff and volunteers?

continued

FIGURE 3–1 concluded

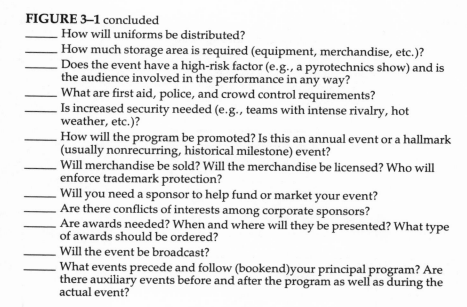

_____ How will uniforms be distributed?

_____ How much storage area is required (equipment, merchandise, etc.)?

_____ Does the event have a high-risk factor (e.g., a pyrotechnics show) and is the audience involved in the performance in any way?

_____ What are first aid, police, and crowd control requirements?

_____ Is increased security needed (e.g., teams with intense rivalry, hot weather, etc.)?

_____ How will the program be promoted? Is this an annual event or a hallmark (usually nonrecurring, historical milestone) event?

_____ Will merchandise be sold? Will the merchandise be licensed? Who will enforce trademark protection?

_____ Will you need a sponsor to help fund or market your event?

_____ Are there conflicts of interests among corporate sponsors?

_____ Are awards needed? When and where will they be presented? What type of awards should be ordered?

_____ Will the event be broadcast?

_____ What events precede and follow (bookend)your principal program? Are there auxiliary events before and after the program as well as during the actual event?

Recruitment and training of volunteers is important in all sport events. A charity or sponsor associated with an event is a good source for volunteers. Another successful way to recruit volunteers is to mention the need for volunteers in your promotional materials. Popular events such as the Cherry Blossom Run in Washington, D.C., which requires a lottery drawing to enter, offers volunteers an automatic registration for the following year. Megaevents such as World Cup Soccer require a very structured volunteer recruitment and training program. A volunteer coordinator is typically hired to develop and oversee such programs. The United Way has developed volunteer coordination into an art that is a model for other organizations to follow. Contact your local United Way for help and assistance.

Training programs typically include a basic educational component followed by specific department training. Simulation exercises should be included in these sessions where potential scenarios are played out as close to reality as possible. Volunteers with radios in hand should sit around a table while a problem is posed. They should then simulate what they would say and do to rectify the problem.

FIGURE 3–2

The Organizational Chart

This chart is an example of the management personnel
involved in planning and operating a sport event.

Event Manager

Event Assistant Manager

Marketing	Sales	Operations	Legal	Financial
Advertising	Direct Mail	Grounds	Contracts/ Licenses	Budget
Media	Merchandise Licensing	Buildings	Risk Management/ Insurance	Payables/ Receivables
Public Relations	Tickets	Other Utilities	Personnel	Investments
Hospitality		Communications		Auditing/ Accounting

Once the day of the event arrives, let the volunteers take charge.
Tell them to do what they have to do (get more ice, water, call
emergency services, etc.) to make the event enjoyable and safe for
participants. Make sure your volunteers understand that the
customer is always right.

FIGURE 3–3

Key Personnel and Important Contacts

Each person in charge is a critical link to the future cohesion of your entire event.

- Admissions Supervisor
- Athletic Trainers
- Box Office Supervisor
- Buildings Supervisor
- Catering Manager
- Civic, Municipal, and Federal officials
- Communications Manager (public address, radios, scoreboard, internal-wireless, and external-public telephones)
- Convention and Visitors Bureau Director
- Emergency Services Supervisor
- Entertainment Coordinator
- Fire Marshal
- Grounds Supervisor
- Housing Coordinator
- HVAC (heating, ventilation, air-conditioning) Supervisor
- International Officials, Delegation Leaders
- Marketing Director
- Media Center Director
- Medical Supervisor
- Military Leadership
- Parking Supervisor
- Police
- Protocol Expert
- Public Relations Director
- Public Safety (signage, non-marketing) Supervisor
- Sanitation Supervisor
- Security Supervisor
- Television Producer
- Transportation Supervisor
- Utilities Supervisors (electric, water, gas)
- Volunteer Coordinator

Whether volunteers or paid employees, you should appoint troubleshooters to supervise the setup of the event, the flow of people, and the breakdown of the event.

UNIFORM DESIGN AND DISTRIBUTION

Have you ever wondered why certain sport event volunteers and staff members are dressed the way they are? Have you ever considered the planning it takes to design, manufacture, and ultimately distribute all those outfits? According to Andrew Marsh, a veteran sport event manager and a Uniform Distribution Coordinator for World Cup USA 1994, this is one of the most challenging yet important pre-event logistic. The uniforms of the staff and volunteers and perhaps even the contractors and vendors should reflect the "look" of the event. Not only will uniforms provide a means of identification and authority for the staff, but they bring class to the event.

Well before the event begins, the style, color, and fabric of the uniforms are selected for specific reasons. For example, the executive staff, interpreters, adminstrators, and hosts and host-esses may be outfitted in a blazer and slacks or skirts and blouses since it is likely that they will interact with the media, sponsor representatives, or public officials. To avoid confusion among the patrons and to build team spirit, each division within the man-agement team should have a unique uniform color and style. The admissions or public information staff may wear a blue polo shirt and matching shorts or pants while the ushers wear a red T-shirt or windbreaker. The operations and support staff are outfitted in more casual attire, such as shorts and a T-shirt so not to affect their work, that is, setting up equipment. The uniforms for security and medical staff must be readily identifiable yet not threatening to the spectator. The security guards for the World Cup wore a khaki uniform complete with purple berets reflecting the international and peaceful flavor of the games. The medical personnel wore white jackets with an internationally recognized green cross on front and back. The uniform fabric must be selected with consid-eration for the weather and temperature. Obviously, you do not want wool uniforms for a summertime event or shorts in the winter.

Depending on the number of staff involved, the style (e.g., elastic waste or button) and number of pieces in the uniform, sizing and distribution could be problematic. It is very important that the staff, particularly the volunteers, get the correct uniform and that it fits well. An ill-fitting uniform would reflect poorly on the event and for a volunteer with shorts three times too big, make it doubtful that he or she will enjoy helping you out. It is important to consider these points when selecting uniforms:

• sizing;
• ordering in time for manufacture;
• in-kind sponsorship of uniform parts;

- simple distribution;
- exchanges/return policy;
- alteration of executive uniforms.

When Lisa Delpy volunteered for the 1988 Seoul Olympic Games, she first reported to a warehouse where she was measured for her uniform and provided a shoe coupon. This coupon was redeemable at certain stores throughout the city that carried the official uniform shoe. Lisa later returned to retrieve her uniform, at which time her credential was scanned and she was checked off as receiving all pieces of the uniform.

FACILITIES

Venue selection is extremely important but may be limited by the type of sport event and availability within your region. Each sport governing body provides guidelines on required venue dimensions and amenities in order for an event to be officially sanctioned. The number and type of permits and restrictions demanded by a venue may also influence your decision. You must also consider the expected size of the crowd. You do not want to hold your event in a 15,000-seat arena if only 2,000 people will attend.

Access to public transportation is another critical factor. Again, one of the most efficient ways of handling these challenges is to find out what others have done in similar situations. If at all possible, select a venue with a suitable area for hospitality. The Reston Town Center in Virginia, where the Muscular Dystrophy Association (MDA) Tour de Bud bicycle event takes place, has a public pavilion equipped for food service. Such amenities reduce the overhead of tents and trailers.

A sport event that requires a great deal of equipment will need a storage facility. Each cross-country skier at the 1994 Winter Olympic Games brought approximately 30 pairs of skis. That meant that between 40 to 70 tons of sport equipment needed to be secured and stored during the games.

Ask athletes for course ideas in sports such as cycling and running. Try to keep participants off the main roads and avoid traffic lights and turns; if the course is straight, you need fewer directional signs. Posting volunteers at major intersections for safety and directional purposes is also important.

WEATHER

When 1987 Super Bowl producer Dan Witkowski scheduled his final dress rehearsal for the halftime show in the afternoon, there was a method to his madness. First, he wanted to have a fallback plan if the anticipated rains actually appeared that night. Second, he wanted the network television crew to tape the show in the same light in which the cast would perform during the game. Fortunately for Witkowski, the rain never came and he was able to have not one but two full dress rehearsals that day.

Scheduling is only one consideration under weather conditions. The number of staff and volunteers required for an event also depends on the weather. More people will be needed to shovel snow and prepare grounds in bad weather. Inclement weather, or merely the threat of it, can clog highways or reduce audience size. Have standby crews in place in the event of inclement weather.

The *Farmer's Almanac* is a useful tool in predicting likely weather conditions; however, as the date of the event approaches, the National Weather Service is a better gauge of rapidly changing meteorological activity. Still another source of weather information is the Federal Aviation Agency located at your local airport. Ask the agency for recommendations on weather conditions and your future activities.

Whether you hire a personal meteorologist or merely raise your index finger to check the wind direction, paying attention to the weather is a major logistical consideration before, during, and immediately after your event.

TRANSPORTATION: SPECTATOR ARRIVALS AND DEPARTURES

Professional parking lot supervisors use the terms *trickle* and *dump* to describe the rate at which spectators will attend your event.

FIGURE 3–4

Traffic Patterns to Consider in Planning

1. Athlete housing → practice field → competition area → media center → cultural/social activities
2. Media housing → media center → practice field → competition area → cultural/social activities
3. VIP housing → competition areas → special requests
4. Spectator pick up points → competition areas

Trickle means exactly what its image conveys. Your guests will come and go from the sport event throughout a given period of time rather than all arrive and depart at the same time. Dump means the opposite of trickle and describes all the guests arriving within a narrow window of time such as 30 minutes prior to the event and within one hour following it.

These arrival and departure activities not only involve public safety but also interact with the entire hospitality experience. A spectator's first impression of your event may be through the automobile windshield upon arrival in your parking lot. The last impression most certainly will be of your parking facility and traffic control.

Determine early on the means by which guests, athletes, and media will arrive. Then design and control transportation and parking logistics to meet their needs (see Figure 3-4). Do you have a jumper cable service in your lot to assist stranded drivers? Do you have adequate lighting, signage, and parking hosts that make the guest feel secure and at the same time help reduce the likelihood of crime? Should you provide a parking shuttle from the satellite parking lot to the front gate to assist your guests and reduce parking congestion? Should you work closely with a municipal transportation agency to encourage spectators to use mass transit by offering an incentive such as a discount admission or a sponsored ad gift specialty? In order to avoid a large rush of traffic to the opening ceremonies of the 1988 Calgary Olympic Games, Maxwell House hosted a community breakfast that attracted many people to the stadium early. The goal of any successful arrival and departure is to ensure a safe, easy, and fun experience for the spectator.

Although the 1994 Winter Olympic Games in Norway was a great success overall, author Lisa Delpy would have improved spectator transportation. Unfortunately, services for the average spectator at major events such as the Olympic Games are low priority. George Dales, former track and field coach at Western Michigan University in Kalamazoo, once said "The games are first for the television audience, then VIPs, corporate sponsors, athletes, media, and finally paying spectators." When the director of transportation for the Lillehammer Olympic Organizing Committee, Osmund Ueland, was asked about the transportation difficulties (e.g., long lines, inconsistent schedules, confusion over the purchase and price of bus tickets), he explained:

> More people were staying in Lillehammer than previously expected so until we were able to reallocate buses from outlying areas a shortage existed. In terms of ticket logistics, when the Norwegians originally purchased their tickets they had the opportunity to buy a discounted reserve ticket for bus transportation as well.

Most foreigners, however, were not aware of this offer and were confused when the bus driver asked for a reserved ticket. Frequently, an event credential or admission ticket allows free access to public transportation. Such is the case for the 1996 Summer Olympic Games to be held in Atlanta.

In order to make transporting guests a fun experience, put yourself in the position of the guest who has had the worst possible time prior to arriving at your parking facility. Perhaps they traveled halfway to the venue and then discovered that they didn't have their tickets and had to return home. Or perhaps the guest ran out of gas and had to walk the rest of the way. What can you do as a sport event management professional to transform their unpleasant experience into a surprisingly positive one? The answer you design will control their behavior and improve their perception and appreciation of your event.

TRANSPORTATION: ATHLETES, MEDIA, AND VIP GUESTS

Transportation of athletes, VIP guests, media and other official needs to be considered for larger events. Depending on your needs, transportation, in some cases, can be contracted out in whole or in part. Transportation, of VIP guests can be as simple as hiring a limousine or as complex as hiring a bus company with hosts and hostesses on each vehicle.

At larger sport events, credentialing and the treatment of athletes, media, and VIPs also becomes very important to transportation issues. Athletes will require transportation to and from their living accommodations, practice fields, and competition arenas, as well as transportation for shopping or sight-seeing excursions. When transporting athletes to and from the airport or to competition and practice venues, remember to request the appropriate type of vehicle (e.g. trucks for bicycles or pole vault equipment) or at least provide specialized equipment such as a bicycle rack for a car. Media may require transportation to and from the main press center, their housing accommodations, and the athletic venues.

Transportation logistics such as the overlap of beginning and ending times in multisport and venue events are very important. Miscalculation and coordination of buses could cause major traffic congestion. At the 1984 Los Angeles Olympic Games, normal traffic patterns were studied and events scheduled accordingly.

Continual monitoring is necessary to either increase or decrease the number of buses in circulation on each traffic pattern. Organizers of the 1994 Winter Olympic Games at Lillehammer had hoped for, but did not actually expect so many people to use mass transportation. Therefore, transportation was inadequate until adjustments were made and buses shuffled to new routes. Although 80 percent of all spectators ended up using public transportation, the organizing committee had to plan for large parking areas. In addition, make sure your limousines and buses have a predetermined area to stage.

Organizing the transportation of event entertainment may also become an issue. When Frank Supovitz had to transport over 1,000 halftime show participants to San Diego's Jack Murphy Stadium for the Super Bowl, he knew he had to have plan A, B, and possibly C:

> When you are moving large groups into a crowded area you must not only work with local police to establish a traffic pattern but also plan for emergencies such as the bus breaking down and other emergencies which require an immediate remedy to keep the schedule on time.

Transportation for high school, collegiate, and professional sport events must also be coordinated and monitored. Monica Barrett, the athletic director at Cactus Shadows High School in Cave Creek, Arizona, schedules transportation one year ahead, but the day before each sport event she always double-checks the exact departure time and the bus driver's name and home number in case of emergency. Professional teams hire travel managers to handle all ticketing, equipment cargo, and local transportation needs.

The checklist in Figure 3–5 will help keep your schedule running smoothly as you plan and execute your transportation manifest.

FIGURE 3–5

Transporting Athletes and Participants Smoothly

1. Identify all transportation and parking needs (athletes, VIPs, media, spectators, entertainment).
2. Make certain all riders have proper credentials.
3. Confirm that the bus company has appropriate parking passes, accurate and the latest manifest listing all riders, schedule of pickup and delivery, and routes.
4. Verify that all bus drivers are connected through communications to a central dispatcher who reports to you.
5. Work with local police, traffic, and parking officials to produce an accurate map showing the confirmed transportation route, including specific drop-off points, pickup points, and parking designation.
6. Prepare with authorities a separate alternate route to be used in case of emergencies (threats, traffic jams).
7. Assign one person to confirm and verify that the entrance gate is accessible to all transportation and that the guard has been briefed.
8. Position one staff person at the transportation arrival area to keep the area clear and to greet riders and direct them to their appropriate entrance.
9. Confirm that the bus company has insurance and has named your organization as an additional insured party.
10. Do not identify buses with specific names. This attracts attention. Instead, use a simple numbering system and give each rider a pass with the same number.
11. Know the phone number for a 24-hour towing service in case any bus requires assistance. Arrange with the operator of the tow truck to be on standby during the transportation period. Always have a spare bus ready to go in case stranded riders must be transferred.
11. Arrange for a security escort if protocol requires it.
12. Provide a rest area with refreshments for the bus and limousine drivers during the event.

When providing transportation, make sure to inform guests of the length of the journey, especially if there are no bathroom facilities on board the vehicle. Also, take advantage of this opportunity to make a first impression by introducing your guests to the area. Ask the transportation hosts and hostesses to provide information and interesting details along the journey. Your guests will also appreciate refreshments if the trip is particularly long. Guests arriving from great distances can be irritable, so you can use this initial greeting to promote a happier attitude. A good first impression is particularly important for the media because you always want positive press coverage. Make arrangements beforehand for special media parking and have a media area or building designated specifically for their use.

SPECIAL ACCOMMODATIONS

"Whether the athletes participating in your sport event are disabled or not, there are a number of reasons to make your venue accessible to all," explains Kirk Bauer, executive director of the National Handicapped Sport Association (NHSA). First, a tremendous untapped market of over 40 million disabled people are interested in attending sport events if they are accessible. Most of these individuals have money and want to enjoy life. Second, disabled athletes who participate in regular sport competitions have become a media attraction. The U.S. Track and Field Association, for example, invites top disabled athletes to compete in demonstration races during their national championships.

Equal Access for the Disabled

With the advent of the Americans with Disabilities Act (ADA) in 1988, the U.S. government has mandated that certain reasonable accommodations be made to provide equal access for persons with disabilities. Throughout the United States, ramps have been built, handrails have been hung, and infrared listening systems have been installed. These reasonable accommodations allow disabled spectators to enjoy the sport event without undue restriction.

The key to ADA is that the disabled spectator must be afforded the same *equal* access as a spectator without disabilities. This means that a spectator in a wheelchair must be able to enter the front door of a restaurant along with other patrons and not be carried in through the kitchen entrance. As you plan your sport event, you must survey the needs of your spectators and identify any individuals or groups who may require special accommodations. Sport events such as the Paralympic Games obviously will have a much higher number of disabled individuals in attendance than football bowl games, which typically attract the nondisabled general public. However, your group sales division may sell a block of seats to a group of disabled spectators. Therefore, you must make plans to provide them with similar accommodations.

The infrared devices available in stadiums, arenas, and theaters allow hearing-impaired spectators to better hear the announcer or entertainers in your sport event. Hearing-impaired guests often have difficulty adjusting to strobe lights or other rapidly blinking lights. To avoid this difficulty, post a sign to notify your spectators that "Strobe Lights Are in Use during This Performance". You may also wish to schedule several sign language–interpreted performances of the event or provide a sign language interpreter during the program to assist hearing-impaired guests. Today, "The Star-Spangled Banner" is commonly signed in conjunction with the vocalist.

Planning for the Disabled

As a producer of a sport event for disabled athletes, you need to identify all venue limitations and remove barriers for the visually, auditorially, and physically impaired. Bobbi Avancena, public information director for the NHSA, says:

> For the 52 events we coordinate annually, we have a program manager who conducts a site visit with a checklist they have created for the specific event. For large events, this inspection occurs eight months before the actual event. Perhaps one day we will establish actual standards or guidelines to provide a uniform assessment for each event.

It is the law to have public facilities for sport events architecturally accessible. In private venues, you may need to build temporary ramps with plywood or remove stall doors. Changing rooms with seats should also be available for athletes who need to remove artificial limbs prior to competition.

The disabled parking plan is also critical for temporary venues. Frequently, sport events held in temporary locations do not always plan adequately to assign parking for disabled spectators. Make certain that you determine how many spaces are required by local ordinance and that you assign them in the correct location with appropriate signage.

Bauer also suggests including the following considerations in the planning of a sport event with disabled athletes.

A certain number of volunteers should be assigned as facilitators to help the blind adjust to unfamiliar territory, aid wheelchair athletes up steep grades not built to code, or help in the transfer from the wheelchair into sport equipment or into the pool. This last responsibility requires the volunteer to have some knowledge on appropriate and safe transfer procedures.

Another unique logistical consideration in regard to producing sport events for the disabled are the various categories that must be included. The National Amputee Summer Games have classifications such as wheelchair, stand up, and blind so that athletes compete on an equal playing field. In addition, there are three levels of visual impairment. In disabled ski competitions, there are 15 different physically and visually impaired classifications. If a wheelchair category is included in a regular run, special consideration of the terrain should be made. Avoid steep and windy hills and try to select hard concrete surfaces over gravel surfaces.

Senior Citizens

As the median age of Americans continues to rise, design the logistics for your event to welcome senior spectators, many of whom have disabilities.

From handrails to large-print programs and adequate lighting, senior citizens require special considerations to cope with the infirmities of age. Do not make senior citizens feel old by treating them as infirm. Instead, plan ahead to provide the necessary accommodations so they enjoy your sport event.

Foreign Visitors

Another population to consider for special services are foreign visitors. A greater number of people travel to distant lands as tourists or for business purposes. A major event during these travels may be a sport event.

The cultural differences among people are melting due to mass communications. However, language can still be a major hurdle for spectators who attend your event. To lower this hurdle, plan to provide simultaneous interpretation systems, multilingual signage, and even live interpreters for groups. Anticipate the confusion and anxiety these foreign guests may feel at your event and elevate their experiences through your careful and thoughtful logistical planning.

When planning multilingual programs remember the transportation system. A multilingual driver or host on board might provide a better first impression for your foreign visitors.

FOOD AND BEVERAGE

Susan Gersten, vice president and director of major events for Ridgewell's, a catering firm in Bethesda, Maryland, first became involved with sport event hospitality in 1988 and has since developed a profitable niche for the 60-year-old catering company. She has truly witnessed sport hospitality escalate and transform into big business. To illustrate the rapid growth, Susan mentioned that "10 years ago there were 6 tents at the U.S. Open and in 1993 there were 47. A tent that cost $12,500 at the Preakness in 1988 would today cost approximately $25,000 plus." Of course, the demand and cost for hospitality varies in different demographic regions. At the 1993 Super Bowl in Pasadena, California, Hyatt's Regency Productions sold one large tent to 80 different corporations and 24 separate ones for a grand total of 6,000 people.

The tradition of food at sport events started during the era of folk games and continues as a strong influence today. At games like the

NFL Super Bowl, the per capita expenditure on food and beverage may climb to $50 or more per person. Food and beverage is not only big business in sport events, it is also a serious logistical concern for a variety of interrelated reasons.

Licenses and Permits

Not the least of these concerns is liquor liability. In this era of mass litigation, concessionaires are rightly concerned about the pouring laws in their jurisdiction and are investing heavily in training programs for their staffs to make certain that the dispensing of alcoholic beverages is in accordance with the law. Beer and sport seem to be inseparable. Therefore, it is important for the sport event professional to work closely with local bottlers and licensing jurisdictions to make certain their event is in absolute compliance with all applicable laws. One major logistical consideration is who will hold the liquor license for the event. Make certain you thoroughly investigate whether beer, wine, or liquor is dispensed free or sold. If the venue "club house" has a liquor license, you may not need to apply for a separate license.

Wherever alcoholic beverages are sold, restrictions that include the legal age of consumption come into play. Check with local officials to determine how individuals are to be carded in order to guarantee that they can purchase alcoholic beverages legally at your event.

The health department will also require your sport event to obtain a license or permit to dispense food. A host of regulations will be required to obtain this license, including in some jurisdictions running water for each food stand and netting to protect food from foreign substances. Some jurisdictions may require food handlers to have individual licenses and to wear specific clothing such as protective headgear. The sponsor, manager, host, or concessionaire dispensing the food or beverage has a responsibility to know the law and comply accordingly. Therefore, before you handle any food or beverage, make sure you learn what is required in order to feed the multitudes who come to your event. This information can be obtained directly through the health department in the appropriate geographical jurisdiction.

Purchasing, Inventory, and Distribution of Goods

Purchasing, inventory, and distribution of goods, and the design of the service counter are other logistical concerns about food and beverage. You must consider the type of event (number of stops in play), time of event (meal time or snack time), capacity of venue, amount of tickets sold, and the weather, particularly if food or beverage is sold outdoors. And you must know where the food and beverage will be warehoused, how it will be transferred, and who is accountable. Placement and design of service stands should also be considered in terms of space allocation for maximum efficiency and spectator access. Quality can only be maintained through continual evaluation of needs and the distribution service.

Determining Final Guarantees

A final guarantee on the number of guests or amount of food is usually required 36 to 72 hours in advance of the event. This guaranteed date and time is critical. If you miss it, you may be obliged to pay for the number of guests you estimated in the original contract. When determining the final guarantee, consider that if the event is free, it is typically safe to guarantee for 15% under the actual number of confirmed reservations. (See Chapter 4 for more information.)

TICKETING AND ADMISSIONS

Admission may include the purchase of food and beverage tickets or merely cover the gate or entry fee. Regardless, the sale of tickets is a logistical challenge that can determine the financial success or doom of your sport event. Your first major decision should concern the distribution network. Will you print and distribute your own tickets? Options include selecting a company such as TicketMaster that prints, sells, and accounts for all tickets for an added premium, doing it in-house, or choosing some combination of the two. In selecting an outside ticketing agency to distribute your tickets, find out who has exclusive rights and how extensive the distribution channels are in your area. Once you have identified the company, negotiate royalties and service charges. Ticket service charges can vary depending on the price of the ticket and the event itself. High-end boxing tickets of $400 or more increase the distributor's risk; thus a service charge of $10 may be added. As the host organizer, you should remain in control of the computer setup and reserve certain sections of seats or earmark seats with obstructed views.

Mark McCullens, director of admissions for the Robert F. Kennedy (RFK) Stadium in Washington, D.C., states:

> Communication is the key to success in sport events. If all advanced specifications are not accurate, ticketing becomes a problem. An example is a pole that was said to be 20-feet tall and turns out to be 40 feet and blocks the view of 15 seats. Or the top lighting shelf of a boxing ring is wider than communicated, and blocks the view of spectators in the upper seats. Or when playing on the regulation-size field for World Cup Soccer, the corner of the field is obstructed in the upper-level seats. Since this does not allow spectators to see the corner kick, such seats must be identified as obstructed seats.

Forgery of tickets and scalping are major concerns for sport event management officials. It is important that you seek expert counsel either from an experienced ticketing firm such as Globe or an accounting firm specializing in entertainment events.

Security for ticketing and admissions is essential to ensure the safe collection, accounting, and deposit of funds. An experienced accounting firm can assist you with developing certain protocols to reduce the risk of your cash management. Make certain that each ticket booth has police or armed private security supervision and that the transfer of funds is made either by armored truck or with a police escort. Vary the time you transfer funds and alternate your route.

All ticketing and admissions personnel or the principal contractor for this area should be bonded to guarantee your investment. In addition, each ticketing and admissions worker should be trained, supervised, and checked in and out of the operation to ensure fidelity.

Glassman secures his financial intake at sport events by keeping more than one person on each money-collecting and counting position. He advises that "no one person should be in charge of collecting, counting, and depositing money. A series of checks and balances should be in place to protect your assets, including dual signatures on checks."

Many sport event managers have successfully used a secret spectator system to catch dishonest ticketing and admissions personnel committing a felonious act. If these persons are aware that secret spectators are being used, they may think twice before committing a crime. Admission losses can also be reduced by using glitter or raised lettering on tickets or boldly printing the date or game number to easily identify the tickets.

Jim Dalrymple, general manager of RFK Stadium, has implemented a number of different admission loss-prevention plans. The placement of plainclothes observers in front and behind entrance gates help in identifying admission fraud. He also rotates ticket supervisors in no particular order—sometimes clockwise every gate, at other times counterclockwise every two gates.

In sport events as in general entertainment, credentialing has grown in importance with increased criminal activity. Make certain that all admissions personnel are thoroughly familiar with the various credentials and test them to make sure they can easily spot counterfeit identification. (See Chapter 6 for specific information on credentials.)

FREE, PAID, GENERAL, RESERVED, FESTIVAL

Each sport event will be defined from either a ticketing or a seating perspective by one or more of these terms. It is important that you become familiar with each and understand the variances.

Free sport event. No admission is charged in this event. Tickets may be issued, however, and some ticket firms may charge a small handling fee for even a free ticket. The handling charge covers the reservation labor and the postage cost. Some free events charge fees for merchandise and food and beverage. When you are told an event is free, investigate further to find out whether any funds are being collected, perhaps through spontaneous donations. This is important because you may be liable to taxation authorities.

Paid sport event. Funds are collected for admission to this event regardless of what the fee covers. At some paid sport events, the admission fee merely buys a seat while at others the fee includes a donation to a charitable organization. At still others, the fee includes a package of goods and services such as parking, pre-event hospitality, and postevent receptions.

General admission.   This does not mean first come, first served. Rather, it is a lower-priced seating with, usually, a lower ticket price. General admission seating usually is a large section with a more distant view of the sport event.

Reserved seating.   This is a premium ticket price with prime seating located close to event activities. The seats are often of better physical quality than general admission seats.

Luxury boxes or suites.   These are usually leased by corporations, require a catering service, and often an exclusive entrance in addition to special ticketing requirements.

Festival seating.   Auditorium and stadium managers in the sport event field do not look favorably upon this type of seating because major riots have occurred as enraged fans have stampeded for seats. Festival seating is also referred to as **open seating**, allowing the spectator to choose his or her seat without prior assignment by ticket number. Obviously, the first arrivals will rush to the front rows, creating a domino effect for the remainder of the audience. Most venues have banned festival seating for safety and security reasons.

The type of admission and seating plan you select will ultimately determine the level of logistical planning required for your event. When free festival seating is offered, more security is required to restrain the spectators. If you select paid reserved seating, less security is needed because of the orderly seating system you have planned. However, each event requires a different level of logistical preparation. You can ease your burden by making certain you match the type of ticketing and plan of seating to the audience to assure your guests of a smooth operation.

SEATING DESIGN AND CONTROL

Stadium-style seating is traditional for the sport event. It uses four sides of the stadium for the spectators to view the event. However, with the high-tech spectaculars planned for the Olympic Games and major bowl games, the sky is the limit. Today, three types of seating predominate sport events. In addition to a stadium style, spectators may experience a thrust style where the action "thrusts" into the middle of the audience seated on three sides. In an auditorium style, the audience is seated out front and the action takes place on only one side of the athletic field (see Figure 3–6).

Not surprisingly, television has had a major influence on the staging of sport events. The Michael Jackson halftime spectacular at the 1993 Super Bowl was, for the most part, staged as a proscenium production to allow maximum control for television production. The proscenium style is a temporary auditorium style combined with the general stadium style in which only one side of the audience gets to view the event. The Pan American Games in Indianapolis, Indiana, produced by the Walt Disney Company were staged in a thrust style to allow for maximum crowd shots. The Barcelona Olympic Games were staged in a combination of styles ranging from stadium to auditorium that involved not only the live spectators but also the billion television viewers tuned in from around the world.

As you prepare your logistical plan for the seating configuration of your sport event, remember that the more angles involved in production the higher the cost. Although the proscenium style is more cost-effective, the stadium style allows spectators greater participation. Consult with your television producer to ensure that your staging and seating will allow the maximization of television viewer involvement.

HIGH-RISK EVENTS AND EMERGENCY PRECAUTIONS

Modern sport events often resemble the Circus Maximus in ancient Rome. The Philadelphia Phillies baseball team, for example, contracted with circus producer Bill Hall to present high-wire and other high-risk acts before or in between the games. One such act is Benny Koske, the "Human Bomb." Koske fills a small box with high-powered dynamite, then climbs in and, blows himself up. While extremely dangerous, promoters are assured beforehand that if Benny does not survive he does not have to be paid! Any act that may require audience participation, including the San

FIGURE 3–6

Diagram courtesy of the 3M Meeting Management Inst. from their 1994 Meeting Manual.

3M Center
6801 River Place Blvd.
Bldg. A145-5N-01
Austin, TX 78726-9000

Design from Berol RapiDesign R-2127 Metric Civil Engineers' Radium Guide

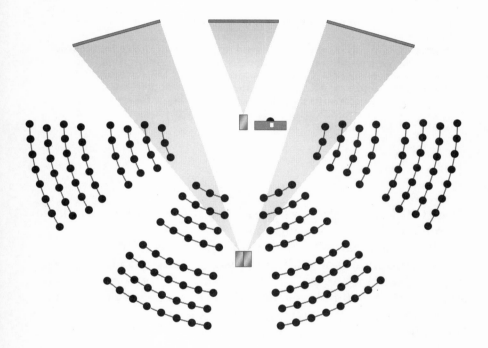

FIGURE 3–7

Emergency Care Procurement Ideas

- Local Red Cross may provide emergency care for your sport event in exchange for a small contribution.
- City or county fire and police are often available at no charge, but they can be called away for emergencies. If fees are charged, they may be waived depending on the relationship the event director or organization has with government officials and the amount of profit made.
- Private security and ambulance companies are usually paid by the hour. A typical fee for a private ambulance company is $150 per hour. Be sure that the ambulance service is used not only for transportation but also is capable of emergency care.
- An organization such as the International Association of Fire Fighters or the Radio, Emergency and Communication Team (REACT) may provide free services as a sponsor. REACT is a nationwide disaster relief organization whose members use events to practice their skills. The organization is especially fitting because its members are local and know the area, have medical and communication training, and provide their own medical and communication equipment.

Diego Chicken or even a Basketball Free Throw Contest, should be planned logistically to reduce risk.

Make certain that performers name you, the event manager, and your organization as an additional insured party on their insurance policies. Examine the policies to determine if the insurance coverage is adequate for the level of risk. The San Diego Chicken may require only $1 million aggregate insurance while the Wallendas High-Wire Spectacular may need $3 million dollars and the Grucci Fire Works Show may need to post a minimum of $5 million. Check with your insurance professional to determine the level of risk and then make sure the appropriate insurance is in place. (See Chapter 6 for more details on insurance.)

Without alarming the spectators, post appropriate signage or make frequent announcements alerting them to potential risks. Document these announcements and signage with photography and recordings. Signage such as "Circus acts are extremely hazardous. Please remain seated throughout the performance as a safety precaution" or "Pyrotechnic Staging Area, Do Not Enter" may protect you from a future law suit. Figure 3-7 provides an emergency care checklist that when implimented will ease concern in this important area.

HALLMARK OR RECURRING EVENTS

A hallmark event presents a particular set of logistical problems due to the erratic nature of the event location and schedule. When the term *hallmark event* is used about a sport event, it usually means a significant historical milestone such as the Olympic Games, the 100th anniversary of Wimbledon, or the World Series. Hallmark events have a particular value in addition to the traditional reason for staging the ceremony. A recurring event may also be a hallmark event, but it presents somewhat easier logistical opportunities because the audience may be comprised of a high percentage of repeat attendees who are familiar with the venue and understand the event process and system in advance of arrival.

When planning logistics for either the hallmark or recurring event, make certain you understand the habits of your spectators in order to plan accordingly. If spectators are likely to arrive early for a hallmark event to avoid parking problems, you must plan for extra staffing at that time. Using the same logic, spectators at a recurring activity may arrive somewhat later and you must staff to meet their arrival patterns.

Keeping precise statistics of the arrival, flow, and departure times of your guests will be helpful for both recurring and hallmark events. You can compare and analyze data for the production of your next event of similar size and scope.

AWARD CEREMONIES

The presentation of awards can be as simple as mailing a certificate or ribbon through the mail to an all-participant gala dinner and dance. "Depending on the size of the school and number of different sports involved (full year or fall/spring), high school athlete award banquets are typically held in the school's gymnasium or at a local restaurant," explains Monica Barrett. In the gym, food is provided either by a caterer or by parents potluck style.

Restaurants will typically offer a choice of menus from which the organizer will preselect for the entire group.

Preceding dinner and prior to the award presentations, a motivational speaker is usually invited to address the athletes. The high school booster organization is relied upon heavily for the recruitment of the speaker and the purchase of awards (medals, trophies, MVP). Frequently, coaches from the local universities are invited to speak. A slide show is also fitting during dinner or at the end of the evening after the awards presentations.

In addition, you may wish to contact the office of the mayor or governor to see if the mayor or governor, or a representative, could attend. If no one is able to attend, request a letter that can be read during your ceremonies.

One of the most difficult chores of an awards banquet coordinator is scheduling a date that does not conflict with any athletic event. The greatest fear, according to Monica Barrett, is that you or one of the coaches forgets someone on the team or an individual deserving of public recognition. As a damage control measure, Barrett always brings blank certificates and school letters (JV and V). The setup and testing of audiovisual equipment, especially the microphone and slide projector, is an important consideration, particularly when using an off-campus facility.

BOOKENDS AND OTHER CONFLICTS

The events that occur before, during, and following your event—bookend events—have special significance for logistical planning. We have previously discussed the first logistical concern about arrivals, parking, ticketing, admissions, and seating. Other events scheduled too closely to the starting time for your event may cause traffic jams and resulting confusion. You need to survey all departments and agencies, including the local convention and visitors bureau, to be aware of all events that will be held near the time of your event.

Another concern with bookend events is housing for your athletes, officials, staff, media, and spectators. When another major event is held in your host city at the same time, there is a risk that this event may consume all available hotel space. Study your hotel agreements carefully to make certain the hotel or hotels are firmly committed to your organization through a specific date and time.

The possibility of a bookend situation for the sport event can also have positive effects. You can purposely select an event to piggy-back your event. You may be able not only to boost attendance but also to share promotional expenses with the management of the other event or the local convention and visitors bureau. Research name entertainments that will be in the area during your event. If you decide to book this act, your costs could be substantially reduced.

Furthermore, when creating a bookend situation, you create a greater economic benefit for the local community because visitors are likely to remain in the area for an extended period and spend more money. Research confirms this. At the same time, be selective so that the bookend event compliments rather than overshadows your event, distracting the media.

These logistical concerns are only a starting part for your overall analysis. To identify other areas, ask your advisors, managers, and other key staff to add to your list so that your concerns are purposely event-specific.

Most international and national sport federations have detailed organizational guidelines outlining logistical requirements for hosting their specific events. (See Chapters 11 and 12 about indoor and outdoor events and Chapter 13 for bid proposal information.)

Beginning the Logistical Planning Cycle

Once you have identified all of the logistical concerns of your specific event, the logistical planning cycle commences. This cycle begins with turning the brainstorm or creative idea into a solid form through a system such as a chart or time line. This has been compared to the difference between a dream and a goal; a goal is only a dream . . . written down. Figure 3–8 lists in sequence some of the steps needed to plan a sport event.

This schedule is incomplete for a number of reasons. First, four months is usually too short a time for a planning period. Missing from this schedule is a date for each activity to both commence and to be completed. You may use "COB" for close of business

FIGURE 3–8

ACTION PLAN		
Date	*Activity*	*Person responsible*
1 Oct. 94	Brainstorm meeting	M. Smith & committee
5 Nov. 94	Select date, contract site	Legal
11 Dec. 94	Site inspection	Operations
21 Jan. 95	Contract vendors	Legal
25 Jan. 95	Design marketing campaign	Marketing
5 Feb. 95	Ad campaign commences	Marketing
15 Feb. 95	Interview schedule begins	Marketing, P.R.
20 Feb. 95	Site setup commences	Operations
21 Feb. 95	Site setup complete, inspect	Operations, legal
22 Feb. 95	Media day at site	Marketing, P.R.
23 Feb. 95	Event date	Operations
24 Feb. 95	Tear down event site	Operations
25 Feb. 95	Accounting, reconciliation	Financial

provided everyone in your organization and vendors agree on the appropriate closing time. Better still, assign a specific time to each activity to ensure a precise and therefore nonconflicting schedule with other activities. For example, the electricity needs to be installed before the caterer arrives and the tents need to be erected before the decorator can begin. When precision planning is implemented, you will find little opportunity for details to slip through cracks in your logistical reasoning.

SYMBOLIC REASONING

The ability to convert your creative ideas into symbols such as charts and graphs in order to produce a reasonable outcome for your sport event is the very essence of logistics. (Appendix II-I contains a thorough production plan using symbols created by Robert Hulsmeyer of New York City.) Hulsmeyer has managed many sport events and understands the value of using symbols to make reasonable decisions based upon all available information. The logistical plan plays an increasingly important role as the event date draws closer and you begin to layer your organization with new team members who may not know how they fit into the big picture. Dennis Gann, executive director of the Sioux City Convention Center and Auditorium Tourism Bureau, recommends that when you organize your sport event committee, no more than three people should have final decision-making power. A good mix is to have one person responsible for legal and government entities, one for finance, and another for logistics. The purpose of the event also determines the level of logistics. For instance, charity sport events are typically more concerned with the bottom line and do not plan for as many amenities as the high-profile sport event geared to attract media attention.

This picture of your event is an essential tool in helping your staff and volunteers understand how they can use their skills and talents to help the organization achieve the desired outcome. The ancient Greeks understood the value of reason in planning their society. To advance your organization through sport event management, use logistical planning as a tool to produce a well-defined work of art: your sport event.

Lillehammer Logistical Case Study

The importance of detailed logistical planning can be seen in the opening ceremony at the 1994 Winter Olympic Games in Lillehammer, Norway. Although the performance itself was brilliant, many ticket holders were unable to get to their seats in time to enjoy it, and by the end of the ceremony 11 spectators were hospitalized with broken bones. The reason for such complications are multifaceted.

First, all spectators were funneled through one entrance. No direction was given to general standing admission ticket holders and reserved seat ticket holders about their seating location. The result was a mad crush of people in one area not knowing what to do. General admission ticket holders stood in the stadium aisles blocking the way for reserved ticket holders trying to get to their seats. Everyone in the stadium area, including security and ushers, was wearing a white plastic poncho for television aesthetics, so it was difficult to identify persons with authority. Lisa Delpy recognized an official volunteer and asked, "Why aren't you checking tickets?" The reply was, "It won't help anyway." As the rush became more intense, security and ushers simply merged with the spectators.

FIGURE 3–9

Cardinal Rules for Planning Large Scale Productions for Major Sport Events According to Dan Witkowski

The First Commandment: The Show Must Not Upstage the Sport

No matter how great your show may be, the primary reason that people are buying a ticket is to see a sport being played.

Pete Rozelle, the brilliant commissioner of the National Football Leagues and the genius behind the Super Bowl, successfully made the last Sunday in January the unofficial American holiday. (Actually, the Super Bowl is observed by more people than many official holidays.) Rozelle and his staff were careful to have a balanced mix of sport and entertainment to appeal to a huge audience. Even if you are not a football fan, chances are you have attended a Super Bowl party or watched the spectacular pregame or halftime extravaganzas. Keep in mind that while the show is important, people ultimately come to watch a sport event.

Second Commandment: Plan, Plan, Plan

There is no such thing as overplanning. If your event is outdoors, you had better know the exact time of sunrise, sunset, dusk, when the sun will be in the spectators' eyes, what direction the wind will be from, and what the average wind speed is in the stadium at that time of year. However, compiling these facts does not mean your event is a sure bet, but it forces you to think of all the contingencies you may have to implement.

Before God got his current job, perhaps he was an event producer. I know of very few sport events that have actually been canceled due to rain. A Super Bowl halftime show has never been rained out. No matter how sophisticated the computer equipment for forecasting weather, we rely on the *Old Farmer's Almanac* more than anything else for scheduling rehearsals and performances. It is also consulted every year before the date of the Academy Awards is decided . . . honest!

By thinking "what if?" during your preproduction process, you can deal with those last-minute crises that bombard you the last few days before the live event. Contingency planning forces you to think things through.

Third Commandment: Overcast Your Cast and Crew

Always overcast 25–40 percent more people than you need for your show if you are using volunteers. If your show requires 1,000 people, cast 1,250 to 1,400.

(continued)

Another safety consideration was the steep and icy incline all 40,000 spectators had to climb to reach the stadium. LOOC's environmental efforts precluded putting salt on the grounds. Unfortunately, this left everyone slipping and sliding up and down the mountain. A veteran sport manager, Hill Carrow, recommended that a work crew be assigned to continually spread gravel along the busiest walkways. Although the Norwegians were gracious hosts, they forgot that the rest of the world was not used to such slippery conditions and perhaps not as physically fit to challenge the elements.

FIGURE 3–9 concluded

No matter how much fun a show sounds like in the beginning, it is a lot of hard work for the volunteers. Respect their time and do not waste it. Do not rehearse more than necessary and keep people busy when they are scheduled. If you have a thousand people waiting for rehearsal with nothing to do because the props or costumes have not been taken out of storage, that is the equivalent of wasting one-half year of a working person's time!

Even if you are well organized, people will drop out because of conflicts with work, school, transportation, or other social commitments. Make sure you communicate the total rehearsal schedule and time commitment when you recruit volunteers. However, have plenty of understudies ready to step in so you are not caught short.

Fourth Commandment: Use Technology to Improve the Show

The most important tools of a sport event producer are a dictation recorder and a camcorder. The dictation recorder should be used to log all your production notes during the preproduction and rehearsal stage when ideas are coming in so fast you don't have time to write them down.

If you have a secretary or assistant, have this person transcribe the microcassettes or your staff written notes for you. Then the notes will be ready at your next production meeting, that same night after rehearsal, or the next morning.

The camcorder can serve the same function for rehearsals. It allows choreographers, directors, costume dressers, dancers, and so forth to see the problems on tape.

During a big production of a ceremony or halftime show, choreographers are trying to work out small problems, and they don't often see the big picture. However, a camcorder—set up in the bleachers or in the audience and shooting a wide, constant picture of the field or stage—will allow the production team to analyze what must be done to make the show attractive from the point of view of the audience or television.

Final Note:

Following these rules will not guarantee a successful sport event production, but it will greatly increase your chances of success.

Producer Dan Witkowski has summarized the science of logistics into four commandments: "If God gave Moses Ten Commandments to run his life, a successful sport event can be controlled by four key commandments." (See Figure 3–9.)

The myriad of details that affect logistical planning often cloud one's overall view of the purpose of the event. In Chapter 4, you will be able once again to see the forest for the trees as you explore the importance of hospitality and protocol.

GAME HIGHLIGHTS

- Remember that the term *logistics* means "what is reasonable."
- Notice the activities before and after your sport event because they will directly affect your planning.
- Identify the key elements for success and logistical personnel necessary to begin your planning. Athlete, VIP, media, and crowd arrival and departure patterns are critical influences on your logistical staffing needs.
- When deciding on your sport event, consider that the location (indoors or out) and the number of public venues will determine scheduling, staffing, and other critical factors.
- Establish an organizational chart of all staff positions to enable communications.

PLAY BOOK

action plan: The day-by-day, minute-by-minute accounting of each sport event task and the person responsible for each.

Americans with Disabilities Act (ADA) A federal law guaranteeing equal access to venues for all persons regardless of disability. Include the ADA as an addendum to all your facility contracts. This will ensure that the facility is adequately prepared, thus taking the financial responsibility for lawsuits off your program.

hallmark event Staged to mark a special purpose such as a historic milestone.

logistics Details necessary to stage a successful sport event—site location, personnel, uniforms, transportation, security, and marketing.

organizational chart Matrix listing all staff positions in a logical sequential order of reporting responsibility.

recurring annual event Repeated every year, such as the Super Bowl.

seating From festival to reserved, the design of seating determines other logistical factors including personnel and security.

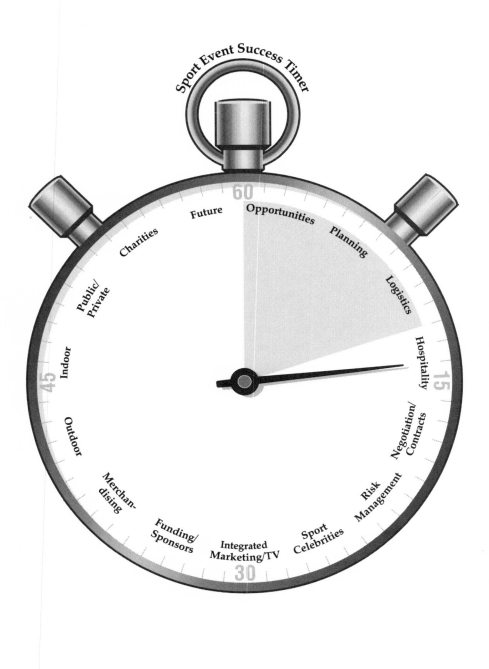

Chapter Four

Hospitality and Protocol in Sport

"Some of us will do our jobs well and some will not, but we will all be judged by only one thing—the result."

Vince Lombardi

W hat is the link between hospitality services and protocol that produces an entertaining, profitable, and memorable sport event?

Coca-Cola's Olympic Games hospitality program is almost as legendary as the much heralded games themselves. Klaus Inkamp, manager of international meetings and hospitality programs for the Coca-Cola Company, is an experienced hospitality professional. Inkamp says:

> When planning international sport event hospitality, the most important consideration is to understand the customs, traditions, strengths, as well as weaknesses, in the host country. This requires months of research and logistical planning to ensure positive, memorable guest experiences.

Indeed, the combination of sport, food, and drink appear to be inseparable elements throughout human history. Professional hospitality encompasses much more than invitations, tickets, food, and beverage. It is a management plan that satisfies the needs and expectations of guests. This plan can be organized by the event producer, a sponsor, or an outside firm, and it can be as simple as a small reception or as complex as a multiple-day sponsor village. The hospitality program should not interfere with the enjoyment of the sport event. In championship events, for example,

FIGURE 4–1

Typical Hospitality Packages
1. Preferred ticket packages, often with reserved parking, special entertainment, and souvenir items.
2. Private hospitality spaces (individual or corporate), carrying with them the preferred ticket package elements.
3. Visibility packages, offering opportunities for on-site signs and product sampling as well as advertising in whatever program-type vehicles are used for an event.
4. Activity packages, such as Pro-Am tournaments or corporate competitions between sponsors, in addition to one or more of the above packages.
---

game tickets alone may satisfy the guest's hospitality needs. Serious fans do not welcome distractions such as live entertainment or special effects when Shaquille O'Neil is facing Charles Barkley in the NBA Finals. Often the hospitality plan is part of a complete package of services (see Figure 4-1).

Hospitality specialists are frequently hired by sport event organizers, or they purchase the hospitality rights to the event directly from the organizers through a competitive bid process. Their responsibility is then to package, sell, and carry out the sport event hospitality program. This is especially worthwhile if the task is large and the staff small.

In Great Britain, members of the Corporate Hospitality Association (CHA) arrange hospitality for both national and international clients. From paint ball to clay shooting, CHA members strive to professionalize their industry. In so doing, they have created minimum standards for health, safety, catering, tents, and other critical elements.

As the exclusive catering company at the United States Open, Ridgewell's major events division, under the guidance of Susan Gersten, is not only responsible for providing the best food but also frequently assists the U.S.G.A. to sell the event year after year to tent sponsors. Some companies, such as Regency Productions by Hyatt, based in Chicago, guarantee in contracts with the organizing body that they will bring a certain number of clients to the event. With all of its suppliers and corporate clients, Hyatt has the necessary clout to succeed in this effort.

As a new sport event hospitality planner, you need to know what your hospitality tent package includes. For example, at some events it includes only tickets and parking, and catering is an additional fee. You will also want to consider extra amenities. Susan Gersten explains that "corporate entertaining is a very personal thing, thus it is important to offer the flexibility for creating unique packages. This is why tents are sold with a standard level of decor and a laundry list of extras."

The cost of a tent alone at sport events can range between $37,500 to $125,000, depending on the exclusivity of the event and its geographic location. Catering charges are extra and depend on the type and amount of food ordered. Options can range from full-day menus to only one meal. All these decisions must be made carefully prior to the event. Many potential sponsors attend an event the year before they plan to sponsor it in order to get a feel for the hospitality possibilities. Inviting potential sponsors to your event may help land a sponsorship the following year.

When working with exclusive hospitality providers of a sport event, do not rest assured until you have personally reviewed the setup and details of the event and know that all contract provisions have been fulfilled. Package hospitality providers do not always maintain the standard of quality that you would expect if you were personally producing the event. Although some revenue and control may be lost, delegation of services can bring peace of mind and professional expertise to your event.

Regency Productions by Hyatt provides hospitality services for the NFL Super Bowl corporate pregame and postgame sponsorship program, the NBA all-star jam, the NCAA Final Four, the PGA Raiders Cup, and the newly formed professional athlete golf league. Mark Donovan, Regency account executive, explains that "These events provide the perfect relationship marketing opportunity. Thousands of people are served a variety of foods in individual settings, which allow them to network while being entertained." If not located indoors, as in the World Congress Center in Atlanta, massive tenting for shelter is erected on a creatively landscaped parking lot. Decorations embrace unusual themes and are specifically designed to incorporate the sponsor's logo to maximize corporate visibility and investment.

Virginia Wolf, president of Virginia Wolf Inc. of Chicago, provided decorations for the Chicago World Cup celebration at the famed Navy Pier. This event, for over 7,000 fans, required Wolf and her staff to provide large-scale floral displays and landscaping to create a proper ambiance. When planning decor for sport events, Wolf advises that planners concentrate on location, theme, and budget. "These three factors, more than any others, influence the final outcome of the event." She adds, "double-check that the freight elevator is present and operational." In addition to this good advice, be sure to double-check the sound system, sample the catered food, be satisfied with security procedures, review the decor and placement of signage, and attend to any other details described in a contract.

Carl Bach, managing director of Reliance National Insurance (UK) found à la carte hospitality to be more compatible with his needs and less expensive than prepackaged hospitality for the American Bowl in London, England. Bach explains:

> Together with my secretary, we personally invited 20 of our customers and asked them to meet at the Dug Out sport bar, reserved a table at the establishment which was serving a preset Game meal, hired a luxury bus to pick the group up from the bar, bring to the game, and return at the end of the competition. Team caps were distributed on the way to the Game and once inside the gate, souvenir programs were provided and refreshments offered to all guests. On the return bus ride, results of a football pool contest conducted earlier in the evening were announced and prizes were awarded.

A recent trend is to offer individual sport event ticket purchasers an opportunity for a more upscale concession. Two examples include the Pavilion at the Kemper Open in Maryland and the Hunt Club at the Gold Cup in Virginia. These tickets allow the holder to enter a special area with an open bar and private restrooms.

WORKING WITHIN A BUDGET

You can find ways to be creative and put on a first-class hospitality event without overspending. First, consider the time of day that you plan to host the event. If you want quality but can't afford quantity, schedule the event before or after mealtimes This timing allows you to serve light, elegant hors-d'oeuvres.

If your guest list is extremely long and you want to reduce the number of RSVPs (please reply), consider hosting the event at an odd time or inconvenient location. For example, if the sport event ends at 6:00 P.M., start the party at 8:30 P.M. If the sport event is held at the Madison Square Garden, host the reception at the World Financial Center in lower Manhattan. These strategies force the guest to make a conscious decision whether or not to attend.

Richard Perelman, an event management and information services consultant with Perelman, Pioneer & Company in Los Angeles, suggests comparison shopping among competitors on price, quality, and service if planning time permits. For larger programs, set up a bidding process by circulating a series of detailed, written specifications among a group of handpicked vendors and invite responses by a preset date. A winner is then selected using the criteria set out in the specifications.

Event producers should also be good value engineers. Value engineering means working within a budget to select the quality and quantity of items that best meet the guests' expectations. For example, the requirements for cowboys on vacation at a rodeo are not the same as those for corporate guests attending Wimbeldon. If the decision is between swizzle sticks or more food, which would you select for the cowboys?

WINNING THE HOSPITALITY GAME: FOUR STAGES OF SPORT EVENT HOSPITALITY SUCCESS

From the invitation through the departure of the guest, the four stages of your sport event must be maximized to provide the guest with a thoroughly positive experience. Refer to figure 4-2.

FIGURE 4–2

Four Stages of Success

Stage 1: Knowing your guests' needs and expectations. Be aware of the guests' view of your event from designing your theme to developing your guests' last impression of the event.

Stage 2: Amenities: the extras that matter. Create a series of strategies to exceed expectations while accomplishing the event's goals.

Stage 3: Observation and adjustment. Build flexibility into your hospitality program to ensure that the sport event continually satisfies the needs of your guests through constant change.

Stage 4: Evaluation and measurement. Set goals for the sport event and establish measurement and evaluation devices to identify gaps in your planning so that you can improve your performance next time.

KNOWING YOUR GUESTS' NEEDS AND EXPECTATIONS

To understand the needs and expectation of your guests, determine in advance if they are Doers or Watchers, Participants or Spectators. The Doers want to attend a sport event where they can participate fully in the activities. The Watchers want to relax and be catered to. Sometimes, the sport event must satisfy both types of guests.

You can identify the needs and avocational interests of your prospective guests by asking their friends or co-workers or by sending a questionnaire to a random sample of prospective attendees. According to Richard Perelman, "the concept of 'taste' is very much in play here." Your program should please your audience, not put them off. Questions of alcoholic beverages, smoking, specific forms of entertainment, and foods all come into play. Ham sandwiches for a Jewish audience are never appreciated, while meatless entrees on Fridays during Lent will be gratefully acknowledged by practicing Catholics. Perelman's two rules of thumb are "If in doubt, find out and if still in doubt, throw it out."

For frequent invitees, create a file listing their educational background, social profile, allergies, and medical history, even their golf handicap. If a specific group has been hosted before, it is especially critical that you find out what worked and what did not.

At annual events, each year's activities should build upon those of the previous one.

Once you know the avocational interests of your guests, you can begin planning for those activities that will not only please them but also drive their actions and feelings toward your predetermined goal. For example, if your survey reveals that your guests are golfers, you may wish to rent a portable miniature golf course and hold a putting contest at your hospitality event. Or perhaps your guests are volleyball fans. Setting up a portable volleyball net with a Nerf volleyball provides not only an interactive activity but may create considerable excitement as the other guests enjoy food and drink watching your championship players having fun.

The technique of finding out what guests like to do for fun is an important step. Marketers are increasingly concerned with understanding the psychographic profile of potential buyers—an analysis of consumer lifestyle interests.Through telemarketing, direct mail, and other survey techniques this can be accomplished.

EFFECTIVE HOSPITALITY STRATEGIES

Western culture is dominated by mass media. Consumers are bombarded with a never-ending litany of advertising that competes for their attention. The guest or consumer is affected by this mass media syndrome, so your planning must match precise strategies with needs in order to exceed expectations.

To accomplish this goal despite the guests' short attention span, the sport event planner must structure the hospitality program in specific segments.

1. Understand the arrival patterns of your guests.   Will they trickle in or all arrive in one wave or in several waves. Your staffing for food and beverage must match the arrival times of guests.

2. Plan according to what has preceded or will follow the guests' arrival.   For example, it is unlikely that guests will have eaten supper before an event scheduled at 6:00 p.m. Consequently, your planning must allow for food substantial enough to satisfy

FIGURE 4–3

The Guest's Bill of Rights

By accepting this invitation . . .

• I am entitled to arrive at and depart from this sport event easily, safely, and efficiently.
• I am entitled to be greeted as soon as I enter the event site.
• I am entitled to be introduced to other guests by the host.
• I am entitled to be comforted with a beverage, food, or other tactile experience within three minutes of my arrival.
• I am entitled to enjoy pleasant surprises to establish a favorable memory of this sport event.

---

their hunger yet light enough to keep them from snoring through the event that follows. Make sure that athletes on your guest list understand the schedule and the menu. At the World University Games, athletes invited to a reception at 5:00 P.M. assumed that they would be fed a dinner. Instead, they were served only snacks. When the group returned to the athlete's village, the dining area was closed.

3. Plan with the understanding of what this sport event is expected to achieve for the guest. Is the goal networking for bisiness purposes? Is the sport event an incentive award for high sales productivity? a promotional activity to build brand awareness of a new product? a vehicle for entertaining prospective customers or thanking them for previous orders? or simply to create goodwill between the guest and the corporate sponsor?

By understanding the precise purpose of the sport event, you can develop strategies to achieve specific goals. A specific program that supports two or more goals may make things more complicated but still possible.

The host of a hospitality sport event serves as the bonding agent who glues the guests to one another and the entire group to the goal of the event. Station greeters at the entrance to the hospitality event to welcome each guest and offer directions to the first of a series of event activities.

Asked how she makes sure everyone feels important at a sport event, Stephanie Eaden of Party Planners West replied, "by being prepared and continually evaluating the scene."

Each guest is entitled to certain rights when they accept an invitation. Figure 4–3 is a guide to guarantee that each guest will enjoy the sport event.

Attending a sport event is a privilege. However, the host must accept the responsibility. It is not unusual today for the celebrity or VIP guest to receive numerous invitations to attend events on the same date as your sport event, increasing the pressure on the host to ensure an enjoyable and memorable occasion.

YOU'RE INVITED: INGREDIENTS FOR SUCCESSFUL INVITATION DESIGN

Since the invention of the printing press, the graphic arts have been a major resource in conveying the excitement of the sport event to prospective guests. Line drawings, photos, text, or any combination should be used to design an invitation that attracts attention, engages the imagination, and ultimately solicits a positive response.

Invitation design in the 1990s places a much greater emphasis on substance than style. Whatever the final design of your invitation, you must include a number of key ingredients to achieve success. Refer to Figure 4–4 as a reference.

FIGURE 4–4
Key Ingredients of Invitation Design

1. The mailing container (envelope, tube, or other packaging).
2. The quality of the paper (bond, weight).
3. The style of the typeface and use of raised or traditional printing.
4. The who, what, where, when, and how to respond to information. Easy RSVPs are also very important.
5. Artwork or other pictorial information to engage the imagination of the prospective guest. Sponsors' names should be prominent.
6. The delivery system (mail, hand delivered, overnight messenger, electronic).

Types of Invitations

Nontraditional mailing containers—tubes, boxes—capture the attention of the prospective guest. The Lower Delaware Chapter of the International Special Events Society (ISES) used a brief videotape including messages from the mayor of Philadelphia and the former governor of Delaware to invite its guests to a fifth anniversary celebration for the organization. The videotape was labeled "A Personal Message for_____" with the name of the recipient. From a bottle containing a secret map with directions to the regatta, to an imprinted headband with the instructions to the starting line of the 10K run, to an imprinted golf ball with the date and time of your hole-in-one shoot-out, the possibilities for innovation are endless. Avoid loose glitter, scents, or other items that may leave behind an unwanted residue when opened.

Quality and Innovation in Design

Typically, the heavier the weight of the paper and the finer the *bond*, the greater the importance of the event to the guest receiving the invitation. In addition, select a typeface appropriate to the theme of the event. Using traditional Times Roman for a newspaper headline announcing "Extra! Extra! You're Invited to the Big Game!" or a more theatrical style such as a Broadway design that proclaims "SRO at Sport Spectacular! Reply Now to Guarantee Good Seats!" are some good examples.

More formal invitations are generally printed with raised letters by a process known as *thermography*, which is similar in cost to traditional printing, or by engraving, which is more expensive. In addition, foil imprints can attract the eye with their reflective quality. Embossed printing conveys a sense of permanence. One innovation in invitation printing design is the use of the die cut to create a geometric shape such as a football or basketball cutout with the text revealed underneath.

The authors of the ancient Chinese proverb proclaiming that "one picture is worth more than a thousand words" could not have foreseen the tremendous influence television has had on our ability or inability to communicate. In this world of visual impressions, it is important that your guests see the type of program you are planning in order to build excitement about attending the sport event.

Award-winning special event designer Sue Ann Drobbin of Washington, D.C. designs invitations to attract attention and produce a high RSVP ratio. She advises you of the following important factors when selecting the style of your invitation: "Try for cleverness. A successful invitation grabs the prospective guests' attention and also sends a subliminal message that generates positive excitement about the event." An invitation imprinted on a jigsaw puzzle may become the talk of the office as prospective guests seek help in piecing together your message. The more people start talking about your event the greater the potential response. Drobbin also recommends that the invitation be visually pleasing and of high quality regardless of cost. "Even an inexpensive invitation should be exquisitely designed and executed," adding that the invitation must accurately represent the client and set the stage for what will happen at the event. Perhaps the best advice is to design the invitation so that it becomes a souvenir of the event, a keepsake to remind guests of a wonderful experience for years to come.

To convey your message, use clip art of a related sport activity and desktop publishing software that include sport graphics and photographs. When staging a hall of fame event, include photos of the honorees and perhaps the symbolic trophy to be bestowed upon the most honored individual. You might consider holding a contest for best invitation design and recognize the winner during your event.

Delivering the Invitation

The delivery system is often taken for granted as an incidental process and expense, but it is probably the most important step in getting a positive response from prospective guests. Like comedy, timing in invitation delivery is everything. Select a day for mail delivery when your invitation is not likely to compete with dozens of other mail items. Midweek deliveries are generally better than Mondays.

Early morning is usually the best time to hand deliver invitations because it is easier to find recipients in their office then, and the invitation has a longer time to attract attention through word-of-mouth endorsement. Always call first to confirm that the recipient is at the delivery site and let the receptionist know that you will be delivering a special invitation to your sport event. You do not want to surprise the receptionist. Instead, you want the receptionist to become part of your sport event team and help arrange the successful delivery of your invitation.

Do not forget systems that allow for faster invitation delivery including courier, rush, second-day or priority mail, and overnight. Delivery firms will usually provide a substantial discount for large numbers of invitations sent rush or overnight. Private couriers costumed as referees or umpires make a big impact entering the traditional office setting.

The newer technologies including E-mail and even satellite transmission also allow for a quick response to your sport event. While not as formal as a printed invitation, these invitations—with proper verbiage—can succeed in motivating your guests to respond quickly and positively. E-mail and faxes are also great for sending reminders.

Invitation Components

Who should attend? What is being offered? What day and time will the event be held? Where will the sport event be produced? What driving or other travel directions should you include? How should the guest respond and is there a deadline after which reservations are no longer accepted? The answers to all these questions are critical items that must be included in your invitation. Appendix II-M provides examples of successful sport event invitations that can serve as models in developing your own effective product.

Finally, have the courage to be creative in planning your invitation design. Why not send your invitation as a teaser on card made of coated stock with the message: "Hurry! Call this toll-free number to attend the hottest sport event this month! Operators are standing by with more information. Call Now!" The prospective guest who calls will get a recording with the voice of a famous sport personality who invites them to the party, provides them with the necessary details, and asks them to RSVP when they hear the beep.

After guests confirm, you mail a second postcard to each confirmed guest with travel directions and other critical information.

The creativity you demonstrate can ensure a positive response to your sport event.

YOU NEVER HAVE A SECOND CHANCE: FIRST AND FINAL IMPRESSIONS

In times of tight budgets, it is especially important to concentrate your hospitality planning on areas that will have the greatest impact on your guests. The second greatest impact is the first impression. The greatest impact is the final impression as the guests depart your event.

Transport your sport event guests through a sport time tunnel where, with black-and-white slides and taped voices with music and cheers, they can recall fond memories of one of baseball's dream teams. Then as they exit the other end of the tunnel, in living color are some of the team members assembled to sign autographs and pose for photos. This transition from a low-key to high-key event can be very effective and inexpensive to produce.

Likewise, the final impression can be even more important than the first. Suppose your guests arrived in an agitated state having fought heavy traffic caused by bad weather. They may have missed the first impression entirely as they sought out that first liquid refreshment to help them relax. However, through proper planning, you can turn this around so that the final impression will be more positive and meaningful—and the one they go home with. In a musical sense, this impression is the crescendo of a successful sport hospitality event. Whether you introduce a surprise sport hall of famer as guest speaker, stage an elaborate aerial fireworks and laser show, or simply present each departing guest with a special souvenir of the occasion, the final impression is an opportunity that should not be missed to sustain, support, and signify warm memories of your sport event's success.

AMENITIES: THE EXTRAS THAT MATTER

Whether you are managing sport event hospitality for a few friends or thousands of prospective clients, Perelman's assumption is correct. Guests want to be treated as individuals no matter how

FIGURE 4–5

Little Things That Matter

1. Personal assistance at entry and/or parking gates through the stationing of a person from the host company or group clearly identified by badge or clothing.
2. Personal services in the arena or stadium through conciergelike assistants: binoculars available for use; cellular telephones; host service for food orders; message delivery to seats; provision of programs, statistics, or other items to help follow the action—anything to help guests follow the action and make him or her feel well informed and important.
3. Information desks in the guest's hotel lobby providing event schedules and general information, activities and dining in the city, and maps and directions. Remember to prekey your VIPs and have a special area such as the assistant manager's desk secured for their registration.
4. Welcome signs (conforming to local, state, federal ordinances) in the airport, train stations, bus depots, city streets and buildings, hotels, sport and entertainment venues.
5. Gifts and complimentary items for guests as they leave the sport event to remind them of your appreciation.

many attend. Therefore, design and manage each guest experience as though you were hosting a reception for close friends. Satisfy their needs, exceed their expectations, and watch the success equity in your sport event grow proportionately in size and scope (see Figure 4-5).

Novelties, advertising specialties, and souvenirs are a traditional part of many hospitality programs and serve as a reminder of the host and the experience shared. For the greatest impact, the item should mention or reflect the company or group giving the gift and have a useful life well beyond the event itself. Depending on the item, the name or logo of the sponsor may be emblazoned or imprinted (hats or T-shirts), or may be noted by a small insert or tag (crystal or jewelry). Novelties or souvenirs should also be distributed when they will have the greatest impact and offer the least burden to the receiver.

Reliance Insurance Company in England, for example, invited 20 guests to the 1993 American Football Bowl between the Dallas Cowboys and the Detroit Lions. Prior to the game, Reliance provided a choice of hats to its guests so that they could wear them during the game. At the end of the evening, the company awarded contest prizes of sweatshirts and jackets that were much bulkier to carry.

For major events such as the Olympic Games or the Super Bowl, identification badges, limited-edition clothing, and souvenir pins can become sources of great pride for the wearer. During the 1960s and 1970s, ABC television raised this concept to an art form with its identity packages for guests attending the Olympic Games. ABC's VIP guests received specially designed clothes and pins that continue to be high-priced collector items. At international events like the Olympic Games and Pan-American Games, souvenir pins featuring the logo and name of the organizing committee, national teams, and sponsors in varying combinations are as good as gold. Upon arrival at the games, guests of sponsors receive a handful of special-edition pins, which they can barter for others. For many people, this is the most exciting event of the games and an unforgettable memory.

As the host of a sport event, you must also purchase gifts for the participants. Rings are the most common gifts at major contests such as bowl or all-star games. A choice of an alternative gift must be offered in case recipients have too many of one kind of gift and prefer something different. Your creativity will determine the best gift for your event.

OBSERVATION AND ADJUSTMENT: FLEXIBLE PLANNING FOR NONSTOP FUN

Sport event planners frequently err in planning so rigidly that they cannot satisfy guests' last-minute whims and changes in attitude. For example, if the sponsor's representative asks for the band to play music from a particular era or to speed up the food service, the flexibility of the event planner is the key to success.

Too often planners are solely concerned with the tools of the event (music, food, decorations) and ignore the sole purpose of the event, the guests' response. Professional sport event managers should circulate among the guests throughout the event, asking "How's the music? How's the food? Having a good time?" This frequent check will ensure that they can correct any problem immediately.

At a sport event for Xerox Corporation, Joe Jeff Goldblatt circulated among the tables of guests at the final banquet inquiring "How's everything?" Some irate diners were disappointed because they had ordered prime rib and were served chicken. According to the diners, the waiters told them that the kitchen was out of prime rib. Goldblatt immediately reported this to his client and the thoughtful host, accompanied by Goldblatt, apologized to the dissatisfied diners. Wine was also delivered to the table immediately to appease these unhappy Xerox employees who had traveled halfway around the world from Asia to enjoy this event in Virginia.

Consider what might have happened if Goldblatt had not taken a temperature check? The guests would surely have complained about their dissatisfaction in their written evaluation and perhaps grumbled to others about the poor service or even written letters to their superiors. By intervening early, the likelihood of guests resorting to this activity was possibly reduced. More important, the guests had their displeasure recognized, and it is hoped that they enjoyed the rest of the event.

When planning catering for the media, do not forget that journalists work long hours and that food service should be readily available as long as the press center is open. Ed Hula from Atlanta, Georgia, editor of *The Hula Report*, a bimonthly newsletter on the business, politics, and events of the world of sport, commented that during an IOC session in Monaco he could not get any food after 9:00 P.M. without the major inconvenience of going outside the press center.

Another common mistake that event planners make is to ignore the needs of guests during the sport event. For example, some guests may require more physical activity after a long trip or desire a quieter location to escape the noise of the stadium or to conduct business through networking.

Diagnose attitudinal alterations by standing to the side and observing the body language of guests. Are they straining to hear one another? Do they appear physically restless? When the event requires a new element, use the guidelines for change shown in Figure 4–6.

Your sport event closet should be filled with ideas like this just in case you have to make a last-minute adjustment to guarantee

FIGURE 4–6

Changing the Game Plan

1. When guests appear fidgety, add a physical activity such as dancing, games, a slide or video program, entertainment, or some other activity to engage them.
2. To calm guests, open a room or area where quiet conversation can be held.
3. To keep things interesting during a lengthy banquet or seated dinner, use a different service style when waiters pass the desserts among guests. Have the waiters appear every 15 minutes with a new dessert delicacy to keep the guests interested while they convere with one another.
4. Use a live video camera to provide instant pregame reports from the sport venue. Closed-circuit technology enables you to be sure your guests are on the sidelines right up until game time.
5. Introduce a surprise element such as a cheerleading team, high school marching band, or team mascot to liven up the proceedings when the energy level lags.

---

nonstop excitement, fun, and success. Likewise, don't be afraid to cancel a scheduled activity or entertainment that is unsuitable to the current mood of the event.

EVALUATION AND MEASUREMENT: HOW DID WE DO?

Always find out from your guests how you can improve your event to achieve greater success the next time. This can be accomplished through a formal written evaluation, telephone interview, or more informal exit interview. You also should conduct an internal review with your staff.

Marketing organizations will of course take this process several steps further and determine through sales reports whether the sport event contributed to the sponsor's productivity. In addition, an examination of the morale of the sales force and other employees who helped plan and produce the sport event may determine some key information that will be useful in planning future programs.

Publish the results of your survey and share this information with prospective clients or sponsors and your own staff.

PROTOCOL FOR SPORT EVENTS

Hugh Wakeham, event marketing director for Live Entertainment of Canada, Inc., has a rich background in sport event protocol. According to Wakeham, "precedent, or the ranking of dignitaries, guests, and VIPs is most important." (See Appendix II-L for specific rules of precedence for your sport event.)

During the closing ceremonies for Expo '86 in Vancouver, British Columbia, Wakeham discovered that sometimes protocol must be waived to accept changing traditions, and sometimes events take on a life of their own (see Figure 4-7).

> The closing ceremonies were designed to introduce the various countries in alphabetical order. However, seconds before the planned entrance one of my colleagues reported that he could not locate the Soviet Union delegation. Rather than delay the program, we continued the procession and were both surprised and delighted that these two archrivals, the United States and the Soviet Union, had decided to enter the stadium arm in arm, with the U.S. delegation carrying the Soviet flag and vice versa. They had overturned protocol, precedence, and tradition in favor of world peace. We could not have been more

FIGURE 4–7

**Protocol Guidelines
According to Hugh Wakeham**

Entrance of Athletes

• Two teams (e.g., at a football game): guest team enters first, followed by the home team.

• Multiple teams (e.g., at an international game): guest teams enter the stadium in alphabetal order according to the language of the home team, followed by the home team. For the Olympic Games, Greece enters first, followed by all other teams in alphabetical order with the exception of the host country, which enters last.

Anthems

• Two teams: guest anthem first, followed by host anthem.

• International event: official anthem only.

Flag Raising

• Host flag center: guest flags placed alternately right and left according to precedence of flags.

• Olympic flag (or other international flag) takes the central "host" position, with other flags arranged either alphabetically (the flags of participating nations) or according to precedence (if they are made up of flags of the host country, state, and city).

---

delighted and the 65,000 spectators confirmed our excitement with their emotion-filled cheers.

The following guidelines will help you better understand and manage protocol in your sport event hospitality activities.

A FINAL WORD ON SPORT EVENT HOSPITALITY

Producers of corporate hospitality programs at the Super Bowl and Olympic Games share the same secrets of success with Little League baseball fund-raising dinner organizers or 10k fun-run award ceremony organizers. To achieve success through sport event hospitality, know the needs and expectations of your guests, plan a series of activities or strategies to satisfy these needs and exceed their expectations, and, above all, make your planning flexible enough to allow for last-minute adjustments to ensure that each guest is enjoying a nonstop positive experience.

Whether you are serving hot dogs and beer or prime rib and champagne, the challenge is the same. Plan and deliver a level of hospitality that the guest would not normally experience. Use your imagination and creativity to transform your basic program into a sport special event. Richard Perelman suggests that extra services that can make the difference between an ordinary experience and a memorable one do not necessarily require great financial resources. Sometimes, the extra edge lies in working harder to meet the needs of guests beyond their expectation—what is called "sweat equity." Hospitality involves many steps and critical factors. Figure 4–8 is a checklist to assist you in developing the hospitality for your event.

Hospitality and protocol issues are often derived from customs or traditions rather than rules of law. Chapter 5 examines standard contracts and typical negotiations that will further ensure a hospitable sport event for you and your guests.

GAME HIGHLIGHTS

- Know the needs and expectations of your guests and develop a plan to satisfy these needs while exceeding their expectations. Use flexibility to continually fine-tune this process.

FIGURE 4–8

Sport Event Hospitality Checklist

1. Decide whether to produce the hospitality activities internally or externally.
2. If external help is required, create and disseminate a request for proposal (RFP) to qualified vendors. Qualify the vendors by determining their years of experience and the type of events they have produced previously. Most important, find out the typical number of people in attendance at their events. A vendor who is well qualified to provide hospitality for 50 may be ill-equipped to handle 5,000. The reverse is often true as well.
3. Identify your goals and objectives and include these in a position paper with your RFP to circulate to your staff.
4. Produce a detailed plan book or manual of operations.
5. Identify and secure appropriate insurance, paying special attention to host liability coverage.
6. Identify and secure all necessary permits from local municipality, police, fire, or health departments in order to put up temporary structures such as tents and provide food service.
7. Develop a practical budget and amend as needed during the development of the hospitality program.
8. Once you have solicited vendor bids, review them with expert guidance, negotiate fairly, and seek approval from all parties.
9. Select a menu appropriate to the time of the event and the dietary requirements of the guests.
10. Establish an estimated attendance number and a price per person.
11. Determine when the final guarantee will be required by the caterer (usually 36 to 72 hours in advance of the event). Remember, when determining the final guarantee, typically 20 percent of guests who have confirmed for a free event will not show up. In addition, 10 percent of the guests who did not confirm will arrive at the last minute. Therefore, you are ready to guarantee for 10 percent under the number of confirmed reservations. But wait! In most agreements, the caterer will automatically provide a 5 percent overage (excess) clause. This means that the caterer will provide enough food to serve 5 percent more guests than you have officially guaranteed. Therefore, guarantee only 15 percent under the actual number of confirmed reservations. Also take into consideration weather, conflicting events, and major world events that might keep guests from attending. Remember, the guarantee means you are guaranteeing payment for a specific number of guests. **Using this formula could save you thousands of dollars.**
13. Identify and contract appropriate gifts, amenities, advertising specialties, and souvenirs to give to your guests. Depending on the complexity of the design and the location of the manufacturer, allow 6 to 36 weeks to have these items ready for distribution.
14. Create printed materials including invitations, passes, confirmation notices, maps, signs, and programs. Schedule mailing operations.
15. Schedule all transportation needs, confirm insurance coverage, and provide communications for drivers to handle any last-minute changes.

- Remember that the first impression is not necessarily the most important. However, the final impression is critical to creating a positive memory of the sport event.
- Design and deliver invitations that attract a positive response from the guest. Be creative! Produce a unique product that will capture the guests' imagination and make them want to attend.
- Measure and evaluate your success through regular temperature checks of the guests' "fun quotient" during the sport event and through a more formal process afterward.

PLAY BOOK

bond The grade of paper, also indicates strength and durability.

embossing A printing process that produces in paper products an indented impression of images such as a corporate seal or hallmark.

foil A modern printing process that uses reflective foil to attract the eye to various areas of the invitation.

hospitality The four-step process of satisfying all the needs and exceeding the expectations of guests.

invitation The verbal, written, or electronic communication that captures the prospective guests' attention and persuades them to attend your sport event.

measurement The final step in the hospitality process by which the sport event planner measures, evaluates, and interprets the hospitality experience from the perspective of both guests and planners.

RSVP Please reply—a request for confirmation that the guest will attend your sport event.

thermography A printing process using heat which produces raised letters at about the same cost as regular printing.

container The package within which the invitation is delivered.

weight The cumulative weight of the mailing product. Used with size and shape to determine postage costs. Also used to describe the basis weight of paper products; for example, 80-pound cover weight, which refers to the heavier paper used for shells and covers for invitations.

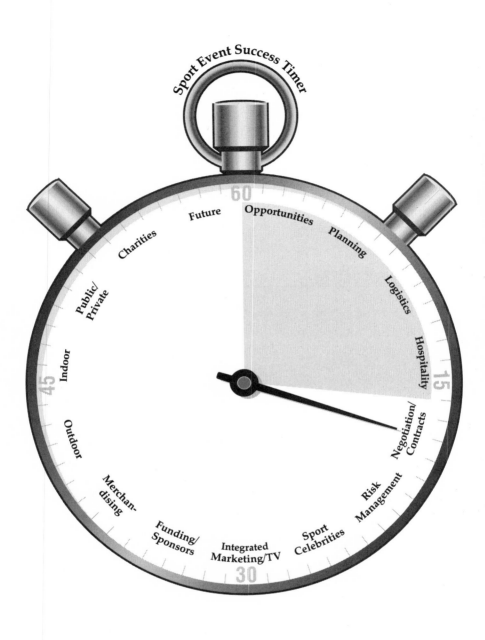

Chapter Five

Negotiation and Contracts

"I ask a player, 'Are you happy with this contract?' He'll say, yes, he is. 'Fine', I tell him, 'I'm happy too. We're both happy. But I have one provision before we sign this contract. There will not be any renegotiation."

Arnold (Red) Auerbach, former general manager, Boston Celtics

What is negotiable, who do you contract, and how do you find your way through the sport event legal jungle?

Former heavyweight boxing champion, Riddick Bowe, explains that he is able to concentrate solely on his sport inside the ring because he knows that Rock Newman, his manager, and Jeff Fried, his attorney, are handling the many business and legal considerations outside the ring.

It is estimated that Washington, D.C., has one lawyer for every seven people. This means that if you are attending a sport event and someone is injured, you won't have to look very far to find legal counsel. Just count to seven, ask for a lawyer, and legal help should come running with briefcase and retainer letter in hand.

The legal jungle can be treacherous, even for experienced attorneys, in the new field of sport event management and marketing unless they have extensive experience in this developing profession. These attorneys must possess expertise in many different areas connected with sport events. They may be asked to perform tasks that include performer contract negotiations, financial and tax considerations, venue concessions and merchandising contracts, sponsorship deals, domestic and international television rights, spectator litigation, insurance, and related hospitality issues.

In each of these categories, early managemen decisions and philosophy concerning control, size, and goals of the event, and the potential legal and commercial exposure for the promoter of the event, typically determine the number of negotiations conducted and contracts to be drafted and executed by the respective parties. If the event director and management team wish to promote a single event, make a one-time profit, and control all aspects of the event, they may veer away from vendor and subcontractor agreements. On the other hand, a host committee interested in running a well-organized event for athletes, sponsors, spectators, television broadcasters, and the community at large—all within a balanced budget—may subcontract to a number of experts to ensure the success of the event for both short-term and long-term benefits. From a practical viewpoint, most established event promoters now include a variety of professionals on their staff to address issues typically associated with a large-scale event.

The fact remains that when promoting any sport event, some standard negotiations will take place about the responsibilities of the various parties and the corresponding financial considerations and contracts that need to be executed. Always remember that contractual agreements protect the respective interests of all parties involved.

EXCLUSIVITY

The most important item in contracts between sponsors and the sport event organizing committee is exclusivity—the exclusive sponsorship right per product category or service. This matter should also be discussed with potential licensees, television partners, and service subcontractors such as caterers and hospitality providers. Refer to Figure 5-1 to help develop your exclusive action plan. The importance of exclusivity is illustrated in professional basketball. The NBA has certain rights that it sells, and the team, the venue, and perhaps broadcasters have specific rights that each can sell. With all these different rights, a sponsor must consider the various possibilities for ambush marketing and close the holes as much as possible. Ambush marketing is the strategy employed by nonrights holding companies to create an appearance as if they are an official event sponsor. Another term for this

FIGURE 5–1

Exclusivity Action Plan
1. Determine what rights require exclusivity and list them in order of priority of value to your organization and the event as a whole.
2. Identify the rights that are negotiable and those that are not.
3. Assign a value and negotiating range to each item where exclusivity is absolutely required.
4. Use competent sport event legal counsel to assist you with the contracts governing exclusivity (i.e., sponsorship).
5. Distribute exclusivity agreements to all critical parties and ask for their feedback prior to concluding negotiations.

---

activity is parasite marketing. At the 1984 Olympic Games in Los Angeles, Kodak tried to ambush Fuji, the official film of the Summer Olympic Games by using the slogan "Official Film of Summer." They also tried to confuse consumers by marketing their official sponsorship of U.S. Track and Field, for which they did purchase the rights. Nike employed ambush marketing techniques during the 1994 Goodwill Games in St. Petersburg, Russia, by decorating the city with flags, banners, and hats while Reebok was the "Official Footwear" of the Games. To protect its rights for the 1996 Olympic Games, the Coca-Cola Company has developed an anti-ambush plan. Control over exclusivity is easier for less developed sports where one sanctioning body is largely responsible for the entire show. Another illustration of the difficulties related to exclusivity is the California State High School Associations, which sold an exclusive sponsorship to Reebok for specific state championships while signage at individual schools and championship venues was purchased directly from Nike. Simply put, exclusivity is difficult to control, but it would be impossible without contractual stipulations. As a general rule, sponsors will require exclusivity related to its particular industry category (e.g., sportswear, soft drinks).

TERRITORIAL BOUNDARIES

This issue is not as important for local events as it is with national and international events. For the Olympic Games or World Cup

FIGURE 5–2

Territorial Action Plan
1. Assign a value to territorial trademark usage rights.
2. Defend this assigned value with relative data including television viewership and market share.
3. Decide whether the territorial rights will be international, national, and regional or by destination and a fixed-mileage circumference (e.g., within a 500-mile radius of the sport event site).

Soccer, sponsors are solicited at all levels—international, national, and local—so if specific categories and boundaries are not identified and preserved, exclusivity may be lost. International sponsors have the authority to use the sport event trademarks in all consenting countries whereas national sponsors are restricted to using the trademark within the host country. With international contracts, it is important to specify in writing that any fluctuation in the currency exchange rate will not adversely affect the amount due in U.S. dollars. Territorial restrictions that are important in the area of television and merchandising will be discussed later. Figure 5-2 provides suggested steps to create a territorial action plan.

OPTION TO RENEW AND RIGHT OF FIRST REFUSAL

According to sponsorship guru Lesa Ukman, whose Chicago-based newsletter—IEG Sponsorship Report—tracks the industry: the option to renew gives the existing sponsor the option to extend the sponsorship agreement when the initial term of the contract expires. The right of first refusal allows a window of opportunity for the existing sponsor to make an offer to retain sponsorship rights. The event producer can accept the sponsor's offer or find an offer of greater value. A lower offer cannot be accepted. Most importantly, however, the right of first refusal allows the sponsor to walk away from negotiations with the option to match any competitor's offer. Depending on the length of the initial contract, a specific time frame—usually eight months to one year before a contract expires—should be designated in which a sponsor must notify the sport event owner of intent to continue involvement in the event. This agreement allows the sport event owner ample lead time to secure another sponsor. Some sponsors may also demand an approval clause for certain sponsorship categories. Coca-Cola, for example, may not want Taco Bell or Kentucky Fried Chicken to be a sponsor because of their affiliation with Pepsi.

TERMINATION AND ARBITRATION

When all else fails, divorce is inevitable. The domestic courts have a procedure for separation, annulment, or divorce. The same is true in the civil courts for legal agreements. Make certain your written instruments outline reasonable cause for termination and a time frame after which all terms are null and void and the parties are free to negotiate with others. Also significant, considering the possibility of high legal costs, is to include dispute-resolution provisions such as arbitration pursuant to the rules of the American Arbitration Association.

RISK MANAGEMENT AND INSURANCE

In order to limit your liability, your master agreements must incorporate language pertinent to risk management and minimum insurance requirements for all parties (see Figure 5-3). From naming specific parties as additional insurers to providing certificates of insurance by certain dates and times, these important considerations should be spelled out carefully in writing and checked by your attorney and insurance broker for compliance with your current policies. In any sport event, insurance plays a very significant role in ensuring appropriate protection to the promoter, venue, sponsors, television broadcasters, and performers. Examples of typical insurance coverage for an event include general liability insurance, performer medical insurance, cancellation insurance, television mechanical breakdown insurance, worker's compensation, prize indemnity, and so forth (see Chapter 6 for more information about insurance).

FIGURE 5–3

Risk Management/Insurance Action Plan

1. Describe the parties' responsibilities requiring safety compliance with federal (e.g., Occupational Safety Health Administration[OSHA]), state, and local codes.
2. Determine the minimum amount of insurance required by each party, the names of the additional insureds, the date and time that certificates are to be delivered to the sport event manager, and other items required by your current insurance coverage. Ensure that your existing policy conforms to any special event you are promoting.
3. Include a clause requiring each party to exercise due care in the administration of duties to ensure the safety of its organization's employees, your personnel, and the public at large.
4. Determine if waivers of indemnity are required as attachments to the agreement.
5. Determine through legal counsel the wisdom of each party indemnifying the other. Always receive indemnification from the other contracting party because you do not want to be responsible for its actions or inactions.

SPONSOR AND SUPPLIER AGREEMENTS

Category exclusivity is the most important aspect in a contract between sponsors and an organizing committee. A specific description of the category, with the names of particular competitors and products, must be included. In the financial institutions category, for example, the description does not include credit cards; these are considered to be a separate category. This means that even if the sponsoring financial institution may promote its own credit card, it cannot promote the product. In the fast-food category, McDonald's may want pizza and Pizza Hut to be mentioned to avoid confusion about pizza as a category of fast food.

Trademark Rights

Identification parameters and procedural details must also be included for event trademark approvals. All promotional and marketing material, including premiums produced by a sponsor, must be examined and approved by a representative within the organization. The purpose of this scrutiny is to control the quality of the trademarks and to avoid possible abuse or infringement of rights. To avoid excessive delays in the approval process, contracts should specify a turnaround time and contingencies if conditions are not met. A design handbook is provided to each sponsor with guidelines on appropriate trademark and logo usage. It is important that the guidelines specify promotional time limits on the use of the trademarks and logos and where they can be used. M&M Mars continues to sell boxes of M&M candies displaying the Olympic rights, and Olympic stickers remain on U.S. Postal service trucks despite the end of Olympic sponsorship contracts for both organizations.

Territorial Rights

You must also see that territorial rights for promotions are defined. Home Depot, a sponsor of the 1996 Atlanta Olympic Games, was allowed the right to offer its vendors the opportunity to use the Olympic logo on their merchandise and packaging but only on inventory sold in Home Depot stores. Black and Decker products sold in Home Depot can therefore promote the five rings on its packaging even though Black and Decker never paid a rights fee to the Olympic Organizing Committee. Black and Decker products carried in other stores are not entitled to this right.

Sponsorship Fees

The sponsorship agreement should clearly define the specific amount of cash and in-kind services, and it must be accepted by all parties and include payment schedules and delivery or service dates. Requests for additional contributions are never welcome after contracts have been signed.

In sport events that need promotion, corporations typically have some leverage in contract negotiations which allow them to offset a large portion of their cash fee with a promotional fee. But it's going to be all cash for sport events that do not need promotion and sell out their tickets.

Specific rights and privileges included in the sponsorship fee also should be clearly defined. The opportunity for accommodations, hospitality, signage, and tickets are frequently provided. For smaller, more low-profile events, these are frequently included as a benefit in the sponsorship fee.

Typically, your sponsorship fee simply entitles you to the right to spend more money on such items. It is important for a sponsor to ask about the type, location, and cost of tickets, accommodations, and hospitality. World Cup Soccer sponsors, for example, were not aware that the tickets allocated to them were not premium seats and only discovered later that premium seats could be arranged for an additional charge. On-site sales, samples, or pouring rights should also be outlined in the contract.

As far as working with other sponsors or licensees, a best effort clause is typically included in the contract to encourage the purchase of premiums or goods from official sponsors or licensees. Best effort infers that companies involved in the event will utilize each others' products or services as long as prices are competitive. VISA, for example, uses UPS exclusively for overnight delivery. Both companies are sponsors of the 1996 Summer Olympic Games.

TELEVISION

Television negotiations are becoming more complex—and lucrative—with the increase in cable and satellite options and the rapidly increasing international interest in U.S. sport events. Most television contracts include exclusivity and territorial stipulations (see Figure 5-4). The television rights holder can then opt to sublicense certain amounts of the programming but generally needs written consent of the licensor. For example, the Winter Olympics offered so many hours of programming that CBS granted a license, for an appropriate sum, to TNT for specific days and hours of Olympic coverage. Certain contracts must also include specifications for satellite rights if a rights holder has the capacity to produce both feeds.

Another common element included in television contracts is the preferential treatment given event sponsors regarding commercial time slots. According to Howard Stupp, Director of Legal Affairs for the International Olympic Committee (IOC), "This is especially important for Olympic sponsors since there are no advertising billboards allowed in the competition areas." The agreement basically offers sponsors right of first refusal at negotiations but not necessarily any price discount. Other contract stipulations in a television agreement include the control of "on-screen" or "super-

FIGURE 5–4

Television Action Plan
• Determine whether to have territorial or exclusive stipulations in your contract.   • Decide whether sublicensing is desired.   • Determine whether event sponsors will require preferential treatment.   • Find out if other restrictions need to be considered.

imposed" credits during coverage, the location and number of cameras allowed, the basic technical support provided by the host committee, and copyright credit.

The issue of appropriate "news access" for competitors should also be delineated to protect the rights holder. The IOC established the "3 × 2 × 3" rule whereby Olympic coverage can be aired by non–rights holders three times per day, in two-minute excerpts, and spaced a minimum of three hours apart.

PERSONNEL: FULL-TIME, PART-TIME, AND SUBCONTRACTORS

The most important part of a personnel contract is the specific, detailed responsibility of the individual, including when the employee is to begin and end work, payment schedules, tax withholding, reporting procedures, and provisions for changes in the contract (e.g., extension or increased responsibilities). All contracts should also specify the state where contract litigation is to be carried out. It is in the best interest of employees to be identified as secured parties, meaning that they will be paid first if the event goes bankrupt. Secured parties are typically paid 25 percent up-front, 50 percent with satisfactory progress, and another 25 percent upon completion of the work contracted. A variety of employees are necessary to produce a sport event as outlined in Figure 5-5.

SPORT CELEBRITIES

Chapter 7 will discuss the reasons for hiring or including a sport celebrity in your event. However, you need to spell out the details

FIGURE 5–5

Sample Sport Event Legal Payroll Terminology
• Independent contractor/Employee
• Part-time worker
• Full-time employee
• Consultant (may also be independent contractor)
• Hourly worker
• Day laborer

in personnel contracts for sport celebrities. Frequently, a corporation may employ an athlete for a set number of hours, say 300 hours per year, and specifics on how the hours are to be scheduled and accounted for must be delineated. Does the celebrity have the right to refuse an engagement? How far in advance must the engagement be scheduled? Is there a minimum and maximum amount of time the celebrity must spend at an event? What type of travel and hotel accommodations will be provided? All contracts also should include a termination clause for immoral behavior. Some contracts include specific athletic achievements for the contract to remain in full force (e.g., the athlete must remain ranked in the top five in the world). (See Appendix I-C for a sample endorsement contract.)

NOT-FOR-PROFIT BENEFICIARIES

Chapter 14 discusses sport events and not-for-profit charities in detail, but it is important to highlight certain contractual agreements between for-profit event organizer and not-for-profit beneficiaries. Charitable organizations should be careful not to provide services far greater in value than the dollar amount to be received. Check the number of volunteers requested and the number of work hours required from each. If the contract requests the use of the not-for-profit postage benefit, check whether you are also responsible for the packaging of the materials to be mailed. Contract inclusions like this can cause a great inconvenience for not-for-profit organizations and may eat away any potential revenues. Since not-for-profit beneficiaries typically do not have

direct control over the management of the event other than providing necessary services, many request minimum guarantees
from the sport event producer to protect their interests.

VENUE CONTRACTS

Suppose that the venue is not clean, meaning there is existing
permanent signage, and your organization requires a clean venue.
Then negotiations about covering up existing signage may be
necessary or existing contracts should be renegotiated. One can
also apply for a variance of contract (wherein the agreement is
amended), suspending all other agreements for a specific period
of time while the venue is occupied by the sport event tenant. The
lease rate, security responsibility, other personnel responsibility,
concessions, and indemnification are the principal provisions to be
covered in a venue contract.

LICENSEES

Category exclusivity on licensed goods depends on the size of
the market for an event and the amount of income desired from
license fees. Obviously, the price for a license will be less if the
category is nonexclusive (more than one licensee may purchase
this product category), but sometimes the sum of two parts is
greater than one. The Lillehammer Olympic Organizing Committee (LOOC), for example, decided to grant exclusivity because of its small market, whereas the Atlanta Committee for the
Olympic Games (ACOG) opted for nonexclusive licensing
agreements because of the large demand anticipated for licensed
products. Nonexclusive licensees should request that the contract include a limit on the number of licensees per category. A
licensee contract should also stipulate the minimum guarantee
required and the royalty payments (a percent of proceeds paid
to the owner of the rights) beyond that point.

Restrictions prohibiting licensees from selling official licensed
items to nonevent sponsors are also included in some contracts. This
protects sponsors from ambush marketing. Nonevent sponsors like
to provide customers with licensed premiums (a prize, bonus, or

reward given as an inducement) to associate with the event. Refer to Chapter 10 for more information on merchandising, and see Appendix I for a sample licensing contract.

HOSPITALITY

On-site sport event hospitality may be offered as an exclusive benefit included in the corporate sponsorship package or marketed to sponsors as an additional revenue stream for the event. Either way, someone must provide the services and more often than not an external management company specializing in hospitality either purchases the on-site hospitality rights or is employed as a subcontractor. Contracts for subcontractors were covered previously under "Personnel: Full-time, Part-time, and Subcontracters" and contracts for hospitality rights are discussed under "Sponsors and Supplier Agreements." Important points in hospitality negotiations and contractual details are discussed below. (See Figure 5-6 for Hospitality Action Plan.)

Before beginning negotiations with either the host committee, their hospitality subcontractor, or the exclusive hospitality rights holder, corporations seeking hospitality services at a sport event should first investigate the selection criteria for corporate invitations and the protocol for space allocation. Frequently, only sponsors of the event are offered the opportunity to purchase hospitality packages, and site selection is based on first come, first served, the extent of the sponsorship, or tenure with the event. If this is not the case, request information about hospitality packages and their availability. Check whether the package is comprehensive or if power, water, and catering are additional charges. Once a package is selected, be sure to stipulate in writing that your hospitality space should not be adjacent to any industry competitor. Jockey for the best location in terms of closeness to the event and visibility, if this is a corporate objective. Again, first come, first served is the industry rule of thumb, but it never hurts to inquire.

When working with exclusive hospitality providers, it is also wise to include in your contract the right to quality control of the provider. Thus, if you are dissatisfied with the level of service,

FIGURE 5–6

Hospitality Action Plan

- Determine who is responsible for purchasing hospitality services (e.g., event planner, sponsor, venue).
- Decide what company will provide hospitality services.
- Determine if the hospitality package is comprehensive.
- Make sure the hospitality package is not in conflict with current sponsors (e.g., the hospitality company serves Budweiser while your event sponsor is Miller).
- Include a quality control clause in the contract.

---

selection of food, decor, or any other item, you have the option of requesting reasonable changes, which if not fulfilled entitle you to a refund. (See Chapter 4 for more information on hospitality.)

WHEN TO UTILIZE LEGAL COUNSEL

The involvement of an attorney depends entirely on the originality and complexity of the event and, correspondingly, the contract terms. Sample contracts for standard events are available in the *International Event Group's Legal Guide*. Jennifer Jordan, an attorney working in sport events, explains:

> If you are creating a new event with unique features, then it is advisable to hire an attorney trained to identify potential pitfalls and prevent any loopholes in the contract. The attorney should also understand what state laws are applicable if a conflict occurs.

Lesa Ukman warns that "If selling title to a new event, it is especially important to establish ownership because if the event is successful, your sponsors can easily do it themselves in year two or three."

Ukman suggests that you create your own contract and present it to sponsors. This will eliminate the time and expense of hiring a lawyer to go item by item through each new sponsor's contract. Lawyers will advise you that it is better to work from your contract and begin negotiations, rather than rewrite the contract from your negotiating party. Some corporations, like Kodak, always generate their own contracts and send them out before they are even interested in your property in order to lock things up. You must be careful about this action. Look at your own skills and abilities to see whether you can handle the negotiations yourself or need an attorney or agency to represent you.

An attorney is not always recommended for repeat events with relatively few changes and when both parties are satisfied. The general attitude of sport event managers toward attorneys is appropriately conveyed in the statement, "We are short on time and lawyers are long on words."

WHEN TO CONSULT A SPORT MANAGEMENT/ MARKETING CONSULTANT?

Unless you have specific and extensive expertise in the sport event being negotiated, it may be a wise investment to hire an individual or firm with expertise in this area. This expert can bring more negotiating power to the table and, at least for the first time around, help manage and showcase your sponsorship activities. Companies unfamiliar with the intricacies of sport more often than not find themselves overextended in fulfilling their sport event contract.

Electronic Data Systems (EDS) of Dallas, Texas, was contractually bound to produce all the results of the Barcelona Olympic Games. Whoever signed the contract, however, did not fully understand the extent of the Olympic event program (e.g., men and women, individuals and teams, the various swim and running distances and heats) and did not stipulate the type of hardware that they needed. Instead, EDS was provided a less powerful machine that required additional programming and staffing resources.

Agency Agreements

Michael Jordan's agent, David Falk, was quoted in the Marquette University *Sports Law Journal*:

One type of negotiation tactic is to literally walk away. I do not recommend this unless the negotiations are fruitless. Instead, I prefer to set a rigid time frame to keep the pressure on. In one situation, I purposely scheduled my return flight in such a way to imply that time was of the essence.

If you decide that an outside agency is necessary to help manage your event, be sure the agency's role is defined in the contract. Is the agency's role simply that of an adviser or one that proactively finds properties to sponsor? How will the agency be compensated—by retainer or commission? What happens if you release the agency after the first year of a multiyear contract? Will it continue to receive a commission and, if so, for how long? What if it does not perform at the expected level?

LITIGATION, ARBITRATION, AND ALTERNATIVE DISPUTE SYSTEMS

Whether a contract is written or verbal (and it should always be written), if one party performed a duty that it would not normally provide and could prove that its work benefited the other party, then its case for litigation is considered strong. In the same vein, if a plaintiff can provide that he or she is the injured party because the defendant did not complete the work specified in the agreement, the plaintiff may be able to file a legitimate complaint against the other party.

With the U.S. court system gridlocked in civil litigation, injured parties in increasing numbers are taking their complaints to a certified arbitrator who is trained to issue a nonbinding judgment. This saves both parties 50 percent or more of the cost of a trial and is much more expedient. It is not unusual today for a civil case to take upwards of five years to go to trial whereas arbitration can find both parties sitting face-to-face in a few months trying to reach a solution.

It is recommended that you include an arbitration clause in your master sport event agreement with all parties. The clause states simply that in the event of a dispute the parties agree to seek arbitration. Make sure to use a trained arbitrator recommended by a reputable group such as the American Arbitration Association. The location of the arbitration will be a negotiable issue.

CLOSING ARGUMENTS

Although verbal agreements confirmed through a handshake between two top-level people can be upheld in a court of law, a problem exists when one of these individuals leaves his or her place of employment and the terms become lost in confusion. For this reason alone, you should insist on a formal written contract. Jennifer Jordan suggests that you remember the four corners rule: if the terms are not within the four corners of the contract then they are not agreed upon. Unless there is a clause referring to another document, the contract represents the entirety of agreements.

William "Woody" Woodruff, a former Xerox employee and now a consultant in event marketing, highly recommends that you "take the time to review the final written contract in detail as this version does not always reflect previous editions or reflect changes that you verbally thought were agreed upon." Woody adds, "Do not rely on the organizing committee to really understand what it takes from a sponsor's point of view, particularly in the area of service."

Contracts may range from 1 to 500 pages, but the important consideration is not the length but to have all parties clear on their role, responsibilities, rights, and the consequences of any breach in contract. (See Appendix I for sample agreements.)

Negotiations and agreements cannot prevent a catastrophe. That is why Chapter 6 on risk management must be used in tandem with this one.

GAME HIGHLIGHTS

- Make sure your sponsorship agreements include clauses related to exclusivity, territorial rights, option to renew, first right of refusal, termination options, arbitration, insurance provisions, time frames for trademark and logo use, guidelines for trademark approval, and the rights and responsibilities of the sponsor if applicable.

- Provide for guidelines in your television agreements on coordination with sponsors, sublicensing privileges, and news access coverage for non–right holders.

- Include in your personnel agreements time periods of employment, specific responsibilities, reporting procedure, payment schedule, and provisions for change. These terms are also applicable to agreements you draft for sport celebrities.

- All parties should be in full agreement before signing any legal contract.

- Stipulate in contracts the state in which all litigation is to be carried out and include an arbitration clause to avoid the court system.

- You may want to hire an attorney to review first-time or very complex or original contracts. However, developing your own contract is more cost-effective over time.

- Do not rely on the host organizer to serve as your corporate sponsorship consultant. If you feel that you are not prepared to negotiate effectively, seek external advice, at least for the first round of negotiations.

PLAY BOOK

ambush marketing When a company markets and promotes itself as an official sponsor when it has paid no rights fees. Another term is parasite marketing.

arbitration Submitting a contractual dispute to a third party for determination.

best effort clause An encouragement for event sponsors to support each other by utilizing each others, products or services as long as at fair market value.

contract An agreement between two or more parties enforceable by law.

exclusivity One sponsor per product or service category.

litigation: A dispute or lawsuit.

mark approval The process in which sponsors submit all promotional and advertising work to the event organizer for approval.

mark or trademark A name, slogan, graphic image, or other property registered with the U.S. government and owned entirely by the registered agent holder.

negotiations A discussion designed to produce agreement on terms.

not clean A venue with preexisting sponsor signage.

option to renew The existing or current sponsor has the option to renew the agreement when the initial term expires.

responsibilities Obligations such as cash payment, in-kind services, or goods imposed on a sponsor in return for specific rights.

right of first refusal The existing sponsor has the option to submit an offer or match any competitor's offer in order to retain sponsorship rights.

rights The ownership of something of value such as the event title, logo, trademark or broadcast signal.

termination The act of ending a contract by declaring all terms null and void.

sublicensing selling off part of your rights to another company.

venue A sport event facility.

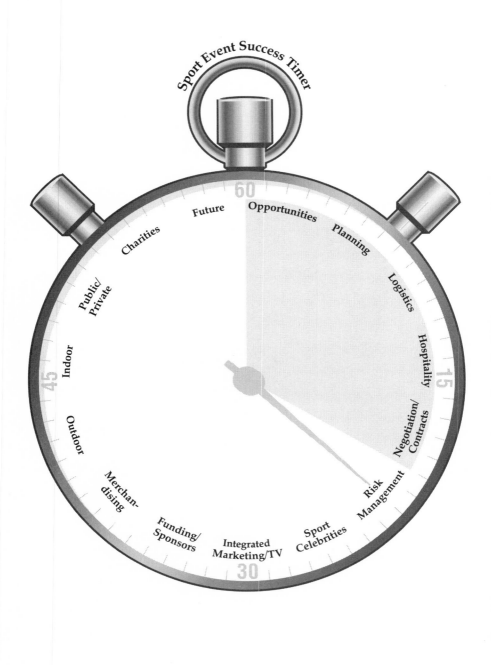

Sport Event Success Timer

60

Future
Opportunities
Planning
Charities
Logistics
Public/
Private
Hospitality
Indoor
45
15
Outdoor
Negotiation/
Contracts
Merchan-
dising
Risk
Management
Funding/
Sponsors
Sport
Celebrities
Integrated
Marketing/TV
30

Chapter Six

Risk Management:
Protecting Your Investment

"Sometimes the light at the end of the tunnel is an oncoming train."

Lou Holtz, football coach

How can you reduce the risk of injury to spectators and participants, prevent inventory or personal theft, limit potential financial losses from promotional contests, and protect your event from catastrophic losses due to acts of God?

Sports Illustrated reported in 1989 that at Cleveland Stadium a group of fans sitting in an area known as "The Dawg Pound" threw dog bones and dog biscuits onto the field. These woofing bleacher creatures also threw eggs, rocks, and batteries. The barrage forced the officials to move the Browns/Bronco game to the other end of the field.

During the late 1980s, newspapers around the world described in vivid detail the massive injuries and casualties at soccer matches in Great Britain. During this same period, stadium officials throughout the United States braced for their own increased troubles with out-of-control spectators and legions of lawyers leading them into courtrooms on a daily basis.

During the last decade, and for a variety of reasons, the topics of risk management, loss prevention, and safety have been addressed continually throughout the sport event profession. There are many reasons for this increased interest.

Mira Koplovsky, a seven-year veteran of the operations staff at the George Washington University's Charles E. Smith Center in Washington, reports, "We are in the service business. As sport events have grown, so too has the need to provide well-trained, competent, and courteous personnel to welcome and direct our guests."

STANDING ROOM ONLY

The number of spectators attending sport events has increased beyond the physical capabilities of many venues, and stadium officials, team managers, parking officials, and others are working hard to handle this demand. One major problem is that the challenges of crowd control are greater than the current ability of professionals to handle them in conventional ways. In addition, the infrastructure at many venues is insufficient to accommodate the expanding number of spectators attending these events. Still another major challenge is the increasing trend for fans to act out their passions in an often dangerous manner. Fans storm the playing field, hurl objects at the players and each other, and even bring weapons into the venue. This complex web of too many people in oftentimes inadequate facilities with increasingly aggressive and uncontrollable behavior requires additional security personnel, and more sophisticated equipment. This means that teams, promoters, and venue operators spend more money to pay for these essential defensive strategies. Unfortunately, the public ultimately absorbs the cost of fan misbehavior as each profit and not-for-profit entity passes along the increased cost of doing business to the customer.

TELL IT TO THE JUDGE

The most dangerous development that is strangling sport in the United States is liability litigation. Jim Dalrymple has witnessed an increase in liability claims over the past few years. He believes that these are directly correlated with the leniency of courts in awarding damages against cities and sport venues. "When spectators travel to a stadium in the snow and ice, you would think that there is an inherent known risk, but somehow claims for slippage are continually awarded." The astronomical awards that have become commonplace have increased insurance premiums and these costs too have been passed directly to fans through higher admission costs to sport events.

BETTER NEWS

Sport event professionals are well aware of these challenges. In an effort to reduce the risk, stem rising losses, improve safety conditions, and keep costs in line so fans do not suffer financially, they have taken many positive steps. Professional education programs such as the Crowd Management Seminar sponsored by the International Association of Auditorium Managers (IAAM) and the annual risk management programs offered by the International Special Event Society (ISES) Conference for Professional Development address the most recent developments in this field.

Both private and public entities are assessing the infrastructure of their facilities to determine how to accommodate present and future fans. More important, public/private partnerships are helping these costly capital projects move from goal to reality.

A Super Bowl official was quoted in *Amusement Business*: "The biggest problem we have is that at a Super Bowl, 90 percent of the people have not been in the stadium before." The official added that "the more knowledgeable our 800-member security force is, the more helpful we can be."

For Super Bowl games, the NFL hires a national security firm, Contemporary Services Corporation (CSC), known for its experience in sport events. This firm hires some of the best local security personnel but heavily supplements the staff with people who have no affiliation with the city or local friends who might want to attend. Finally, arbitration is slowly but surely being introduced as an alternative to lengthy and expensive traditional litigation. Recognizing that there is an implied risk when a spectator attends a sport event, some fans are satisfied with the arbitration process as an efficient way to mediate their complaints.

WHAT YOU CAN AND MUST DO

The challenges and solutions we have described affect the big picture in sport event safety and risk management. Whether you are the organizer, player, vendor, or even a spectator, you are potentially liable when someone is injured at a sport event. Therefore, you must take and document basic precautions prior to the final organization of your sport event. See Figure 6–1 for an effective risk analysis.

FIGURE 6–1

Eight Steps of Effective Risk Analysis
According to Alexander Berlonghi
1. Planning and preparation
2. Gathering written information
3. Preliminary review of documents
4. Conducting interviews
5. Site survey
6. Reviewing and analyzing information
7. Designing risk-reduction recommendations
8. Writing a risk analysis report

Risk Assessment Meeting

Alexander Berlonghi, author of *Special Event Risk Management Handbook*, believes the first step in identifying potential risks is to conduct a detailed risk assessment of the event. Berlonghi, who handled risk management for Pope John Paul II's visit to Denver, Colorado, says that event managers either may hire a professional risk management consultant or use the internal expertise of their staff. When you use your own staff to identify potential risks, it is important to involve not only horizontal management positions but also vertical staff. Ticket takers, grounds keepers, security guards, and parking lot attendants as well as mid- and top-level management should participate in this process. (See Figure 6–2 for the format to use for this meeting.)

The risk assessment meeting serves several important and related purposes. First, it is an excellent way for you to empower your line staff and volunteers to take responsibility for identifying and managing risks. Safety is everyone's responsibility but unless you assign, train, and monitor this activity it may not become part of each person's job function. Second, you will benefit from the combined expertise of the members of your organization as they share their observations with you in a nonthreatening environment. Finally, you will have taken a significant step toward achieving a standard of care in your industry by convening this informational meeting.

FIGURE 6–2

Risk Management Assessment Meeting
According to Alexander Berlonghi

1. Assign a knowledgeable person with excellent communication skills to facilitate this meeting. This may be the event director, the director of security, or someone else who has the knowledge and experience to achieve the goals you desire.

2. The facilitator should distribute a meeting notice less than two weeks before the scheduled meeting to alert participants that they should come to the meeting prepared to identify risks in their area and throughout the event.

3. At the beginning of the meeting, the facilitator should briefly describe the seriousness of the agenda and ask for everyone's help in staying focused on identifying real threats that could jeopardize your event.

4. The group may be timid about beginning so the facilitator should suggest one or two risks he or she has identified through research. "The parking areas need more light for the night events in order to help prevent criminal conduct, and the ticket booths need rope and stanchions to establish a lineup area for day-of-event sales. What do you think about that?" This kind of inquiry will promote discussion that helps begin the dialogue and, with continuous facilitation, ultimately help you identify dozens of real risks that can be easily reduced at little or no cost.

5. This meeting is a mind-mapping exercise. List every potential risk, real and imagined, on a flip chart. This is similar to the SWOT analysis described in Chapter 2. Ask the reporter to explain how the risk was identified and what the potential risk is (e.g., injury, theft, bad public relations). Do not criticize any risk at this point. Instead, dutifully list them all and collect as many as possible before ending this step of the exercise.

6. Once all risks have been listed, ask each reporter to estimate the total financial cost of his or her risk. With the understanding that this is an exercise, encourage your associates to assign real dollar figures to each potential risk. This helps the entire group recognize that each risk has the real potential of reducing your bottom line revenue from the event. If the risk is one that is covered by insurance, list an estimated dollar increase in your premium due to the identified exposure.

7. Now that you have identified and assigned a cost to the potential risks, encourage the group to act as risk management consultants and make recommendations that will reduce these risks.

8. Before the meeting is adjourned, get agreement from the members of the group that they have, to the best of their ability and with the most recent information available, identified as many risks as possible. Ask them to remain vigilant in reporting other risks that may emerge before, during, or after the event.

9. Assign independent groups from this large group of risk managers to handle the next stage: the actual risk management phase. Ask each small group to design a variety of strategies that will effectively eliminate or reduce the risk at the lowest possible cost to your organization.

continued

FIGURE 6–2 concluded

10. Make certain that you document every step of this risk assessment meeting from keeping an accurate attendance roster to creating an action plan of activities you will undertake to reduce the risks. Make certain this document is prepared immediately following the meeting so that you can use it as a measuring stick of your progress in managing the risks.

If you should become the defendant in litigation, you will be able to demonstrate in writing that you showed due care in working with your team to identify and correct as many risks as possible to ensure the protection of your valuables and the safety of your guests.

ATHLETE PROTECTION

Since the stabbing of tennis star Monica Seles and the attack on Olympic ice skater Nancy Kerrigan, sport event managers have made security for athletes a key area of concern. Barbara Perry, director of events for the International Management Group, emphasizes the importance of walking through the sport venue—tracing the route of an athlete from the locker room to the competition or media and hospitality areas—and looking for vulnerable areas. Perry found that older buildings in particular have many nooks and crannies to secure. (See Figure 6–3 for tips concerning athlete protection.)

LOSS PREVENTION

Theft of property or money is a significant problem in sport event management. The explosion in attendance at sport events has brought a significant increase in criminal acts.

These acts range from box office robberies to pickpockets, from pilferage of souvenir merchandise to theft of automobiles and their accessories such as audiocassette tape decks from parking lots. At the RFK Stadium in Washington, D.C., Jim Dalrymple discovered that children would sneak under the end zone bleacher seats and steal bags and purses. To prevent this, fences with gates had to be

FIGURE 6–3

Athlete Protection Considerations

- Inspect the venue for vulnerable areas.
- Keep security discrete.
- Heighten the awareness of athletes toward the value of security precautions (e.g., credential checks, metal detectors).
- Ensure that credentialing criteria specify reason for and location of access to athlete (i.e. coach allowed in dressing room while family members restricted to hospitality area to meet with athlete).

FIGURE 6–4

Loss Prevention Considerations

1. Where will cash, receipts, and valuable inventory be stored?
2. How will access to cash and valuable inventory be provided?
3. Who will supervise your loss prevention program?

---

constructed to close off the ends of the bleachers and ushers were placed at each gate.

Each sport event management organization has an implied responsibility to prevent the loss of money and property at the sport event. Three critical considerations must be reviewed prior to commencing operations (see Figure 6–4).

STORAGE

The identification of a secure location not only for counting money but also for selling tickets, storing inventory, and conducting contests and prize-related activities is an important consideration for your loss prevention program. By establishing a secure location for these high-risk tasks, you will automatically reduce the opportunity for a burglary or robbery resulting in a severe loss. To provide a secure location for these tasks, follow the simple guidelines shown in Figure 6–5.

FIGURE 6–5

Securing Your Valuables

1. Select a location with one entrance that is away from the usual spectator traffic.
2. Secure the storage area with a door that has a double bolt lock.
3. When possible, make sure the area is an interior room with additional perimeter walls and a concrete floor.
4. Do not identify this room as a storage or counting room. Identify only box office areas.
5. Find out who has access to this room, including previous occupants who may still retain keys. When possible, change the lock or use additional locking devices as safeguards.
6. When using collection boxes to accept admission or concession tickets, make sure these boxes are secured and that only an appropriate authority has the ability to unlock them.
7. The opening through which the ticket is passed should be the same size as the ticket itself to prevent padding the box with bogus tickets.
8. When possible, chain this box to a secure location in the box office, admission area, or concession operation unit.
9. Involve law enforcement experts in your planning.

Access to your valuables is an issue that also includes the proper credentialing of your personnel, media, athletes, trainers, coaches, judges, staff, VIPs, and spectators (see Figure 6–6). Also, there is information that must be included on the credentials (see Figure 6–7).

ACCESS TO EVENTS

Early in your planning, determine how access will be set up to ensure that only the proper persons enter secure areas. Security guards at each entrance area must be fully briefed on different types of credentials and specific access privileges. Figure 6–8 is a checklist to assist you in developing a secure access plan for your sport event.

According to Terry Cooksey, a 10-year veteran of ticketing operations in Nashville, Tennessee, each ticket must contain at least five basic pieces of information: pertinent event information, seating information, policies unique to the event, applicable legal disclaimers, and the price. Cooksey suggests using a checklist

FIGURE 6–6
Credentialing Procedures

1. Review previous credential procedures from past or similar events to determine requirements and areas of improvement.
2. State in writing all credential procedures for each group (e.g., staff, volunteers, athletes, officials, media, participants, VIPs, corporate sponsors).
3. Establish a secure credentialing area with ample space for waiting lines, equipment, security, and other departments. Make certain electricity is available to operate cameras and other equipment and that telephone lines are available for communications.
4. Identify and contract a photography vendor to provide cameras and film for credentialing.
5. Conduct an orientation program for all staff issuing credentials.
6. Consider contingency plans for particular situations such as cameras becoming nonoperational, loss of communications, gridlock among crowds in the credentialing waiting area, theft, and other threats.
7. Keep all credential area signage low key to avoid attention.
8. Provide a separate line or area for athletes, VIPs, and media in recognition of their status.
9. Maintain and protect a computer system that stores credential requests and distribution information. Only persons with proper credentials or authority should have access to this information. Use passwords and backup, and store information in a secure place. If necessary, use the services of a security expert to determine any loss of your information through telephonic or even satellite transmission.

FIGURE 6–7
Critical Credential Information

- Name of credential holder.
- Photograph of credential holder.
- Code letter(s) for the credential purpose (e.g. press, VIP, official, volunteer, athlete, coach, technical staff, medical staff, administrator).
- Code numbers and symbols detailing event access (e.g. VIP Hospitality area, athletes village, media center, competition area, locker rooms, box office, warehouse, all events or specific events).
- Date of expiration or specific usage dates.
- Country of origin.

FIGURE 6–8

Tickets, Please!

1. Use a focus group composed of experts in ticketing, security, admissions, concessions, and other tasks in which loss prevention through admissions is an important issue.
2. Ask for the ideas of these experts and then show samples of tickets and credentials used at other successful sport events.
3. Create a draft policy that covers how credentials are granted, where they are issued, how day-of-event changes in credentialing and lost credentials are handled, and how fake or forged credentials are recognized.
4. Integrate your signage program with your credentialing process. It causes confusion, for example, to accept only VIP passes at Gate E when the sign above the admissions personnel reads "General Admission Only."
5. Establish a process for challenging tickets at the entrance and determining how to resolve these problems. Who has the ultimate authority to grant admission or change the procedure?
6. Remember that passes or credentials should be required for entry to all secure areas such as the box office, the counting room, the warehouse or storage areas, and other areas where valuables may be stored.
7. Does your organization or state or local laws prohibit scalping of tickets or sale of unlicensed, unauthorized merchandise at your sport event? Make sure you have a written policy to handle this possibility. If necessary, create signs to warn individuals who may consider engaging in this activity.
8. Modern sport events often use an advanced ticketing program that has sophisticated printing of the event logo to prevent duplication. Regardless of the technique you use, it is essential that all admissions personnel receive thorough training on how to recognize individualized credentials and tickets.
9. Future credentialing processes may ensure closer scrutiny by including a fingerprint or retina sensor device that matches the recorded computer database image. No two sets of fingerprints or retinas are exactly the same, so this technology may finally end the rash of forgeries that have plagued sport events.

when designing your draft ticket (see Figure 6–9). Remember that if you will be mailing tickets, first send a letter of confirmation asking for any correction in address and/or ticket purchase. High profile events such as World cup Soccer use two-day mail service to secure ticket delivery.

HIRING AND TRAINING

The Los Angeles Olympic Organizing Committee needed a volunteer skin diver to place bolts in the bottom of Lake Casitas to secure lane buoys. An executive pleaded, "Please hire someone covered by a workmen's compensation policy." A few years later,

FIGURE 6–9

Critical Ticket Information
According to Terry Cooksey

Pertinence
- Name of event/opponent
- Location of event
- Day/date/time

Seating
- Section/row/seat
- Gate, portal information
- Facility map

Unique Policies for this Event
- Refunds/exchanges
- Lost tickets
- Prohibited items
- Weather (rain checks)

- Date/time subject to change
  (televised events)

Applicable Legal Disclaimers
Example: The management reserves
the right to substitute performers.

Price
- Base amount
- Amount including applicable taxes
- Amount including applicable taxes
  and service charges
- Percentage of ticket price going to
  charity (if applicable)

another executive, Michael Gerber, author of *The E Myth*, said that "hiring employees is problematic to say the least. Most entrepreneurs are not prepared for the training process."

Finding and keeping good, honest employees is a challenge. Add to this the responsibility for being alert to theft and for resisting the temptation to skim profits—and you have a nearly impossible burden.

The good news is that while this burden may be more difficult than it was two decades ago, it is not impossible. Barry Silberman reports that "the key to hiring staff is to continually be on the lookout for quality individuals." He adds, "We typically hire interns who have served us well and have caught on to the business. Rarely do we advertise."

You should personally select the individuals to supervise your loss prevention program and its individual components, including ticket sellers, concession merchandise supervisors, and other people who collect, transfer, or sell valuable items.

Despite all of the mechanical means to guard property, the final responsibility lies with the personnel entrusted with these tasks. The selection and supervision of personnel is the most critical step

FIGURE 6–10

Guardians: Selecting and Supervising Loss Prevention Personnel

1. Use background checks before hiring employees or acquire personnel through firms who use this method to screen their employees.
2. Spot-checks ensure the integrity of your loss prevention staff. Spot checkers are trained individuals whose sole responsibility is to roam—dressed like typical spectators—among ticket sellers, admissions personnel, and concessionary staff to prevent profit skimming from your event through illegal activity. Notify your personnel in writing in advance of the potential presence of spot checkers at the sport event.
3. Undercover spectators are trained individuals who may display fake credentials in an effort to proceed through admission personnel without careful scrutiny. Remember, lost ticket revenue is a tremendous source of lost income for your sport event. Therefore, the admission process must be checked periodically to guarantee that security has not been breached.
4. Undercover customers may be used to attempt to purchase alcohol products without displaying proper ID or by using an obviously fake ID.
5. Make certain your training program for all personnel includes how to notify the proper authorities when an unusual occurrence is taking place. An authority may be a direct supervisor, a law enforcement agent, a private security official, or anyone who has the responsibility of investigating and preventing a potential loss.

to master in order to ensure superior loss prevention practices (see Figure 6–10).

At a festival in Fort Worth, Texas, Joe Jeff Goldblatt was asked to review all operations. As part of his assignment, he interviewed ticket sellers and asked them if they maintained change for $100 bills. Within seconds of leaving the ticket booth, two festival volunteers and a police officer stopped Goldblatt for questioning. Obviously, the loss prevention process at this festival received high marks from the event consultant.

Training before, during, and following the sport event must be well developed and appropriate for the learning styles of the personnel. Allow for the continuous input of supervisors and personnel to develop a loss prevention training system that will be effective for your sport event.

TRANSPORTING THE GOODS

Lisa Delpy, a veteran of numerous sport megaevents, states that designing a smooth transportation strategy for goods and valuables is critical. Delays and losses can incur costs that will never be recovered.

The preparation, packaging, shipping, receiving, approval, and inventorying of cash and valuables is too often a last-minute consideration by loss prevention personnel when planning sport events. Private companies realize the importance of this aspect of a sport event and have begun to specialize in this kind of logistics. FMI, for example, has orchestrated the delivery, warehousing, distribution, and protection of licensed merchandise for Super Bowls and World Cup Soccer, and will do so again at the 1996 Olympic Games in Atlanta.

Not every sport event requires the services of a private firm or an armored truck to transport cash, but every event does require a confidential plan to ensure the safe accounting of the event's cash and other valuables. Your plan should be developed with the assistance of local law enforcement personnel, your own security director, and line personnel who will participate in the activity. As a further security precaution, the number of participants who craft this plan should be limited only to those who will be directly responsible for its execution. (See Figure 6–11).

SAFETY FIRST

Most successful sport event professionals admit that safety is a paramount concern. Steve Schanwald, vice president of marketing and broadcasting for the Chicago Bulls, says:

> Some of our players have always received escorts to and from their cars and the locker room. We also have security people positioned intermittently throughout the court area. There is nothing more important to us than the safety of our players and fans. It doesn't make sense to bury your head in the sand and not take precautions.

The night before Nancy Kerrigan was attacked at the ice rink, her agent Jerry Solomon feared for her safety because the only transportation provided by the organizing committee to a midnight practice in the middle of Detroit was a hotel shuttle van with no security.

Safety generally involves three areas: fire, medical, and crowd control. Official procedures and protocols are most likely to be encountered in those three. High school coach Tom Hilton states,

FIGURE 6–11

Safe Transport

1. Establish how the cash or valuables will be transported and by whom.
2. Create three routes to transport the protected materials to the final destination. Alter the route for each delivery so that patterns are not established which might be followed.
3. Vary the time the transport is made to further avoid creating a regular pattern that can be monitored by those with bad intentions.
4. Determine whether a uniformed armed guard will be required. Then secure this person through either a private security firm or off-duty police personnel.
5. Plan for backup of personnel if the armed guard does not appear at the appropriate time to transport your materials or if you need to make an early shipment because of a large accumulation of cash.
6. Do not let large amounts of cash accumulate at individual box office locations. Establish a signal for notifying your counting room when pickups must be made to prevent the theft of large amounts of cash.
7. When receiving concession merchandise, make sure a bill of lading accompanies the goods and that you inspect and accept the inventory prior to off-loading the delivery vehicle at your facility. Determine in advance who has the authority to sign for acceptance of this merchandise.
8. Make prior arrangements for secured storage and inventory of merchandise.
9. When transporting goods to individual booths at the sport event, determine who will pull items from inventory and load delivery vehicles, who will accept these goods for transport, and who will sign for acceptance at the final destination. Receipts should match in order to prevent loss.

"Crowd control is essential. We always hire a uniformed off-duty police officer and make certain the police car is highly visible in the parking lot. This acts as a deterrent."

Hot topics for sport event planners are new issues such as the use of drugs by athletes and spectators and the potential transmission of the AIDS virus through athletic competition. It is important, however, to understand that safety is a global issue to which every department concerned with planning and operating the sport event should be committed. (See Figure 6–12.)

Watching a video of a Huntington Beach, California, riot at a surfing contest prompted an experienced law enforcement officer to comment, "There was little respect for police or security then and less now. We must plan better to counter this propensity for crowd violence." Security must be tight at all levels or it creates a domino effect. If tickets are not checked for appropriate seating, a rush of people could enter a section close to the field and players, overburdening the security personnel in that area.

FIGURE 6-12

Safety as a Global Concern

1. At the first planning meeting, include the word *safety* as a benchmark for producing a successful sport event. Without overall attention to safety, no event can possibly succeed.
2. Remind your event team that everyone is a safety consultant and that you want the input of all personnel in devising a successful safety plan.
3. Establish a safety committee to formulate final plans and set a time frame for its development.
4. Locate a first aid station on your sport event site. In the case of larger events, locate as many stations as medical and law enforcement officials recommend.
5. Determine through consultation with medical personnel or from reviewing other sport events of similar size, attendance, and scope, the number of medical personnel that your event requires. To ensure complete coverage, remember to staff these positions from the time personnel arrive for the event through the time the venue is shut down.
6. Utilize the services of the fire marshal to inspect the venue, confirm the capacity allowed for the event, and to help you determine proper signs for crowd control.
7. When using special effects such as pyrotechnics, check with the fire department about requirements for special permits and/or personnel.
8. Check with the fire department to determine requirements for concessions, decorations, and special areas that may require separate inspection.

Although not all states or jurisdictions require training for private security guards, most venue operators and sport event promoters agree that with the many new challenges confronting this industry, it is a critical need. Training may result in increased costs but the added value will result in a more consistent level of protection from these important sport safety and security professionals.

Risk management preparation is crucial to any event and relies heavily on the ability of event managers to communicate the venue's emergency medical system (EMS) to staff, spectators, and participants. The following scenario illustrates the elements involved in an EMS and how—through oral, visual, and physical means—the emergency system is communicated and implemented.

Scenario: Emergency Medical System

The Super Bowl is in progress and a middle-aged man clutches his heart and falls over. His wife remembers reading a notice in the program (visual) and hearing an announcement over the loud speaker (verbal) giving directions on what to do in an emergency. The wife immediately asked a neighbor to call an usher, security guard, or the medical team. An usher was easily identified by an orange vest (visual). He immediately notified the central communication center (CCC) by portable radio and gave an assessment of the situation before beginning CPR. The CCC then contacted the emergency medical team (EMT) on location and the doctor and nurse on duty to prepare for advanced medical care and transportation. The CCC also alerted other ushers and security to maintain crowd control. After the usher's initial contact to the CCC, all communication was carried out by the CCC to keep radio lines clear. After the victim was safely cared for and taken away, all individuals completed written reports. Supervisors read this documentation to evaluate the effectiveness of the system, after which the reports were stored in case of litigation.

Note: Prior to this event, the facility manager conducted an EMS in-service training for all employees. Each employee was also certified in CPR and given a copy of the policy handbook.

SECURING ADEQUATE INSURANCE

The best laid plans often are circumvented due to circumstances beyond your immediate control. This is why maintaining adequate levels of insurance is critical. This issue is of such importance that members of the International Special Events Society (ISES) are required to have adequate levels of comprehensive liability insurance in order to maintain their membership.

There are four preliminary options to consider before purchasing insurance: retention (self-insure), avoidance (don't do it), transfer (insurance/risk), and reduction (safety audits). A careful review of these four options will lay the foundation for proceeding with insurance decisions.

Indeed, most venues require that the promoter, sponsor, or organizer of the event maintain a minimum level of insurance. Insurance coverage that is typically required is shown in Figure 6–13.

The premiums for these types of insurance are based on the level of risk. Obviously a tennis event is at greater risk of cancellation due to player injury or weather than a rugby match. With a reduction in gate receipts, the burden of proof is on the policyholder to quantify the loss and justify the anticipated attendance. For this type of insurance, it is best to agree upon values, based on average historical records, prior to the start of the event.

FIGURE 6–13

Types of Insurance Coverage

1. *Comprehensive General Liability*
   A package policy that includes fire, theft, and injury also typically includes several exclusions such as pyrotechnics, aerial or participant activities, and other high-risk activities.
2. *Cancellation or Contingency*
   Provides coverage for the cancellation of the event. A comprehensive cancellation or contingency policy will provide adequate coverage for nonappearance of celebrity performers and rain, lightning, or other acts of God.
3. *Prize Indemnity*
   Indemnifies the sponsors against loss of income due to prize fraud or contest awards. Often used for hole-in-one golf tournaments.
4. *Workmen's Compensation*
   Required by most states to provide reimbursement of medical expenses for workers injured on the job.
5. *Automobile Liability*
   Provides compensation to those who are injured by automobiles used for the event covered under the insurance policy.
6. *Property Insurance*
   Insures sets, props, and other material items.
7. *Participant Accident Coverage*
   Provides coverage for the accidental death or dismemberment of an event participant.
8. *Inland Marine Insurance*
   Provides coverage for risks related to marine activities.

Cancellation Policies

Cancellation insurance requires that the criteria for canceling an event be specified in advance. A hot-air balloon race or air show may be canceled because of low clouds and high winds, while other events may be canceled if the humidity level is too dangerous or if players fail to arrive because of travel difficulties. Cancellation insurance also should cover loss of merchandise sales with the merchandise vendor's costs and expenses typically guaranteed for loss of profit.

Prize Indemnity

The conditions for prize indemnity must also be stipulated in advance. These include the type of technology that is allowed in the contest or the prior experience of the contestant. Premiums are based on the number of attempts available to win the prize and the probability of success. A lawsuit over possible fraud is currently pending between a race car driver and an insurance carrier. The race car driver won three races and alleges that, according to the contest rules, the driver is due a cash bonus. However, the insurance company inspected the vehicle and discovered that it was an enhanced version of the technology initially approved by the insurance company; therefore, the underwriter alleges that the coverage is null and void.

UNDERWRITING: AN ART AND SCIENCE

When purchasing insurance, the best advice is to select an agent who is knowledgeable about your business and can thus suggest the most appropriate coverage. Most event management firms purchase an annual policy covering all business activities. In the case of high-risk events such as skiing, however, it is advisable to purchase a separate policy in order to keep premiums to a minimum.

LeConte Moore, senior vice president of Marsh & McLennan, one of the world's largest sport and entertainment insurance brokerage firms, says that it is essential for the sport event professional to seek expert, experienced advice when determining the type, amount, and length of coverage required to manage the risk of financial loss. Moore, a 15-year sport and entertainment insurance industry veteran, states that "the broker's technical expertise and experience, examples and references of past events, and access to a large group of specialized underwriters should provide the purchaser with enough information to make an informed and confident decision."

Moore describes the professional insurance broker's function as "providing the transactional capabilities to link clients with appropriate insurance companies that can adequately underwrite the risks presented. Typically, the broker receives a fee or commission from the insurance company based upon a percentage of the premium paid."

Fewer than 10 insurance firms, by Moore's estimation, have the knowledge and experience to accept the coverage for a major sport event—a great contrast with other forms of insurance where the purchaser may have dozens of options. Therefore, the relationship between the broker, client, and insurance company in sport event management is critical. Paramount in this relationship is the level of understanding between the client and the broker. The broker must listen carefully to the needs of the client to best evaluate the risks involved in the sport event and then properly communicate these needs to the insurance company to provide appropriate coverage.

SAFETY, SECURITY AND RISK MANAGEMENT IMPLICATIONS

The sport event management safety universe will continue to expand rapidly. It will involve not only those who plan the methods that help ensure a safe sport event but also will include feedback from the beneficiaries of your planning: the participants and spectators. Involve these key groups in your planning to make certain you have considered as many safety hazards as possible and that your final plan is practical and can be easily used by the participants and spectators. Your internal planning team may select a seemingly perfect location for your first aid station only to find out that neither the participants nor the spectators elected to use it because of its inconvenience. Their input is essential to creating a workable safety plan.

The effective and continuous use of internal and external communications in planning sport events is the single most important factor in reducing risk, preventing loss, and increasing safety for your sport event. Whether your event involves 100 people or 100,000, the attention given to risk management, loss prevention, and safety are of crucial concern when prospective insurance underwriters, investors, sponsors, and spectators evaluate the benefits of their participation.

THE FINAL SCORE

The most important final tally is not the score recorded on the athletic field. The tally that will be recorded in a great number of record books will be that of your professional management of the risk, loss, and safety. A good record here is one truly to be proud of and is the most important championship of all.

One area where risk is increased and opportunity expanded concerns the celebrity in your sport event. As you will see in Chapter 7, the right celebrity can be an excellent addition to your sport event.

GAME HIGHLIGHTS

- Risk management, loss prevention, and safety are effective management tools to use in producing profitable and successful sport events.
- Use a focus group comprised of event staff to help you identify a wide range of potential threats and plan for their efficient management.
- Provide effective oral, visual, and physical communications so that employees, spectators, and participants will know what to do in an emergency. Use one central control center for EMS so miscommunication will not occur and radio lines are left open. Write a report after each incident for litigation and evaluation purposes.
- Select an insurance broker knowledgeable in the sport event field who can advise you wisely about the amount and type of coverage you need.
- Involve external groups such as athletes and spectators in the safety review process to ensure universal acceptance and usage.

PLAY BOOK

armed security Security professional who carries a licensed firearm.

credential Badge, pass, or other visible document that allows entry into a specified area. Usually includes a photograph for identification.

fire marshal Representative from the fire department who determines the official maximum capacity for your sport event, inspects fire safety equipment and procedures, and grants permission for pyrotechnic effects.

insurance broker Professional who understands the needs of clients and the risk of the events, and shops for an appropriate insurance company to provide coverage.

off-duty police officer Sworn police professional who is hired privately for the sport event while off duty.

password Confidential and individualized code used to gain access to information data through a computer system.

private security Individual contracted through a private agency to provide guard duty or other security services.

risk management Job function responsible for identifying and determining which methods to employ against potential threats that may negatively affect the sport event.

spotter Trained individual who roams the sport event site seeking illegal or unethical activities.

transport Preparation, packaging, transportation, and documentation of cash and valuables.

undercover spectator Trained individual whose task is to interact with sport event staff to identify weaknesses in the loss prevention system.

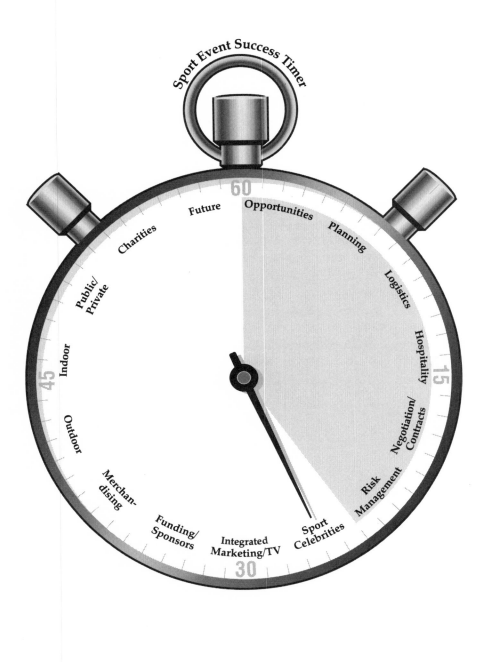

Chapter Seven

The Athlete as Sport Celebrity:
How to Find, Acquire, Contract, and Maximize the Involvement of a Professional Athlete

"On the day of the race, a lot of people want you to sign something just before you get in the car so that they can say they got your last autograph."

A.J. Foyt, race car driver

W hy does a sport celebrity help attract attention, build excitement, and lend credibility to your sport event? (See figure 7-1) How can you locate and manage the right "star" cost-effectively?

Charles Brotman, CEO of Brotman Communications in Washington, D.C., and an expert in sports public relations, says:

> Politicians in Washington, D.C., are considered next-door neighbors and movie stars in Hollywood are not a major attraction, but athletes in their hometown or out of town are like lightning rods. Athletes are viewed as untouchable, only seen from the stands, so when there is an opportunity to shake hands, take a photo, or simply be close to a sport superstar, it is a real turn-on."

As long as they are well managed, using celebrity athletes is a great way to advance your sport event. Ask the sport celebrity to arrive one or two weeks early to have breakfast with one reporter and lunch with another. A single mention by the celebrity of how great the upcoming tournament or event will be immediately builds credence and enthusiasm among ticket purchasers. When a casino in Las Vegas or Atlantic City books a boxing match, the boxers are most often required by contract to appear at a minimum of three publicity events and certainly in the casino with the high rollers the night before the match.

To promote Father's Day sales, for example, a regional shopping center marketing director may contact the Washington Redskins football team office (most often the public relations or marketing department) to obtain a player to sign autographs. The Redskins office refers the marketing director to a player contact list that includes agents, managers, and publicists for each player. Now the fun begins. Who does one contact first to hire the player at a reasonable cost? What is the most effective approach? More important, how does one use the player to raise funds or boost sales?

The late artist Andy Warhol was correct in predicting that every human being would experience his or her own 15 minutes of fame in the waning days of the 20th century. There are more celebrities than ever before so effective sport event management and marketing professionals must decide early on why, when, and how to best use a sport celebrity to accomplish their stated goals and objectives.

Marc Goldman, president of Damon Brooks Associates, a celebrity acquisition firm in Hollywood, California, says "More and more corporations want sport celebrities to mix with their associates because, bottom line, this investment is good for business, builds corporate image, and serves as an incentive to employees or clients."

Whether you are responsible for hosting a corporate golf tournament and want to recruit a celebrity pro to schmooze with your best customers, or you are managing a charity event to raise funds for a local children's hospital and need a sport celebrity to boost attendance, the rules of the game are essentially the same.

CELEBRITIES AT CHARITABLE SPORT EVENTS

Local professional sport organizations often work on a regular basis with charities. One example is the annual Toys for Tots Campaign sponsored by the U.S. Marine Corps Reserve in Washington, D.C. During the campaign, the Washington Redskins collect toys at one of their home games. This generates not only thousands of new toys for needy children but also much needed

FIGURE 7-1

Ten Reasons to Use a Sport Celebrity at Your Sport Event

1. A sport celebrity who has prior participation in a charitable endeavor or affiliation with your cause may lend further credibility to your own event.
2. A sport celebrity, such as a golf pro, may attract serious participants who recognize the value of contact with this individual.
3. A sport celebrity who is a spokesperson for a licensed product may help boost sales by making an in-store appearance on behalf of that product.
4. Television and radio appearances, agreed to in advance by the sport celebrity and managed effectively, will ensure positive publicity for your sport event.
5. Newspaper and magazine interviews given by the sport celebrity will not only boost visibility for your event but provide a lasting record for sponsor follow-up and future solicitation.
6. Sport celebrities can provide services ranging from an autograph signing to a keynote speech. These services can build internal morale among your employees and reward and recognize your customers.
7. Developing collateral materials—such as brochures, videos, audiotapes, and licensed products such as T-shirts and caps—with your sport celebrity can provide a new income stream for your event. They can also provide signed memorabilia for silent auctions.
8. When creating contests such as sport trivia, the involvement of a sport celebrity as part of the program or prize will develop consumer and employee interest.
9. Tying your event into the sport celebrity's other appearances will generate greater publicity to a wide audience. Other appearances may range from the sport celebrity's weekly coach's show to the pregame show itself. During these events, the sport celebrity mentions his or her involvement in your event.
10. Establishing the potential of a long-term agreement with the celebrity helps amortize your investment and provides greater security for developing a major campaign.

publicity for the charity during the busiest time of the year. Furthermore, warm and fuzzy photos may be staged of giant football players collecting and distributing new toys to tiny tots. This is a win-win for both the charity and the sport organization.

Stedman Graham, no stranger to celebrity experiences, says "It is fairly easy to recruit a sport celebrity who has a vested interest in your cause. Do your homework and you'll deliver an 'A' list of names for your event."

Research is the first step in recruiting a sport celebrity to your event. Find out whether any athletes are currently serving on the national board of the charity or have been linked historically to the cause. It is always easier to attract someone who has a personal interest in your cause. In some cases, a celebrity or a member of a celebrity's family may have benefited from the work of your charity. The charitable donations and services that quarterback Boomer Esiason has contributed toward cystic fibrosis, a disease that has afflicted his son, is a recent example.

Check also with your major sponsors for contracts they have with any sport figures. Many major companies retain sport celebrities on their payroll. You could cut the costs of appearance fees if these celebrities are required to make several appearances annually.

After a careful analysis of the most logical choice of celebrity to participate in your event, you should call the appropriate contact, identify yourself clearly, and then check the athlete's practice and game schedules to make sure there are no conflicts with the date of your event. Again, a call to an affiliated sport organization or team can help you identify the best contact for the athlete. It is also important to check the athlete's history of fulfilling obligations. Make sure the celebrity is an acceptable role model for your event and will be easy to work with in developing his or her appearance. To confirm this information, check organizations with which the athlete has made previous appearances, sport journalists, and others who are knowledgeable about the athlete.

Next, draft a brief letter to the athlete stating your request and mail it in care of the athlete's contact person. If you or a board member has a personal relationship with the athlete, agent, or a close family member, a preliminary telephone call is in order.

In most cases, the athlete will refer you to his or her manager or publicist. At that time, you must really begin to exercise your selling muscles. List in descending order the benefits the athlete will enjoy from participating in your event. Then state the purpose of the event, the beneficiary of the athlete's charitable participation, and why this participation is critical to the success of the overall event strategy.

Todd Christensen, a former professional football player and NBC sport commentator, admits that most athletes are chiefly concerned with compensation. Next, they want assurance concerning the credibility and possible media exposure of the event. Many players are committed by contract to participate in a certain number of charitable or publicity events each year and realize that it is part of building their résumé and public service. Christensen personally supports the Children's Miracle Network (CMN) and was the master of ceremonies for a Sports Memorabilia Auction and VIP reception hosted by CMN during the 1994 Super Bowl. This event was an official charity of the NFL Quarterback Club and NFL properties. Mary Lou Retton and Bo Jackson were honorary chairpersons.

Always include a suggested response date to remind the athlete's representative that your publicity is being developed and requires confirmation to proceed.

Unless you are involving multiple athletes in your event, contact only one athlete at a time. Do not send out simultaneous letters to a dozen athletes hoping that one will respond as honorary chair of your event. The world of celebrity athletes is a small one; publicists and athletes get extremely upset when they learn that you have sent multiple invitations. Examples of successful charitable appearances by a sport celebrities are reported by Marc Goldman:

> The sport celebrity has become one of our most popular requests among charities in recent years. Because the celebrity may serve as a positive role model and can be used in multiple ways (print, TV, PSA's, personal appearances, or use of their name in publicity), charities like to work with them. Recently we secured Rollie Fingers (major league baseball Hall of Famer) for St. Jude's Medical Center in Orange County, California. He played billiards with community donors who contributed to this worthwhile cause. The key to a successful match is to select a personality who has a direct interest in the cause, product, or sport which is being played. Another example is to use a nonathlete celebrity to enhance a sport event. Richard Dean Anderson, popular star of the hit television series *MacGyver* appeared at the Des Moines, Iowa, Grand Prix to benefit multiple sclerosis and Special Olympics as a celebrity race car driver. Media attention soared and the female market for this sport expanded rapidly.

Subsequently Goldman has been successful in placing among others, Eric Braeden, star of *The Young and the Restless,* at the Dallas Grand Prix, and Dwight Yoakum at the National Hot Rod Association Celebrity Challenge in Pomona, California. The typical fee for Goldman's services is between $1,500 and $3,500 plus the celebrities' first-class airfare, hotel, and other expenses including a stipend if negotiated. Some celebrity athletes may request financial compensation for their appearance and the turn around and donate it to their own special charity. Often celebrities may request a percent of the gate. Such a profit sharing contract may be valuable if your event is short on upfront cash, but needs a key performer.

CORPORATE SPORT CELEBRITY INVOLVEMENT

The annual sales meeting needs a major lift and your president suggests hiring a motivational speaker. After reviewing dozens of audiotapes, videotapes, and brochures, you remember that this year your human resources vice president is promoting the "new team spirit". What better way to generate team spirit than by inviting a world champion athlete to address your employees?

With the advent of athletes-turned-sportscasters, the number and quality of professional athletes as speakers has greatly expanded. From Terry Bradshaw to Fran Tarkenton, from Mary Lou Retton to Nancy Kerrigan, both current and former professional athletes are now in ample supply as motivational speakers or cheerleaders for your corporate gathering. To obtain a sport celebrity as professional speaker for your meeting, follow the simple steps in Figure 7–2 to select the best value.

Walter Payton, former running back for the Chicago Bears, had a contract with a pharmaceutical company that paid him $75,000 to attend three meetings where he posed for pictures with physicians. When later delivered to the physicians, the photographs served as a continual reminder of the company's products.

Sport celebrities can also be used for question-and-answer programs, conducting sport clinics, serving as emcees at sport hall of fame or awards banquets and even appearing on or off camera in your corporate highlight video. The sky is truly the limit and only your imagination, budget, and the sport celebrity's willingness to participate deters you from achieving your goals. A number of athletes also donate their time to encourage students to stay in school and refrain from using drugs. Tiger Woods, the young professional golfer, is an excellent example of how athletes can serve as role models. Woods, whose charisma with young people is legendary, has worked with numerous outreach programs to

FIGURE 7–2

Finding the Best Sport Celebrity Value as Professional Speaker

1. Obtain the brochure, *Finding the Right Speaker*, from the National Speakers Association in Tempe, Arizona, to learn more about what to look for before contracting for services.
2. Determine what the speaker will be required to do. Will the celebrity be required to speak, sign autographs, or attend a reception? Not all speakers will accept all responsibilities.
3. Identify your budget. If your budget is less than $5,000, you will probably not be able to afford a major name sport celebrity and will have to use a former professional athlete. Fees for those with name recognition range between $7,500 and $10,000, and hot superstars such as Nancy Kerrigan may charge as much as $25,000 or more for each appearance. One way to reduce your cost is to couple your event with a charitable cause that the athlete will support.
4. Most sport celebrities have a canned speech. However, if you want them to customize their talk to your audience, determine in advance from other clients if they have done this before.
5. When contracting a sport celebrity, you must be sure to state all costs clearly in writing. Typical costs are the fee (including the agent's commission), round-trip first-class airfare, accommodations, and incidental expenses for ground transportation, food, and beverage.

introduce youth to sport and healthy living. A nonprofit organization, Athletes Against Drugs, is dedicated to this cause.

COACHES, REFEREES, AND MASCOTS

Too often, sport planners and producers overlook the strong appeal of coaches, referees, and mascots when they design event programs. Not only are these sport celebrities typically less expensive than a major name player, but their message may be of greater value.

For example, coach Lou Holtz of Notre Dame University's Fighting Irish is one of the most popular keynote speakers because of his excellent discussion on leadership. Former NFL referee and past president of the National Speakers Association, Jim Tunney's emotional and often humorous address on "Winning" takes audiences onto the sidelines as he negotiates with giant figures in professional football. And almost every team has a mascot ranging from Benny the Bull of the Chicago Bulls to Whizzer, the mascot of the Washington Capitals hockey team.

Tunney, a 31-year veteran of the NFL uses true stories about the intentions of hulks such as Mean Joe Green and the winning strategies of coaches from George Halas to Joe Gibbs, to illustrate the techniques of winning, leadership, team work, and peak performance. Surprisingly, one of the most important secrets is the use of empathy and understanding. Tunney's insights not only provide gales of laughter but also bring a tear to the eyes of the toughest corporate leaders as he describes what makes the great hall-of-famers human.

Turney has proved that the opportunities in professional speaking for someone with a sports background is great, especially when those opportunities are met with the same focus and commitment as the people he uses in his examples. He speaks for corporations and associations in every field, addressing thousands of people each year. According to Tunney, the opportunities for a professional speaker with a sports background is unlimited.

> Often I am called upon to address school groups that, because of my fee structure, cannot afford this investment. In these circumstances, I ask that they make a donation to the Jim Tunney Youth Foundation, which is my charitable benevolent trust designed to help California youngsters active in athletics. This way I am able to speak to these groups and, at the same time, together we are helping others.

He also states that the opportunity to incorporate video production with live speaking engagements is an expanding area that provides a permanent training system for his corporate offices. Tunney Game Highlights will grow predictably along with engagements by other sport motivational speakers who are as telegenic as Tunney.

At an opening ceremony at the annual meeting for the Religious Conference Management Association in Chicago, producer Mary Ann Rose of TAMAR was asked to select Chicago's most famous personality to welcome the guests to the Windy City. Did she select Mayor Richard Daley, Jr. or perhaps sportscaster and former Bears coach Mike Ditka? Did Michael Jordan offer his welcome? No, the selection, while unusual, was universally praised by the audience of meeting planners.

As the president wound up his remarks, a large costume character bull stampeded from the back of the audience amidst loud cheers, and once on stage, whispered into the prez's ear.

"What's that Benny?" the president asked, and Benny the Bull whispered once again. "Oh, Benny says it's time to welcome you to the home of the world champion Chicago Bulls and open our official meeting. Right, Benny?" Once again Benny cupped his hands and whispered into the president's ear and the president smiled and responded, "And according to Benny, that's no bull!" Accompanied by the president, Benny galloped off the stage leading over 1,000 happy delegates to the exhibit hall where he posed for photos with his many fans.

Mascots such as the Orioles' bird may be obtained through the sponsoring organization for a few hundred dollars per appearance. In some cases, like the Toronto Blue Jays, the mascot is independently contracted through a private firm. Again, if there is a legitimate charitable relationship that will benefit from the event, the mascot's appearance may be donated.

At the 1994 National Hockey League All Star Game in New York's Madison Square Garden, a dozen team mascots appeared in an entertaining opening stunt. Giant replicas of bowling pins were set up in each corner of the rink and the mascots took turns sliding into the pins to see which could knock over the most pins.

The appearance by all mascots on the ice simultaneously was unusual. Licensing agreements normally forbid mascots from appearing with other team representatives. Make certain that you have the approval of the sponsoring teams if you are using multiple mascots to avoid a conflict at your event or you could end up with a new event—the Royal Mascot Battle!

MANAGING THE SPORT CELEBRITY APPEARANCE

Although tiny in height, Mary Lou Retton is a giant in the sport celebrity field. Because of her diminutive size, Joe Jeff Goldblatt notes that specific security arrangements were made during a trade show appearance to ensure her safe passage through thousands of fans.

When engaging a sport celebrity to promote or appear at your event, it is wise to assign a specific staff member to host and handle any unique requests that may arise during the appearance. This is especially important if the sport celebrity is appearing pro bono (without a fee to promote the public good) to benefit a charitable cause, and it may also be included in the contract.

The checklist in Figure 7–3 will provide step-by-step instructions for organizing an effective sport celebrity appearance.

Obviously, you must review many other logistical considerations, including audiovisual (microphones, video) and personnel concerns ranging from the proper training of security in crowd control to the driving record of the limousine or transportation coordinator. Leave no detail unnoticed when coordinating a sport celebrity or you may create a domino effect wherein one small gaffe leads to many others.

SCHEDULING TIPS

Sport celebrities may tend to run late. It is your job to tighten up this schedule as much as possible. Build in flexibility but make sure that things ultimately start and finish on time.

The reasons for this are obvious but you need to consider the potential of cost overruns for security and other labor if the schedule runs long. The reality is that flights can be missed and other delays can be encountered if you don't keep your eye on the clock at all times.

In establishing the schedule, prepare a window of time for each activity that is longer than actually needed so that if the sport celebrity pauses to greet fans, you will still end on time. Figure 7–4 illustrates a typical window of time.

By adding minutes to the published schedule, you can compensate for delays beyond your control. Make certain you add these critical minutes at the front end of your planning to ensure that your stop time is accurate.

Sport Celebrity Challenges

Celebrities are human beings that other human beings celebrate for their achievement. *Sometimes* this celebration misses their heart and goes straight to their head. However, as a professional sport event planner and marketer, you must be prepared to handle the case of the uncooperative celebrity. The most common occurrences include a no show, the tardy celeb, and the difficult celeb.

When a no show occurs, it is important to first determine how the news will be released to your guests. Although you may have pur-

154

FIGURE 7–3

Steps to Produce a Successful Sport Celebrity A

Before the Appearance
- Review all correspondence and contracts to be certain you are in full compliance.
- Set time lines for scheduling air travel, ground transportation, hotel reservations, and other amenities.
- Ascertain whether the sport celebrity has any special needs during travel such as airplane seating preference, food and beverage likes and dislikes, and entertainment or other amusement activities in which they may wish to engage, including sport events.
- Confirm in writing all travel arrangements.
- Check with the celebrity or his or her representative about any specific security arrangements that must be made locally.
- Send a written logistical plan to each venue where the sport celebrity will appear, describing the setup with the help of graphic visuals.
- Confirm that each venue has received plans, understands requirements, and can comply fully.
- Send the final itinerary listing all scheduled activities and ask the sport celebrity to approve, comment, or change with his or her initials. This letter of agreement is essentially your contract and should begin with "This letter is to confirm that . . . ."
- Schedule and confirm in writing all travel arrangements.
- Send confirmation to the sport celebrity and confirm that he or she has received this critical information.
- Assign a person to be available on a 24-hour basis to handle the sport celebrity's last-minute needs upon arrival.
- Notify the hotel that you will be using a pseudonym for the celebrity to avoid pranks or intrusive calls to the celebrity's room.
- Ask the hotel to provide special amenities such as a fruit basket, welcoming gifts, and so forth for the sport celebrity.
- Simulate the travel and walking path of the celebrity to the event venue so that your event plan contains the actual time it takes for the celebrity to get to his or her destination. This will avoid miscalculations and delays later.

Day of Arrival
- Call the airline to confirm flight.
- Call the hotel to confirm room availability and welcoming gifts.
- Call the transportation company to confirm the limousine or shuttle.
- Arrive at the airport one hour prior to flight arrival.
- Stage the limousine or shuttle for prompt pickup.
- Greet the sport celebrity and escort to transportation.
- Retrieve luggage and deliver to the hotel.
- Prior to the sport celebrity's leaving the limousine, retrieve the room key and escort him or her directly to the suite, or have the limousine driver call ahead to make sure the sport celebrity's room key is available upon arrival.

continued

FIGURE 7–3 concluded

- Hand the sport celebrity an itinerary that describes all previously approved and scheduled activities. Ask the celebrity to review and query it.
- Reconfirm the time for pick up and/or transfer to the first engagement.
- Notify hotel security that a sport celebrity is in the hotel and ask for assistance in providing coverage for transfer from room to transportation or lobby.

During Events

- Arrive one hour prior to the sport celebrity appearance to reconfirm all logistics.
- Confirm that the arrival area is secure and free of casual bystanders.
- Confirm that all personnel are standing by for arrival. Personnel may include host, police, security, and other staff.
- Select an escape route if the arrival area fails due to breach of security. Ideally, this will be a nearby room where the sport celebrity can be secured until crowd management is handled.
- Escort the sport celebrity to the appearance area.
- Make sure the crowd lineup is proceeding according to plan and that all personnel are at their posts.
- Keep your eye on the clock and begin checking the departure route for clearance 15 minutes prior to the end of the appearance.
- Do not announce in advance the departure of the sport celebrity. Make the movement as quiet and inconspicuous as possible.

Appearance Physical Requirements

- Use a stage with a height of 24 to 48 inches (48 inches deters guests from sitting on the stage).
- Use rope and stanchion to clearly mark areas where autograph seekers and guests are to queue up to meet the sport celebrity.
- Do not allow guests onstage with the sport celebrity.
- Use a table (eight feet long skirted on the front and two sides) for autographs.
- Use preautographed photos and have the celebrity add initials at the event
- Make certain the area is well lighted with sufficient candlepower for videotaping if required.
- Provide bottled water or other refreshments for the sport celebrity in this area.

Appearance Personnel Requirements

- Make certain private security and police have established communication and are working together.
- Place one guard on each end of the stage and beside access ramps or stairs.
- Place one guard near the front and back of the sport celebrity.
- Place one public relations staff member immediately beside the sport celebrity to serve as buffer for unruly fans or guests.
- Assign one person as gofer to restock autographed photos, bring refreshments, or perform other essential tasks.

FIGURE 7–4

Framing the Window of Time			
Start Time	Activity	Proposed Stop Time	Actual Stop Time
8:00 A.M. (Note: Time extended)	Autographs	8:30 A.M.	8:35 A.M.
8:30 A.M.	Transfer to car	8:34 A.M.	8:39 A.M.
8:39 A.M. (Actual driving time is an estimated five minutes)	Drive to airport	9:00 A.M.	9:05 A.M.
9:06 A.M. (Actual transfer time is 10 minutes)	Transfer to gate	9:25 A.M.	9:25 A.M.
9:45 A.M. Total time lapse	Airport departure	9:45 A.M.	9:45 A.M. 1.45 hrs

chased cancellation insurance to cover such an occurrence, nothing can compensate for the poor public relations effect on your audience. If the cancellation is a legitimate postponement to be rescheduled at a later date, say so and give as much detailed information as possible. If refunds or rain checks are to be issued, describe the procedure simply and promptly. Most of all, continue excellent communications with your guests throughout this challenge.

Tardy celebrities pose additional threats as your planning may suffer both logistically and financially. With perpetual tardiness, explain to your sport celebrity that it is essential that they help you remain on schedule in order to accomplish the goals and objectives to which you have both agreed. When this fails, begin to anticipate their tardiness and arrange for early arrivals, early departures, and other movement strategies to compensate for tardiness. A tardiness clause may be included in the contract stipulating monetary penalties if the celebrity is being compensated.

Finally, a sport celebrity who proves difficult may not be well physically. Ask the celebrity if you can be of assistance by providing refreshments or other sustenance. Do not offer alcohol or medication. Fruit juices, nutritious foods, and even candy will send a message to the sport celebrity that you care about his or her welfare. Remain firm in your planning procedures and try to keep any discomfort on the part of the sport celebrity from spoiling the mood or atmosphere of your event.

FIGURE 7–5

It's Showtime!

- Hire a winning jockey to pose with the roses and your guests for award-winning photos.
- Schedule a bush league star baseball player to provide batting lessons for your corporate sales team.
- Engage a state championship runner to carry the flag into your celebration and have him or her hand the flag to a national running star.
- Turn your shopping mall into a Little League baseball tryout area using a Nerf baseball to avoid damages and invite a former major leaguer to sign autographs.
- Invite a local golf pro to provide putting tips or work with a golf club manufacturer to bring in a PGA pro to sign autographs and answer questions.
- Match a motivational sport celebrity speaker to your theme and develop an entire program around his or her message.
- Introduce the speaker with video clips from his or her best games.
- Take your guests to a major league hockey game and as a surprise arrange for one of the players to drop by the reception after the game to greet and meet your guests.
- Hold your banquet on the 50-yard line of Texas Stadium in Irving, Texas (Home of the Dallas Cowboys), and invite one of the assistant coaches to scrimmage with your team.
- Schedule a clay target shooting tournament at a resort and hire a professional trick shooter to mix with your regulars and keep them on their toes.
- Arrange for an early morning jog for your group and engage a Presidential look-alike complete with five or six Secret Service types to join you.
- Using an Olympic Games theme, engage medalists from 50 years ago to join you in celebrating the golden anniversary of their achievements.
- Commission award- winning *Sports Illustrated* cover artist Leroy Neiman to show slides of his work, speak, and perhaps paint your high-level major donor society event.
- The sky is the limit, remember? While enroute to the big sales meeting on board your 747 aircraft, invite Olympic gold medal skier Tommy Moe to speak to your jet-setting business leaders about never giving up and going for the gold!

It is important to note, however, that most sport celebrities have a popularity cycle. The best investment is in a celebrity who is on the way up rather than one who has peaked or is on the way down. To spot trends, study the popular sport literature and choose a winner for your next event.

There are also professional ratings called "Q ratings" that are available for purchase. These measure the popularity of celebrities.

Steven Levitt, president of Marketing Evaluations, Inc., developed the "Q" rating and finds matches for companies that minimize risk in a scientific way. The Nye Lavalle Group of Dallas, Texas, has developed similar ratings called the NYE ratings.

A sport celebrity can enrich your sport event with talent, marketing power, and ultimately new earnings. Whether selecting a professional athlete to sign autographs, a former championship coach to deliver a keynote speech, or contracting a popular team mascot to meet and greet your guests, numerous opportunities are available to maximize your investment by using creativity in your planning and management process.

IDEAS FOR SPORT CELEBRITY APPEARANCES

The possibilities are limitless for your sport celebrity appearance. Figure 7–5 offers some creative possibilities to illustrate this point. Make a short list of your own sport celebrity possibilities.

The creative use of celebrities in television, media, and marketing has helped spawn a multibillion dollar industry. Next, you will discover how to integrate a variety of marketing techniques to maximize the visibility and profitability of your sport event.

GAME HIGHLIGHTS

- Always determine the goals and objectives of the sport celebrity's appearance before signing a contract.
- Carefully analyze the strengths and weaknesses the athlete can bring to your event.
- Do your homework and find out the sport celebrity's schedules, personal or sponsor affiliations, and previous appearances and their success.
- Use market analysis to determine whether to employ an athlete, coach, official, mascot, owner, film, or television star as your sport celebrity.

- Be prepared for security and challenges. Know in advance how you will handle no-show, tardy, or difficult sport celebrities.
- Use your imagination and creativity to produce successful sport celebrity appearances.

PLAY BOOK

motivational sport celebrity speaker A coach (e.g., Lou Holtz), athlete (e.g., Mary Lou Retton), team owner (e.g., Red Auerbach), official (e.g., retired NFL referee Jim Tunney), author (e.g., George Plimpton) who present motivational speeches using sport analogies.

"Q" or "NYE" rating A measurement of a celebrity's fashionability and popularity.

sport celebrity An individual celebrated by others for his or her positive achievements. This individual may be an active or retired athlete, a coach, a referee, or even a team mascot.

window of time A precise amount of time within which the celebrity appearance must strictly adhere. The outer limits are fixed but the sport event planner may make adjustments as required by allowing for extra time in the planning process.

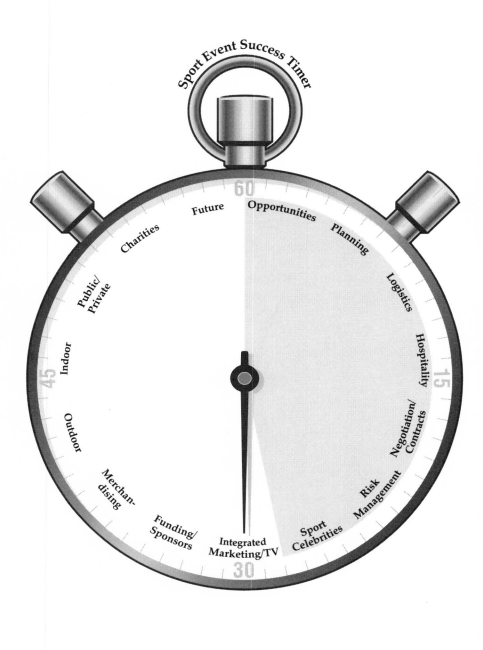

Chapter Eight

Television, Media, and Marketing: An Integrated Approach

"So many sports organizations have built their entire budgets around television, that if we ever withdrew the money, the whole structure would collapse."

—Roone Arledge, former ABC sports director

How do television and other forms of communication and marketing establish the world's perception of sport events and why must you take control to benefit your event?

Greg Gumble, CBS television anchor for the Winter Olympic Games in Lillehammer, Norway, wielded tremendous influence as an estimated one billion pairs of eyes watched him. Every network decision affected the one billion viewers in the CBS Olympic Games audience. This electronic global arena is far more important to advertisers, sponsors, and broadcasting executives than any of the venues built for the games themselves.

Sport events have always held the potential for mass entertainment as well as a medium for marketing. Joe Engel, dubbed the "Barnum of the Bushes" for his antics as president of the Chattanooga Lookouts minor league baseball team, recognized decades ago that fans need entertainment to hold their interest during slow moments of the game. For example, Engle once advertised that an elephant hunt would be conducted on center field on opening day. A parade was held the evening before featuring giant trucks from which the unmistakable roaring of elephants blasted through the town. On opening day, the trucks rolled onto center field, actors dressed as natives aimed their rifles and fired blanks on the costumed elephants Engel had designed. A huge crowd turned out to see this extraordinarily entertaining spectacle. Roone Arledge, a present-day Barnum of broadcasting, expanded this idea of sport as entertainment to television.

Sport event television coverage has paralleled the development of this broadcasting medium. In the 1950s, when television first became commercially available to consumers, sport coverage was limited to major sport events such as baseball's annual World Series. In contrast, today's national and regional sport television channels offer sport programming 24 hours a day. The addition of ESPN II demonstrates that the demand for sport event television programming continues to grow.

A further demonstration of this popularity is the intense competition for the rights to broadcast sport events. Radio and television stations locally and nationally compete annually for contracts to exclusively air sport event competitions in anticipation of potential lucrative advertising revenues. In 1991, *Broadcasting* magazine reported that the National Association of Broadcasters (NAB) held educational sessions that told radio stations how to get the most revenue from sports and special events. The demand for sport programming was further confirmed by Linda Deckard, who wrote in *Amusement Business* that "new leagues need television exposure in order to succeed."

The more popular the sport event, the larger the viewership, the greater the profits. In a sense, the profit potential is tied directly to the viewers and, due to the universal popularity of sport events, that seems to be boundless. Although the amount of advertising broadcasters can sell is restricted by the United States Television Federal Communications Commission (FCC), the advertisement revenues received for selling this time has no restriction.

Despite the continued increase in broadcast rights fees for sport events, a mutual dependency between sport event owners and the mass media appears to be developing. One cannot survive without the other. Together they provide a medium and a message demanded by billions of people throughout the world.

GETTING INTO THE GAME

Today's typical sport fan commutes to the game by way of the media communications highway. This highway includes the following broadcasting and media advertising opportunities:

- Local radio
- Network radio
- Local television
- Cable television
- Network television
- Pay-per-view television
- Satellite television

The FCC is now considering licensing more than 1,000 cable television channels to provide viewers with a wider choice of options. Common sense dictates that viewers will not "channel surf" through hundreds of television stations but will concentrate on a group of channels, such as those related to sport events that best define and satisfy their lifestyle interests. The Golf Channel, the Tennis Channel, and other single sport event media are interesting possibilities.

Interactive media is the most recent technological advance to affect sport event viewers. Interactive television is a service that enables home television viewers to control what they see on the screen. For example, this service allows sport fans to call up specific statistics on a player during a game through the use of fiber optics and computer technology. Although interactive media will become a reality in the near future, the types of broadcasting media in use today are described below.

Local Broadcasting

Many geographic areas with a population of 100,000 or more have two or more television stations and several radio stations. These broadcast outlets often serve a far greater area, depending upon the signal strength of their transmitter, and therefore reach hundreds of thousands more potential viewers and listeners.

These broadcast stations cover not only local, regional, and state sport events, but also national competitions through network affiliations or satellite connections.

Cable and Network Television

When deciding which media communications to pursue for your sport event coverage—network versus cable—you must know your event's appeal to both the TV audience and advertisers. Advertisers may be in search of broader demographics and find that sponsoring ABC's *Wide World of Sports* instead of a local cable channel's sport event is a far better buy in term of cost per thousand impressions.

You should also know the difference within each category of media. SportChannel for example, does not provide ratings to the owner of the sport program. This information is vital when soliciting advertisers. Other cable networks, like ESPN, do provide such ratings.

It is important as well to understand the difference between the terms *broadcasting* and *narrowcasting*. Broadcasting refers to programming designed for the broadest possible demographics while narrowcasting reaches highly targeted consumers in various demographic strata. An example of the difference in demographics is a major television network like CBS and a narrowcaster like the cable channel, The Americana Television Network. Future narrowcasters could be aerobics, running, and other sport-specific media.

Pay-per-View (PPV)

Originally only major boxing matches were broadcast on a pay-per-view (PPV) basis through cable companies such as Home Box Office. Now professional wrestling and other major sport events are increasingly being offered to viewers on PPV at a premium price. Advertisers are carefully watching this trend to determine how best to position their product as a tie-in to the sport event because no actual commercial time is available during PPV programming. Viewers are also watching this development to determine if they will be paying a premium price in the future for those programs they have come to enjoy only at a cost of enduring the seemingly endless commercials that have historically funded these sport events. NFL Commissioiner Paul Tagliabue predicted that by the year 2000 the Super Bowl may be available only on PPV.

Satellite

The launch of the first space satellite revolutionized modern communications. Not since the invention of the printing press have the people of the world been brought together so quickly through a new technology. Now the electronic satellite receiving dish, which might measure eight or more feet in diameter and requires a building permit to install, is being reduced to the size of an ordinary dinner plate that is easily mounted on the kitchen windowsill. Daniel Burrus, author of *Techno Trends*, says "these direct broadcast satellites (DBS) will be digital, giving viewers compact disk (CD) quality sound and super VHS quality picture at a fraction of the cost of your old home satellite system." Ironically, your "old" satellite system, the latest technology, may be only three years old.

This reduction in size and cost and the increased quality of sound and picture will have more and more U.S. fans grabbing Japanese baseball games out of the sky with their very own baseball glovelike star catcher. As exemplified above, this advancement in satellite technology is especially important for sport events reaching beyond traditional borders. Such expansion can lead to increased revenue through broadcast fees and indirectly through increased merchandise sales in new markets. The implications for transnational marketing and banking are tremendous.

Joe Jeff Goldblatt was delighted when he visited a restaurant in St. Louis, Missouri, and noticed that his favorite college basketball team, the George Washington University Colonials, was on television. Each time the Colonials scored, Goldblatt would cheer and was joined by dozens of strangers in the restaurant who were also fans, albeit from afar, of the Colonials. This is but one more example of how television has become the global village of which sport team owner and broadcast mogul Ted Turner dreamed when he conceived Cable Network News (CNN).

MAINTAINING A STANDARD OF PROGRAM EXCELLENCE

With the increased privilege of new broadcasting opportunities comes greater responsibilities on the part of the programmers, executives, and on-air talent themselves. While this is still an emerging science and art form, it is critical that the key players demonstrate respect for their raison d'être: the celebration of sport through the performance of the athlete. Tom Shales, television critic for the *Washington Post*, criticized CBS's coverage of the 1994 Winter Olympic figure skating competition because the commentator talked incessantly and the music accompanying the skaters could not be enjoyed.

With the increase in television rights fees and corporate sponsorship fees, sport event managers are being asked not to jeopardize the integrity of the event with too much commercialization. The recent trend of packaging television and sponsorships will assist event owners, sponsors, and television right holders.

An example was Coca-Cola's sponsorship of the 1989 Super Bowl halftime show. The show featured a magical theme which Coke used to hype its sponsorship by giving free 3-D glasses to watch the show. As the title sponsor for the halftime spectacle, Coca-Cola was featured at the beginning and end of the show and could use its pre-event commercial time to promote and support its sponsorship.

This not only creates a solid message to the consumer but also eliminates ambush marketing opportunities that currently exist between in-stadium sponsorship signage and television commercial advertisers.

GETTING YOUR EVENT TELEVISED

Because of the growing number of broadcast mediums, there is a great demand for sport event programming. Television stations, however, are driven by advertising dollars, and cable stations are driven by both advertising and subscription fees. Your event therefore must meet certain criteria in order to interest a network or cable station in televising your sport event.

FIGURE 8–2

Sport Event TV Evaluation Checklist

_____ Why are you approaching a television station in the first

_____ Will televising your sport event increase your revenues?

_____ Will it enhance the image of your sport and the athletes?

_____ Will it lead to future lucrative arrangements?

_____ How unique and valuable is your sport event property?

_____ Is there enough popular demand and potential for advertising revenue in your sport event to generate the interest of network, cable, or pay-per-view television?

_____ Has the team or event achieved consistent sellout over for the past three years?

_____ What historical television data are available on this or similar sport events?

_____ Has the event ever been televised before and, if so, who aired the program and what were the ratings?

_____ Have one or more broadcast organizations approached the sport event representative about potential purchase of broadcast rights?

_____ Is this a first-time sport event or does it have unique and special features that will attract new viewers and advertisers?

_____ Has the media coverage for the sport event, despite win/loss records, been generally positive?

_____ Are players, coaches, or other official personalities available to offer their talents and services for a weekly highlight show, or pregame, halftime, and postgame programs?

_____ What regulations does the league, association, or other governing body have concerning the sale of sponsorship or broadcast rights?

boost to the tournament in terms of public awareness. The interview was covered by every major television and radio station, as well as all the print media in the area.

Steve Schanwald notes:

Television is like a two-and-a-half-hour commercial for our product. It gives us a chance to reach the people who otherwise would not be able to get inside Chicago Stadium. It gives people the chance to actually see what they are missing by not being a season ticket holder. It gives us an opportunity to grow and develop new fans and to expand our fan base. The more fans we have, obviously, the greater our chances of merchandise and season ticket sales (when they become available again). The objective is to gradually move customers up the ticket buying staircase.

ure 8–3 to increase your like-

NG

added value beyond the basic
e and are seeking ways to fully
s into their overall strategic

Corporate sponsors and ...   ne sport event industry, "We want
it all." They want to control the event, own it, drive it, and position
themselves with a strong integrated marketing approach. Sponsors
also want to know how many people they impacted, how many media
impressions they received, and how much sales increased. Through
the evaluation of return on investment, they will determine if the sport
event was effective marketing for them and what, if anything, needs
to be done to improve their position in the marketplace.

Early in his sport marketing career, Graham identified the need to
offer clients a different way to drive the market other than traditional
media buys. He developed packages that included newspaper
advertisements, radio promotions, special events, direct mail, cross-
promotions, and local retail tie-ins such as sweepstakes and contests.
Today, this approach is called "integrated marketing"—the systematic alignment of a variety of advertising, sales, promotional, sponsorship, and public relations activities to provide greater synergy for
the event marketing program in order to strengthen and stretch the
investor's dollar (see Figure 8–4).

In recent years, *integrated marketing* has become a buzzword
among sport marketing firms, advertising agencies, and corporate
sport event sponsors. As more corporations reallocate their
marketing dollars toward sport event sponsorship, advertising
agencies are finally acknowledging the importance of sport marketing and management. Indeed, sport marketing accounts for the
greatest increase in revenue dollars among advertising agencies.

However, if the total available advertising dollars continue to
decrease, corporate executives will ask, how do we increase traffic
and get more people to purchase our products at a lower cost? How
do companies break through all the clutter and reach their target
audience?

FIGURE 8–3

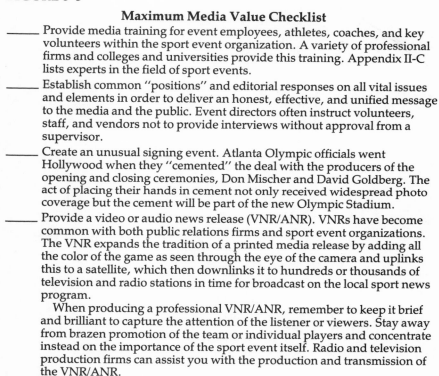

Maximum Media Value Checklist

_____ Provide media training for event employees, athletes, coaches, and key volunteers within the sport event organization. A variety of professional firms and colleges and universities provide this training. Appendix II-C lists experts in the field of sport events.

_____ Establish common "positions" and editorial responses on all vital issues and elements in order to deliver an honest, effective, and unified message to the media and the public. Event directors often instruct volunteers, staff, and vendors not to provide interviews without approval from a supervisor.

_____ Create an unusual signing event. Atlanta Olympic officials went Hollywood when they "cemented" the deal with the producers of the opening and closing ceremonies, Don Mischer and David Goldberg. The act of placing their hands in cement not only received widespread photo coverage but the cement will be part of the new Olympic Stadium.

_____ Provide a video or audio news release (VNR/ANR). VNRs have become common with both public relations firms and sport event organizations. The VNR expands the tradition of a printed media release by adding all the color of the game as seen through the eye of the camera and uplinks this to a satellite, which then downlinks it to hundreds or thousands of television and radio stations in time for broadcast on the local sport news program.

When producing a professional VNR/ANR, remember to keep it brief and brilliant to capture the attention of the listener or viewers. Stay away from brazen promotion of the team or individual players and concentrate instead on the importance of the sport event itself. Radio and television production firms can assist you with the production and transmission of the VNR/ANR.

_____ Find someone to interview you on radio. Select an approach that makes sense for the station so that the interview does not appear self-serving. An example of this technique is to contact a specific radio talk show host who is interested in college basketball's final four competition. Use the host's interest as a way to open the door to discussions about the growing importance of college basketball programs such as yours.

MANAGING INTEGRATED SPORT EVENT SPONSORSHIPS

How does a corporate sport event sponsorship differ from a traditional media buy? From a management standpoint, the most prominent difference is that sponsorships are detail- and labor-intensive. When you are involved in sponsorship management, you may have to provide 24-hour service to satisfy the demands of some sponsors. However, the result can be a winning season financially.

FIGURE 8–4

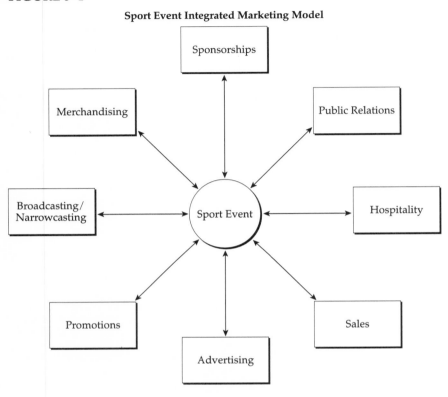

Sport Event Integrated Marketing Model

Susan O'Malley, president of the Washington Bullets, who within one year increased attendance at home games by 30 percent, claimed, "I'm not a marketing genius, I'm a hard worker."

Don Campbell, director of special promotions for MCI, remembers his early years in the business and how challenging it was to leverage a top-notch sponsorship. Campbell explains:

> I did not know what all the opportunities were. We went in with our eyes wide open and our tails wagging. The beauty of a long-term sponsorship relationship is that you can refine and perfect it over time. You keep what works and improve other parts.

Once a company purchases the rights to a sport event (i.e., purchases a sponsorship package), an integrated tailor-made marketing plan must be designed to ensure the maximum return on investment. These plans will be different for each company because the goal for one may be to maximize exposure and image while for another it may be how much product it can sell. A project director should be appointed to coordinate each event and various individuals should be assigned from different corporate divisions to work on the event.

Another example of integrated marketing for a three-on-three basketball tournament is to have entry forms available at one of your sponsor's stores such as Footlocker and then offering each sponsor its own contest to name, such as the "Upper Deck Slam Dunk Open" or the "AT&T Long-Distance Shoot-out."

As the competition for sponsorship dollars continues to increase, it is important that sport event producers assist sponsors in getting the most bang for their buck. Some helpful tips are provided in Figure 8–5.

John Boulter, international marketing director for Reebok, envisions sport marketing becoming more competitive in the future, with only the big players surviving. He believes a total packaged sponsorship complete with television advertising will replace the current à la carte method of sponsorship.

Olympic sponsors, for example, spend approximately $40 million for an exclusive category right and then must negotiate with the exclusive TV broadcaster, for a commercial package around the Olympic coverage worth between $40-60 million. Then add the costs of hospitality, promotions, and public relations efforts.

EVENT MARKETING EXPOSURE ON A SHOESTRING BUDGET

In producing an event, you oftentimes have unexpected costs that will do serious damage to your sport event. It is important to develop a tight budget and stick to it. One way to keep within your budget is to implement inexpensive activities to gain exposure. This works particularly well in a market where it is very expensive to advertise.

In addition to television, you can promote your event through many other avenues. The promotional ideas listed in Figure 8–6 have been collected through years of sport event observations and

FIGURE 8–5
How to Increase Sponsorship Value

- If you purchased the rights to be a title sponsor, turn around and try to sell a tie-in to someone with whom you are conducting business. A perfect example is Home Depot's leveraging of its Olympic sponsorship by allowing its vendors (for a price) to use the Olympic rings on product packaging sold only in Home Depot stores.
- As an event owner, ask one of your sponsors to purchase media for you because it probably has more leverage in this market.
- Develop and keep up-to-date mailing lists and demographic databases. Each of these is an asset and will increase the value of your event.
- Offer a discount for an early sponsorship commitment.
- Offer recognition on the back of the tickets.
- Offer a commission or incentive bonus to existing sponsors who bring another sponsor to the event. For example, if Coca-Cola brings McDonald's to the All-American High School Basketball tournament, it could receive a 10 percent referral fee.
- Offer your media sponsor a category that you are unlikely to sell and as a bonus allow it to bring in a cosponsor.
- Have corporate sponsors identify all they can bring to the table besides cash. Airlines, for example, frequently have the right to sell merchandise in airports. This provides an opportunity for prepromotion of the event and an additional revenue source.
- Consider the following options to expose your company's name in addition to traditional signage: kiosks, park benches, recycle bins, clothing, fanny packs, visors, umbrellas, collector pins, and tables.
- Outfit volunteers and organizers.
- Sponsor an entertainment stage or pin-trading center where spectators and participants gather before, during, or after an event.
- Create a theme for your sport event sponsorship. To promote the "Popwatch," Swatch freely distributed popcorn, lollipops, and popsicles during an event the Swiss watch manufacturer sponsored.
- List the competition results in your entrance office window.
- Road race sponsors could offer a special prize to the first person to pass by a branch office or corporate headquarters (assuming the sponsor has an office located along the course).
- Produce a limited number of specially designed beer and soft drink cans that make interesting collectibles.
- Provide a shuttle bus to and from your place of business to the sport event. Local media will frequently promote this service, which generates free publicity for your company.
- Telecommunication sponsors could make it possible through public or cellular phones for athletes to reach out to friends and relatives immediately after their event.
- Sponsors that fly blimps or hot-air balloons with their name and logo attractively displayed should offer rides to the press, photographers, television reporters and crews, and guests before, during, or after the event.

FIGURE 8-6

Money-Saving Ideas to Promote Your Sport Event

- Organize sport training programs prior to a public event to train and motivate participants. The Los Angeles Marathon, in cooperation with an orthopedic hospital sponsor, provides four programs targeted at different populations—from beginning to elite runners, students to senior citizens.
- Schedule a health and fitness exposition in conjunction with the final days of event registration.
- Sell or give away T-shirts, posters, lapel pins, and stickers before, during, and after the event. The more people wear these items before the event, the more publicity the event receives.
- Organize a communitywide contest to design the logo and mascot for your event.
- Create a theme song or jingle that is connected to the event and can be repeated on local radio stations. Put the name of a star athlete in the jingle.
- Invite schoolchildren to come to the event in their school uniform or school colors.
- Invite the press to meet with a panel of organizers and athletes before the competition, so the public will have the opportunity to know what to look for and what records to expect.
- Hold a press conference or reception prior to an event to promote the competition and athletes involved. Shoe and equipment companies that sponsor individual athletes or teams (e.g., Nike) frequently arrange press gatherings with the athletes in attendance. Press releases and photographs should be made available to the media.
- Ask local movie theaters to show a short clip of some of your athletes in action or highlights of one of your previous events.
- Solicit endorsements from celebrities as well as sponsors. In 1988, the United States Volleyball Association selected Tom Selleck and Susan Anton as honorary national team captains. This not only added excitement and interest for the public but also attracted press coverage and additional revenue. John Davidson and Dionne Warwick also served as board members.
- Put up displays and hold exhibitions in shopping malls and other public places.
- For more visibility, a low-profile event may piggyback with high-profile events. In a recent example, the National Handicap Sport Association (NHSA) worked with the NBA to hold wheelchair basketball games prior to NBA games. The NHSA also schedules educational seminars in NBA cities.
- Print as many flyers as your budget will allow. Hand these out in places with a high concentration of traffic or gathering of people. The flyers should be as interesting as possible and contain just enough material for people to glance at and still remember the event it promotes.
- Use your personal contacts in the entertainment areas of your local club, a favorite restaurant, or a local festival and get the announcer or a participant to say something about your event.
- Posters are excellent ways to let people know about your event, especially if they are designed and produced well. Stores, colleges, and companies may help you advertise your event by allowing you to display the poster on their windows or walls.

continued

FIGURE 8–6 concluded

- Community bulletin boards are always looking for activities to promote. Don't forget the artwork of your local tourist bureau for ways to advertise.
- You can buy advertising space at a reduced rate if you are prepared to take it at the last minute. Space becomes negotiable when it is clear that media outlet does not have a buyer. Something is better than nothing. Find out where these opportunities are in your area and how to best utilize them. Oftentimes, the media outlet will let you know when there is space available if you have developed a good business relationship. Television, magazines, newspapers, radio, and other media are in the business to negotiate.
- Computer bulletin boards and airline computer reservation systems (CRS) are excellent electronic promotional tools.

professional readings. Remember that the cost of most of these promotions should be absorbed by existing sponsors and not by the event organization. In addition, the opportunity exists for promotional materials to double as fund-raisers. A silk screen company, for example, may volunteer to print T-shirts, another company may purchase the T-shirts, and you then sell the commemorative T-shirt.

BIG SUCCESS IN A SMALL TOWN WITH A SMALL BUDGET

If you are a one-person show or are located in a small to midsize city, the challenges of promoting your sport event are great. You must constantly devise new techniques to reach the same audience. See Figure 8–7 for important tips on doing this often, effectively, and inexpensively.

These are merely a few examples of free and low-cost ideas that you can pursue. The key is to constantly review trade publications and find out what is working in other markets and then use these ideas to build your own resource file for future adaptation to the success of your sport events.

TELEVISION, MEDIA, AND INTEGRATED MARKETING WORKS

You have now read how paid advertising, event sponsorship, promotional stunts, and public relations can work together to

FIGURE 8–7

Sport Event Promotion Ideas

- Hold a "name the mascot" contest. Invite local schoolchildren to name the mascot and write a short essay about its past. The Atlanta Committee for the Olympic Games did this in cooperation with *Parade Magazine* and received thousands of responses and international publicity for several months. The resulting name?—"Izzy"!
- Promote a "Crazy About the . . . . Fans" parade. Invite the fans to wear their silliest costume to show their support of the home team. Use local radio personalities as emcees and grand marshals and encourage unusual entries such as the Briefcase Brigade, The Riding Lawnmower Precision Drill Team, and others that are featured in Pasadena's famed Doo-Da parade in California.
- Schedule a look-alike contest to be held right before the game. Award prizes to fans and others who most closely resemble your players.
- Washington, D.C., sports promotion legend Charles Brotman once generated lots of ink and television time holding auditions for an amateur to sing "The Star Spangled Banner" at the opening of a baseball game. Although Roseanne Arnold was *not* invited, those who did show up at Washington's RFK stadium ranged from tin-eared terrors to opera singers, and the media seemed to cover every note.
- Children and animals always generate lots of media and fan excitement. Remember to salute the little fans regularly with photo events, autograph-signing sessions, and even pre-game pet shows in the parking lot.
- Boy and Girl Scout troups may be happy to distribute and post flyers in return for a few seats at the sport event.
- Make sure that each year you feature the oldest fan and host a small reception in his or her honor. Invite the youngest fan to pose for photos with the eldest!
- Invite the local newspaper editor to flip the coin or even say a few words at the opening game.
- Host a local celebrity halftime show in which you feature the television news anchor, weatherpersons, and people performing stunts with your mascot.
- Hold a flea market in your parking lot prior to the game and give the proceeds from booth sales to charity.
- Schedule a postgame charity auction of autographed jackets, gloves, bats, balls, and other memorabilia.

create a successful instrument that will saturate your market successfully. Make certain that each marketing element synergizes with others to maintain the core idea of your sport event. For example, it would be unwise to have a tobacco company sponsor a pre-school sport event and run advertisements with participating toddlers. Use good taste, judgment, and above all persistence to reach as many potential fans as possible with your message.

In Part I you have explored the sport event industry from a macroperspective. You are now well positioned to further examine the practical methods, such as funding and sponsorship, that will help sustain your ideas and promote your accomplishments.

GAME HIGHLIGHTS

- Remember that to reach today's typical sport fan you may want to consider broadcasting because most fans commute to the game via the media communications highway.
- You will use local and network television stations, cable, pay-per-view, satellite transmission, or radio if you decide to broadcast your event.
- Package your television and sponsorships to create a more solid message for the consumer and eliminate ambush marketing opportunities.
- Before you approach a television company, you should first perform an honest evaluation of your sporting event.
- Produce a video/audio news release to promote your event.
- Develop a tight budget and stick to it as much as possible by using low-cost promotional techniques.
- Review trade publications regularly to find out what is working in other markets and adapt these ideas to your own area.
- Integrate sport event sponsorships into an overall strategic marketing plan.

PLAY BOOK

broadcasting Refers to programming designed for the broadest possible demographics.

cable television A series of channels accessible through subscription only that allow you to broadcast your event locally or nationally.

commercial inventory Advertising spots allocated per program.

integrated marketing The systematic alignment of a variety of advertising, sales, promotional, sponsorship, and public relations activities to provide greater synergy for the event marketing program and to strengthen and stretch the investor's dollar.

local television A television station that broadcasts to a specific local market area. Usually an affiliate of a national network.

media/medium A device to communicate information to the public.

narrowcasting Programming that stratifies the various demographics to reach highly targeted consumers.

network television A way to televise your event to many markets simultaneously.

pay-per-view A specific channel on a cable system where viewers pay a special premium fee to watch your event.

satellite transmission A transmission from a satellite that allows you to broadcast your event to select markets throughout the world.

video/audio news release A version of a media release that uses video or audiotape and satellite uplink and downlink to record and distribute your message.

PHOTO FINISH

1.1 Sold-out stadiums are increasingly common throughout the world due to new advances in sport event management and marketing.

Source: Photograph courtesy of Joe Jeff Goldblatt

1.2 Hundreds of sport event details must be considered before the starting pistol is fired at the 1993 World Track and Field Championships in Stuttgart, Germany.

Source: Photograph courtesy of Lisa Delpy

1.3 Integrated marketing combines advertising, sales, promotions, merchandising, hospitality, individual and group sales, media, and sponsorship as well as interactive participation to effectively communicate the sport event's objectives. This Hoop-It-Up tournament is an example of the effective use of integrated marketing.

Source: Photograph courtesy of Global Sport, Inc.

1.4 Television expanded the audience and transformed sport events into multimillion dollar businesses.

Source: Photograph courtesy of Global Sport, Inc.

1.5 Innovative sport event producers must create new and unusual ways to communicate the heritage of host countries as illustrated in the opening ceremonies of the 25th Olympiad in Barcelona, Spain.

Source: Photograph courtesy of Lisa Delpy

1.6 Motor sports demonstrate how sponsorships can be leveraged through both on- and off-site promotions. Oldsmobile motor sports selected the 1993 World University Games in Buffalo, New York, to display its championship race cars and reach an important audience with the company's message.

Source: Photograph courtesy of Lisa Delpy

1.7 The media require extensive logistical and technical planning to produce effective sport event broadcasts.

Source: Photograph courtesy of Global Sports, Inc.

II

PRACTICAL METHODS FOR ACHIEVING SUCCESS

"If you have confidence, you have patience. Confidence, that is everything."

—Ilie Nastase, tennis player

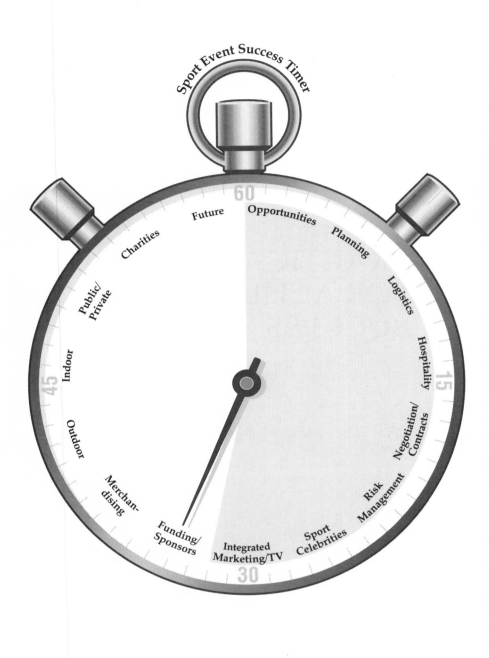

Chapter Nine

How to Achieve Funding, Sponsorship, and Profitability

"The more money you have, the faster you go."

A. J. Watson, car designer,
on the importance of
money in auto racing

W here do you find starting capital? When do you present sponsors with a proposal? What is required to quickly achieve profitability for your sport event?

Streetball Partner, a sport event promotion company and originator of Hoop-It-Up basketball tournaments, began as a self-funded organization. Struggling financially, it solicited an investor the second year who not only brought dollars but also managerial expertise to the company. With this infusion of resources, the business flourished and continues to grow. In 1989, Streetball Partner had 12 people on its payroll. Currently it has 55 employees in the United States and 12 in Europe, with events in 50 U.S. cities, 25 European cities, and 11 Japanese cities. With this success, investors are now at its doorstep.

Streetball Partner has entered into joint equity ventures with the National Basketball Association (NBA) and the National Broadcasting Company (NBC) to produce Hoop-It-Up tournaments, and with Major League Baseball (MLB) to produce Pitch-Hit-Run competitions. The National Football League (NFL) retains Streetball Partner to produce "Air It Out" as does The Association of Volleyball Professionals (AVP) to produce "Spike-it-Up." Kick-it-Up soccer tournaments are also being produced by the company. Such relationships are beneficial in terms of profit-and-loss sharing and promotional enhancement.

"Success in this business is not easy," explains Jeff Ruday, vice-president of Streetball Partner. "It takes a strong financial base, quality staff, lots of determination, and a unique product. We created a niche for ourselves in the production of grassroots outdoor sport events which were underserved."

If the financial success of your event depends on a volunteer committee, it is vital that committee members be selected who can either give or get the resources needed. Dennis Gann, executive director of the Sioux City Convention Center and Auditorium Tourism Bureau warns against "having someone ask for one million dollars if they are not able to give or get that much money themselves. In other words, CEOs need to bring other CEOs to the table."

This may be the most important chapter in this book. That is a bold statement considering the many other excellent resources for building successful sport events. However, *funding* and *profitability* are absolutely essential for your short- and long-term success.

Suppose you are a volunteer who has agreed to chair a local fund-raiser or a road race. Suddenly, you realize you must raise a minimum of $5,000 to produce the charity sport event. Or maybe you are a corporate marketing representative responsible for coordinating your company's spring golf outing and the boss asks, "Why not bring in a celebrity?" but offers no budgetary support. Perhaps you are an entrepreneur who operates a local bowling establishment and want to organize a citywide tournament, but you need capital for marketing and advertising to attract players.

Regardless of your position, the need for cash, support, and profitability are universal challenges faced by every sport event management professional. When preparing a budget for a sport event always over estimate expenses. A margin of 5% is appropriate. It is also advised to have at least 10% of the budget committed before beginning to organize. Once an overall budget is derived, Dennis Gann suggests that individual committees be allocated a budget and held responsible to work within these restraints.

FIGURE 9–1

Elements of a Successful Sport Event Business Plan

- List the key persons responsible for planning and managing the sport event and their relative experience.
- Find people who will vouch for their experience (include written testimonials).
- Briefly describe the sport event including date(s), time(s), location(s), history, and purpose.
- Identify what you have to sell and all of your rights (e.g., merchandise, TV, and signage). Determine the rights that you wish to keep and those that are available for sale.
- Determine how to protect the rights that you have for sale so that competitors or non-rights holders have no opportunity for ambush marketing.
- Briefly describe the demographics of the participants and spectators and the type of economic impact they are most likely to generate. Use examples and be prepared to defend your assertions.
- Describe your marketing, sales, advertising, public relations, hospitality, and promotion plans.
- Explain how you will amortize this capital investment and repay the loan or provide profits for your shareholders.
- Describe your risk management procedures, including cancellation insurance, to further assure your investors that their investment is well protected.
- Name your accountant or chief financial officer and describe the type of record keeping you will provide and when you will distribute periodic statements of income and expenses.

FINDING CAPITAL

A sound business plan is the most direct route to finding investors to provide you with start-up capital for your sport event. As an employee of a corporation, this plan (see Figure 9-1) may take the form of a mem-orandum to your superior; as an entrepreneur, the plan may require a formal proposal. The style may change, but the substance remains the same.

Corporate and Individual Sponsors

Once you have prepared this plan, it is time to shop for prospects to invest in your sport event. After you have exhausted the list of most likely candidates for investing, including friends and family, do your research and identify individuals, corporations, and foundations who may be a good match for your event.

The professional staff of The Foundation Center, an educational organization based in Washington, D.C., confirm that most of the financial giving in the United States is by private, individual donors. However, larger gifts typically come from foundations and corporations. You may wish to use a shotgun approach initially and look at a wide variety of sources for funding. Be aware, however, that it is easier to find $10,000 than $100,000 and that foundations and sponsors want to fund projects with specific goals and objectives.

The *Sport Marketplace* directory lists numerous corporations that regularly sponsor sport events. The *Sports Sponsors Fact Book* also provides up-to-date and in-depth information on more than 1,000 sport sponsors. These two sources and other marketing literature (e.g., *Sport Marketing Letter, IEG Sponsorship Report, Team Marketing, Advertising Age*) can identify corporations that understand the rewards of investing in sport events. You will find this literature and more in the bibliography.

While it is often easier to identify corporations rather than individuals as prospects for investment, it is possible to locate wealthy individuals who may elect to invest in your event. Directories are available which list individuals and the types of business ventures they support. Your sport event may just fit the need and interest of a potential angel.

Foundations

The easiest sources of funding to identify, and the most competitive, are foundations. A foundation is a charitable trust or other tax-exempt, tax-deductible organization whose purpose is to distribute financial grants. The Foundation Center and similar organizations maintain extensive databases of foundation tax forms on microfiche. Also available on disk is the "Sponsored Programs Information Network" (SPIN) that can generate a targeted list of potential sponsoring agencies based on key words (e.g., athletics, education) that you enter into the computer. With a little research, you can quickly identify appropriate prospects to approach for funding.

Before approaching a foundation, make a telephone inquiry about the accuracy of the printed information that you have reviewed and whether any of it has changed. You do not want to mistakenly prepare your grant proposal only to discover the deadline has been moved ahead two months. Simple mistakes of this kind can be avoided by making one telephone call. While calling, also ask if the foundation has any formal guidelines or examples to follow.

Venture Capitalists

Another source of funds is the venture capitalist. This individual or group of individuals specialize in funding small, start-up enterprises. However, it may be difficult to find venture capitalists who are willing to provide financial support for a one-time or hallmark sport event. In order to minimize their risk, the venture capitalists prefer to invest in a growing concern with excellent financial reports and prospects for long-term growth. Your banker, financial consultant, or accountant may be able to recommend venture capitalists who will review your business plan and offer input and perhaps funding.

Financial Institutions

When asked where he went first for sponsorship, one sport event executive replied that he followed the advice of the famed bank robber Willie Sutton: "I go to the banks. That's where they keep the money." Financial institutions are indeed where the money is and an excellent source for sponsorship. As part of a sponsorship agreement, banks may provide a line of credit. NationsBank, for example, is a sponsor of the 1996 Olympic Games in Atlanta and has arranged for a line of credit for the organizing committee based on expected revenue. Depending on your leverage, you may be able to negotiate an interest-free loan to support the organization while sponsorship funds are being solicited. Without a direct relationship to a sport event sponsorship, banks are usually a poor choice for start-up capital because of the expense. Unless your sport event has a long and successful history of financial stability, you will be asked to provide large amounts of collateral (frequently equal to the loan amount) and pay a prime interest rate.

If you do enter into a loan agreement with either a public entity or private investor, be sure to ask what type of loan it is. For example, you could ask for a nonrecourse loan or nonreimbursable loan where you are responsible for paying back the loan only if the event makes a profit. If no profit is made, then the loan becomes forgivable. This kind of financing is usually made through government entities, and the arrangements are negotiated in terms of public security and emergency personnel. If the event makes money, the city where the event takes place will usually expect to be paid for these services. If the event does not make money, the city will write it off as an overhead expense. Most sport event management entrepreneurs can often find a more economical way to obtain start-up funds than bank loans.

Public Entities

The public sector is another funding source that has become more prevalent. Local, regional, and State governments may provide seed money, with or without restrictions. The local sport council, convention and visitor's bureau, or the chamber of commerce may also help fund the event through a bed-and-beverage tax or other reserves.

Other Funding

As a corporate employee who is suddenly faced with the responsibility of finding a top golf celebrity to appear at the spring tournament, you will either have to reallocate your budget to afford this expense or turn elsewhere in the firm for funding. Look at the chairman's discretionary fund or the sales promotions budget, for example, as ways to fund this expense. You may be able to share the golf pro's fee with another department or business unit and also share his or her time to satisfy two similar agendas. Still another way to fund this expense is to ask your vendors (e.g., printer, insurance) to contribute to your effort. Offer them an opportunity to meet the pro and participate in the tournament, allowing them to network with your top corporate officials. Check which among your clients or vendors sponsors a golf pro and, if so, whether a visit of the pro to your event can be arranged as part of the golfer's contract. Even if you do not personally know a corporate sponsor of a golf pro, it may be beneficial to contact this corporation to learn if the exposure at your event would be of value.

As one example of the effectiveness of this strategy, Innisbrook Hilton Resort, the famed golf community in Florida, changed its strategy for promoting the property to prospective customers. Historically, every January the sales department invited qualified meeting planners from large corporations and associations to enjoy one of the premier golf resorts in the United States. But during the economic recession of 1992, the resort decided instead to invite only the corporate meeting planners of the resort's long-time vendors.

Once assembled, Innisbrook staff explained that the lingering economic recession had hit the hotel and resort industry especially hard and that they would welcome any support from these loyal suppliers. This strategy paid off; sales improved as suppliers redirected their corporate meeting business to Innisbrook. The moral of this story is simply, ask your friends first and you may receive.

HOW MUCH CAPITAL DO YOU NEED?

One immediate test of your ability to face stiff opposition from hardened prospective investors is your response to their question, "How much do you think you will need?" In this negotiation, the first person who answers usually loses.

Instead of answering the question directly, show them your business plan. Then carefully walk through each of the steps outlined in Figure 9–1, pausing occasionally to inquire, "Is this clear?" or "Do you want to ask a question?"

Finally, explain that you are seeking an investor or investors who have realistic expectations. *Then* ask for help. A person's love of sport can help your efforts. These people are often prepared to do whatever necessary to make the project succeed. How much help you will need should be clearly stated in the business plan under your expense itemization. If your business plan includes sponsorship, you may state that these expenses could be reduced with sponsorship, but you are not going to bank on this until the funds are actually received.

Whenever negotiating for money, you must walk a fine line. Do not appear desperate, leaving the investor or sponsor uncertain about the security of your organization and the event. Anyone investing in your event will want to feel confident about the individuals in charge and their ability to manage the event successfully.

PROBLEMS WITH OUTSIDE FUNDING

Although outside funding may be essential to the proper capitalization of your sport event, you should be prepared to face some problems that are not insurmountable but nevertheless may cause delays.

Investors may prefer, for tax purposes, to provide their cash investments incrementally over different quarters of the calendar. This may cause difficulties with your cash flow. Other investors may get cold feet and drop out entirely. You should be prepared for this by identifying alternative investors or establishing cash reserves until you have sufficient capital. Still other investors may organize a group that will try to move from its limited partnership to an active partnership position in order to win control of the sport event and ultimately buy you out. If you are willing to sell and the price is right, a buyout may be a good idea. But if the price is low and the potential for future personal gain is great, a buyout puts you in a precarious position.

All of these contingencies must be considered when seeking outside funding for your event. Most sport management and marketing professionals find that a more secure way to achieve full funding is through the sale of sponsorships.

SPONSORSHIP: THE MULTIBILLION-DOLLAR BABY

In the early 1980s, International Events Group (IEG) based in Chicago began publishing *Special Events Report*. For over a decade, this publication has served as the leading chronicle of sport and other event sponsorship.

In 1991, *Special Events Reports* noted that corporate annual spending reached a total of over $3 billion. The vast majority of these dollars ($1.5 billion) went toward sponsoring sport events.

Jean-Claude Schupp, executive director of the General Association of International Sport Federations (GAISF), explains why
corporations financially support sport: "For business, sport is an
easy way to communicate. Sport has existed for years and is
understood by almost everyone." Corporate sponsors are typically
large organizations that wish to reach a mass target market and use
sponsorship as a nontraditional technique to introduce their brand
to new consumers. This becomes more true as traditional media
buys lose value due to fragmentation.

More and more, the media are fragmented. The most recent
example is the explosion of cable television stations beaming their
commercials into millions of households. One advertising executive commented that buying television today is like buying
magazines: one market segment at a time. The cost per thousand
impressions of this advertising has also skyrocketed. As a result,
sponsorship has become even more attractive to both large and
small sponsors.

Cost-Effectiveness of Sponsorship: Virginia Is for Lovers

"Virginia is for Lovers" is but one of many case studies where
sponsorship was far more cost-effective than traditional advertising.

Mary Ann Davies, vice president and account supervisor of
Siddall, Matus & Cughter Advertising & Public Relations in
Richmond, Virginia, represents the State of Virginia Tourism
Commission. Davies is a firm believer in the role of sport event
sponsorship in the total marketing mix. She says:

> We made a commitment to sponsor a NASCAR driver. Over 100
> million impressions later with seven times the investment return,
> we are extremely pleased. So far we are the only state sponsoring
> a race car and this has created lots of interest from the media. Most
> importantly, every time our car places it creates giant waves of
> excitement both in the tourism offices and throughout the state
> itself.

According to Davies, a successful sponsorship means matching
your product or service to the right prospective market for an
excellent cost-benefit ratio. The State of Virginia invested approxi-

mately $250,000 for the race car sponsorship and $1.5 million was returned in measurable public relations. Even more important, the car is dubbed "Virginia is for Lovers." This popular slogan is reinforced on hundreds of hours of television programming annually as race car fans, who are also prospective Virginia visitors, tune in.

When developing your sponsorship package to attract prospective corporate sponsors, bear in mind their motivations. Remember that sponsors are not banks and that sponsorship fees are more than charitable donations.

"The main thing in getting your sponsorship funded is to do your homework and target the most appropriate company," states Don Campbell, of MCI. "Understand the company you are soliciting in terms of profitability, competitors, layoffs, other sponsorship involvements, planning cycle, budget closing date, target market, and strategic marketing plan. A year's notice would be nice. Include as much information as possible in the proposal including a budget and a video."

SPONSOR MARKETING

The four most common reasons to sponsor a sport event are listed in Figure 9–2.

To find additional reasons, convene a focus group of prospective sponsors and probe for answers beyond the obvious. The focus group may ultimately help you write a successful sponsorship proposal.

According to Woody Woodruff, a sport marketing consultant, "Internal corporate negotiations are the first step in getting a sponsorship approved and must continue throughout the contract if a renewal is desired. This is especially true when there are different divisions within a company, some of which see no direct benefit from the sponsorship."

Matching sponsor and events. A marketing director for a leading auto manufacturer explained that in order to sell her company on the sport event, the sponsorship had to be a natural fit. Her upscale car was not a suitable sponsor for the South Georgia Barbecue Festival and Fair; however, the company did

FIGURE 9–2

Sponsor Motivations
1. Brand awareness—to increase and maximize exposure or change perception
2. Sales promotion—to increase and enhance sales volume
3. Opportunities for consumer research—to reach specific or new target audiences
4. Opportunities for sponsor's personnel or guests to have VIP access to sport event—to encourage and reward sales people and customers

sponsor the Jingle Bell Jog, a 10k run held in a number of cities during the Christmas holidays. The Jingle Bell Jog fit and the barbecue event did not.

The reasons for this fit are highly complex. Different formulas are used to evaluate sponsorship proposals to ensure a good fit. Perhaps the most important criteria is audience demographics. The Jingle Bell Jog attracted upscale baby boomers who could afford to purchase this type of vehicle while those attending the barbecue festival could not. The advertising cost per thousand impressions is also an important consideration. The impressions should be made to the correct audience in order to wisely invest the sponsor's dollars. Appendix I–H provides a sample corporate evaluation checklist for sponsorship proposals.

Budgeting. A corporation that enters a sport event sponsorship should not think of the rights fees as the end of its commitment or view this event as a one-time involvement. Companies should adequately support their sponsorship agreement by budgeting at least one to three times as much as their initial sponsorship fee for promotions, advertising, and hospitality, and another 3 to 5 percent for market research. Companies also need to allow equity to build over time. Research has shown that it takes from 10 to 50 images to make one impression on a consumer.

Contracting outside agencies. Corporations may chose to coordinate their entire sponsorship in-house or hire an outside sport marketing firm that has the expertise to make strategic suggestions and to carry out sponsorship plans. Olympic event marketing has

FIGURE 9–3

Checklist for Selecting a Firm to Promote Sponsorships

Prior to selecting a marketing firm, sport organizations should:

_____ Solicit bids from different companies.

_____ Ask for references and speak with previous clients.

_____ Consider the company's historical sport involvement and reputation.

_____ Know what services they offer.

_____ Feel comfortable with the account representative.

---

been a fast-growing field for Advantage International, a major sport marketing firm headquartered in Washington, D.C., with four Olympic sponsors signing up for advice and assistance in implementation. Contracting to an outside agency is especially important for an inaugural event, for the company short on manpower, or for the event that will be in multiple cities over an extended period of time. From the beginning, job descriptions must be extremely clear on role responsibilities, reporting, and follow-up. Some firms offer a variety of services including strategic planning, event management, sponsorship marketing, publicity, hospitality, minority marketing, merchandising rights negotiations, athlete endorsements, sales promotion, sport facility consulting, quantitative sponsorship analysis, and promotional products. (See Figure 9-3.)

Working with the sport event organizer. Before a corporate sponsor can move fully ahead on its sport event marketing plan, it must receive guidelines and direction from the event organizer. These include schedules, a design handbook, and all requests for in-kind services and donations. If the organizing committee continually changes its plans and builds roadblocks, credibility will be lost and the potential for the corporate sponsor's future involvement will be minimal. Sponsors should not be viewed as a "necessary evil" but as a partner. The organizing committee and sponsors should work together to eliminate opportunities for ambush marketing. Both parties should pursue relationships with the event city to attain its cooperation.

Since billboards in Atlanta are under the control of the city government, it may have been wise for the Atlanta Committee for the Olympic Games to request that the city give first right to purchase the billboards to official Olympic sponsors. Unfortunately, timing is often an obstacle in these deals because the city began selling billboard space prior to the time most sponsors signed on. Each billboard is priced at $330,000 and requires a three-year commitment. To purchase two billboards within the area designated as the Olympic Ring, a company must purchase five billboards in outlying areas.

Getting an early start. If possible, corporations should get an early start on sponsorship. Corporate sponsors who sign up in the fourth quarter may receive a discount on their sponsorship fee (e.g., half price this year if they sign a full-price contract for the next two years), but they usually do not have enough time to plan appropriately and eventually pay premium prices for their advertising, hospitality, and promotions. Another problem with signing on late is that decisions on themes and the design of the event have already been made without your input. Thus, you must adapt to ideas that are already in place. Bell South, for example, became a sponsor of the Women's Final Four in Atlanta late in the planning stage. The company would have preferred a different theme for the "Welcoming" night but could not change it.

In the course of several interviews, author Lisa Delpy found that an ideal lead time is 12-18 months. Any agreement reached three to four months prior to the event will almost surely encounter difficulties.

CROSS-PROMOTIONS

One advantage of sport event marketing is the opportunity to tie in with other sponsors and share advertising costs, reach a different market, and possibly recover some sponsorship fees through new business opportunities. For example, if Hilton Hotels promotes a sweepstakes using the product of a cosponsor like United Airlines, then new business is generated for that cosponsor, offsetting its original sponsorship costs.

Another example of cross-sponsorship is McDonald's relationship with Coca-Cola. The two companies utilize each others' network and outlets to advertise their products. McDonald's runs a special promotional program that involves getting a free Coke with each purchase of a hamburger. Coke would run a similar offer using a coupon for a free hamburger at McDonald's with the purchase of a specified amount of Coke.

NationsBank and VISA have teamed up to offer special Olympic VISA credit cards. Each time NationsBank Olympic VISA credit cardholders uses their special card, they are eligible to participate in a variety of Olympic promotions. In turn, VISA will donate a percentage of each card purchase directly to the U.S. Olympic team.

Some corporations are taking their sports sponsorship one step further and intertwining it with sport ownership. Examples include the St. Louis Cardinals baseball team and Anheuser-Busch; the Atlanta Braves, the NBA Atlanta Hawks, and Ted Turner cable stations; Seattle Mariners and Nintendo of America; and the NHL Anaheim Mighty Ducks and Disney.

CAUSE-RELATED MARKETING

Cause-related marketing is becoming the way to market for the 90s. Corporations are driven to give something back to the communities in which they reside. The infrastructure of our cities is whittled away as our environment and quality of life is challenged. People and consumers are less tolerant of large companies coming in, reaping large profits, and not giving anything in return. The result has been the emergence of socially responsible corporations which set up programs that help people. This is a holistic approach to doing business. Employees feel good about the people for whom they work. Dollars traditionally spent for advertising that is no longer so effective are directed to promotions and community marketing where they are much more effective. Everyone wins.

3M, a former Olympic sponsor, used to invite Olympic athletes to its factories to encourage the staff to raise funds for the United States Olympic Committee (USOC). An employee who raised the most money received an all-expense-paid vacation to the 1992 Summer Olympic Games. VISA donates a percent of all customer purchases to the U.S. Olympic team.

WHO DO I ASK FOR THE SPONSORSHIP?

This is becoming an increasingly difficult question to answer because of the accelerating changes in U.S. and international corporations. However, through the secondary literature mentioned earlier, specifically *Sports Sponsors Fact Book*, and follow-up telephone calls, specific contacts can be identified.

Some corporations have an entire department dedicated to sport marketing (e.g., Anheuser Busch, Coca-Cola), others assign to the field one employee who scrutinizes incoming proposals and forwards the best to appropriate departments. Others simply funnel requests through the sales promotion or marketing department. After all, a sponsorship is a marketing investment, not a gift, so those individuals responsible for coming up with new marketing programs should be interested in your sport event. Still other corporate areas to research are human resources, public relations, advertising, brand promotions, special events, and ethnic markets. Check as well to see if the company has a nonprofit foundation with money to support your event.

WHAT DOES A SPONSOR EXPECT TO SEE?

Yvonne Lumsden-Dill, director of industry affairs for the Miller Brewing Company, says that "in today's competitive marketplace, we look for logical opportunities to showcase our products to well-targeted consumers."

Once again, this depends on the organization to whom you are making the presentation. It is wise to first send a letter of inquiry or establish telephone contact to confirm the correct names, titles, and other pertinent information. Be sure to ask whether the company has any sponsorship guidelines. M&M Mars, for example, will provide this information to you upon request. *Amusements Business, Performance*, and publications mentioned previously list the types of sport and entertainment events various corporate sponsorships are supporting.

All sponsors expect you to do your homework and to present not only a great idea but a detailed marketing plan to support it. Sponsorship has become a complex process involving signage,

FIGURE 9-4

Sponsorship Proposal Blueprint

1. Overview paragraph to describe proposed event, managing organization, and those who will benefit.
2. Event facts and history:
   - Title
   - Date
   - Location
   - Participants (names of athletes and/or artists)
   - Attendance—previous and expected
   - Media coverage—previous and expected (include examples)
   - Benefiting charity or cause (name benefactors and level of charitable contribution
3. Demographics of participants and spectators
4. Benefits Available to Sponsor (refer to Figure 9-6). Note: It is important to propose to a sponsor only those benefits that can be confirmed as available for execution prior to and during the event. Be aware of event site restrictions. Many municipal locals require permits that can limit display and promotions during events. Event contracts are generally based upon the proposals as were offered to the sponsor during initial contact and presentations. It is always better to underpromise and overserve.
5. Sponsorship fee—Be sure to identify what costs are *NOT* included in this fee (e.g., catering, accommodations, transportation, tickets, artwork for signage, and merchandise)
6. Summary
   - Target market (Who is this event going to reach?).
   - Benefactors (Who is this event going to benefit?[e.g., local charity, the community]).
   - Corporate benefits/opportunities (Why is this event a good match for the company?).

hospitality, ticketing, merchandise, sampling, point-of-sale and in-store promotions, celebrity appearances, bounce-back coupons, video news releases, and other devices to help the sponsor maximize their sport event investment. Describe in detail how your marketing plan will put their sponsorship in front of the qualified buyers they are seeking. Josephine Sherfy, marketing vice-president for ProServ, suggests that a number of key elements be included in any proposal (see Figure 9-4).

The following warnings will help you to avoid rejection of your sponsorship proposal (see Figure 9-5).

Lisa Delpy further explains that the best way to lose a sponsor is to exude the attitude of "Thanks for the money. Now please go

FIGURE 9-5

Three Ways to Get Your Sponsorship Proposal Rejected
1. Focus on *benefits to you*, not benefits to the sponsor.
2. Focus on *how much money you need*, not the value to the sponsor.
3. Present your proposal in an unorganized, hard-to-follow *format* or think a "teaser" is sufficient. This type of proposal leaves the reader asking, "How good are these people anyway?" and "How do I justify spending this much money?"

---

away." The best way to keep a sponsor is to "treat them like they are your most precious asset. Maintain a client service attitude, look for ways to enhance the relationship, and remember that your sponsor's product is *your* product."

An excellent source of information about the art of sponsorship is the *International Festivals Association's* (IFA) *IFA's Official Guide to Sponsorship* published by the *International Festivals Association*. Author Bob Gobrecht advises you to "always barter." In addition to asking for cash, ask for in-kind goods or services. This might include the sponsor providing its employees as volunteers for the sport event or some other low-cost but helpful service. Another example is to ask your local utility company, an event sponsor, to put a discount ticket coupon in their monthly bill statement. This easy in-kind and virtually no-cost activity could help you sell hundreds or even thousands of additional tickets.

PRICE WARS: SETTING YOUR SPONSORSHIP LEVELS

Peter Ueberroth, president of the Los Angeles Olympic Organizing Committee, states in *Made in America* that the Lake Placid Olympic Games had many in-kind sponsorships but received barely $10 million in cash. He decided to set his sights considerably higher and aim for $200 million in total cash sponsorships. Ironically, the total retained earnings from the LA Olympic Games was slightly more than $200 million so in this case sponsorship was directly related to providing a lasting legacy of goodwill in the community. Ueberroth set a floor of $4 million for an exclusive

FIGURE 9–6

Example Sponsorship Benefits

- Title rights: Sponsor's name to appear in the title in the following manner: The XYZ Sport Event presented by ABC Sponsor.
- Print advertising: event program, event stationary, fliers, posters, T-shirts, tickets, media releases with sponsor's name included.
- Television and radio exposure (if applicable) and the right to use the event footage in the future.
- On-site recognition during event: banners, blimps, booths, and other signage. Provide details on the amount, size, location (especially important for news photo opportunities and television impressions), responsibility for production, placement, and associated costs.
- Pre-event promotions: venue open-house, media day, autograph signing, athlete and/or coach press conference.
- Promotions during event: Booth displays, product sampling, public service announcements, interactive experiences, sponsors name on athletes, and volunteer uniforms.
- Entertainment opportunities: Box seats, reserved seats, sky suite, VIP parking passes, hospitality tent, catering, VIP reception, sport clinic, athlete personal appearances in hospitality area, transportation, and hotel accommodations.
- Relationship building between sponsor, spectators, and charity (cause related marketing).
- Logo use in corporate advertisements and promotions.
- Merchandise rights.
- Direct mail lists.
- Market research opportunities as approved by sport event manager.
- A summary report detailing media exposure and results of any internal research (e.g., sponsor recall or event public image).
- Renewal option—right of first refusal to retain sponsorship.
- Marketing plan prepared by sport event account representative to assist sponsor in extending its sponsorship and merchandising of its product or service.

beverage sponsor and invited Pepsi and Coca-Cola to submit proposals. When he opened the Coca-Cola bid of $12.6 million, Ueberroth tried to maintain his composure! Today the ante is up to $40 million for an Olympic sponsorship.

When determining sponsorship levels, you must first estimate the value by examining all data available to you, including television rating points, newspaper column inches, the value of cost per thousand attendees at the event, seeing a banner, or sampling a product. According to Ukman of the International

Events Group, "one of the primary factors in the determination of sponsorship fees is the cost of media in your market. The same property in Cleveland is not worth nearly as much as the same in Los Angeles. Then you look at the competitive marketplace." Is your sport event the only such event within 200 miles, or are there five others? Is your event a first-time event or is it established? What is the cost to sponsor other properties similar to yours? Is there more value for one product category over another? For example, if the event entitles the sponsor to on-site sales rights of soft drinks or hot dogs, then it may be worth more to some sponsor in that category than to a bank. However, when you ask corporate management for $50,000, their first consideration will be, What else can we do with this money? How much other media time can we buy? How many people will we be reaching? How many trade deals could we cut?

Although tangible benefits are important, do not completely discount the intangibles of your event. As pressure increases on companies to be socially responsible, your event worth also increases with the number of intangible and cause-related images. Ukman explains that "where sponsorship can beat out measured media is its ability to increase a company's share of heart, its qualitative as opposed to quantitative impact."

Once you have assigned a total value, then begin to segment the sponsorships in the manner shown in Figure 9–7 to involve as many potential sponsors as possible. In today's lean and mean sponsorship environment, it will be easier to identify more sponsors at individual exclusive categories than major event-wide sponsors. This is especially true if the time frame for your solicitation is short.

To market these sponsorships, successful sport event marketers often title the levels as Gold, Silver, Bronze, President's Club, Infield, Sky Box, Major Leaguer, Hall of Fame Club, MVPs, Platinum, or Diamond, or they use other terms that convey value. Regardless of the title of the sponsorship, it is important that you describe in precise detail the key benefits the sponsor will receive.

Figure 9–8 is by no means a final description of the myriad of possibilities available to sponsors. However, it does represent the general categories for which you may wish to seek support.

FIGURE 9–7

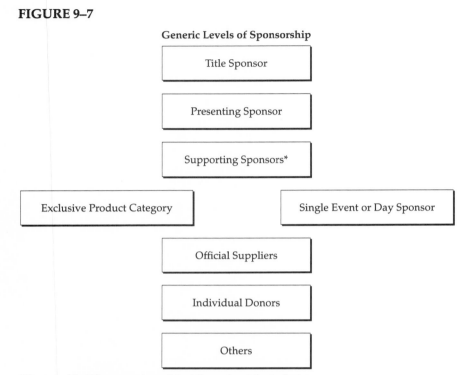

Generic Levels of Sponsorship

Title Sponsor

Presenting Sponsor

Supporting Sponsors*

Exclusive Product Category

Single Event or Day Sponsor

Official Suppliers

Individual Donors

Others

*Sponsorship titles are not consistent throughout the industry.

SPONSOR AGREEMENTS

Key components of a typical sponsor agreement are shown in Figure 9–9. Make certain you consult with legal counsel in crafting an agreement that adheres to the law in your jurisdiction. Refer to Chapter 5 and to other texts that provide sample agreements. One of the most useful texts is *The IEG Legal Guide to Sponsorship* published by the International Events Group.

FOLLOW-THROUGH

The major area where sponsorships fail is the follow-through that is *not* provided by the sport event manager or sponsor. The rule is simple. Provide everything for which you are legally responsible and, with the sponsor's permission, a little bit more. By being

FIGURE 9–8

Specific Types of Sponsorship

Title sponsor: The primary sponsor whose investment allows its name to be listed within the event title; for example, Kemper Open golf tournament. All sponsorships are typically product category exclusive, which prohibits competing companies or product lines from also sponsoring the event.

Product category sponsor: A sponsor whose cash, product and/or services investment is less than the title sponsor.

Single event or day sponsor category: This sponsor has usually directed its sponsorship toward a specific category of the event program such as the torch run, award ceremonies, a stage where entertainment may be featured (e.g., The Bud Bandshell), opening, half, or closing ceremonies (e.g., the Pepsi Halftime Spectacular), one race (e.g., 100 meter dash) or one day of a multi-day event.

Official supplier: This sponsor may provide both financial and in-kind support through the donation of products or services crucial for the sport competition (e.g., balls, mats, gymnastic equipment, timing devices).

flexible with your ticket exchange policy, paying attention to a sponsor's dietary considerations, and providing extras such as valet parking, you will create a memorable impression that will help you in continuing the relationship.

MULTIPLE YEAR AGREEMENTS

Let's imagine for a moment that one of your sponsors inquires about a five-year exclusive agreement. You smile and ask, "What do you have in mind?" The sponsor replies that a significant discount for this long-term commitment would be satisfactory. You take a deep breath and ask, "Are you prepared to pay all five years in advance?"

Your sponsor does not faint but smiles and says, "Let's sit down and work out the details." In fact, a long-term multiyear agreement is desirable to both parties from the perspective of fixed overhead. This means that you and the sponsor can reduce the annual labor of courting one another and negotiating the terms of the sponsorship. Furthermore, both of you will know what is required financially and can thus budget more precisely.

When negotiating a multiyear deal, make sure you allow for an increase in any direct costs associated with the sponsorship that are linked to the consumer price index (CPI). This ensures that the

FIGURE 9–9

Sponsorship Agreement Checklist

The Parties

Who are the legal parties responsible for executing the agreement and how will they be referred to throughout the agreement?

Category Description and Exclusivity

What specific product or service category is being purchased? Is it exclusive? Will sponsor have approval over other sponsors or suppliers?

Performance Responsibilities

What specific tasks is each party to perform? Ambush marketing protection, signage, promoting/marketing the event, hospitality, competition schedule.

Date, Time

What is the date and time of the sport event(s) activities during which the parties are liable for performance of their duties as specified in the agreement.

Location(s)

Where will the sport event take place and what is the official name and address of this venue.

Financial

What are the financial responsibilities of each party.

Terms of Payment

When is payment due, what happens if payment is late, and is there a benefit for early payment?

Risk Management

Who is responsible for insurance, bonds, permits, and other risk management procedures? Who is to be named as additional insured? When must certificates of insurance be received? What types of insurance are required and in what amounts? Who indemnifies whom?

Trademark/Logo License

Under what circumstances and during what time period can a sponsor use the event trademark logo?

Expiration Date

When does the sponsorship offer expire if it is not accepted?

Execution

Who are the official signers?

Date of Execution

When was the document jointly executed?

sponsorship will not cost you money each year despite the discount you have offered for a multiyear commitment.

Ukman discourages long-term agreements with locked-in fees for start-up events. She sees that your main problem is to avoid getting stuck if the event takes off. As a new property, you also want to find sponsors who are interested in promoting the event for you. Sometimes it is better to go with a sponsor such as Coke, which is doing truck backs and co-op ads, than someone who gives you more cash but no promotional commitment. Sponsorship priorities may change as the event grows.

A warning should also be made about keeping sponsors informed yet at a distance, particularly in terms of budgets and production. On more than one occasion, major sport event sponsors have taken complete control of their event by removing the entire promotional and event organization or replacing the original promoter for a less expensive one. In one instance, a major bottler "stole" an event from a major charity—just another example of the competitive nature of the sport event business.

UNRELATED BUSINESS INCOME TAX (UBIT)

If a not-for-profit organization receives money contingent upon services rendered (e.g., product advertising and promotion), this income is considered unrelated and taxable at the corporate rate. With increased IRS scrutiny of sport event sponsorships through Unrelated Business Income Tax (UBIT), not-for-profit organizations should seek the assistance of a tax lawyer when packaging and selling sponsorship packages. Refer to Chapter 14 on charities for additional information. Too much unrelated trade or business income can also cause a not-for-profit organization to lose its tax-exempt status. A current example of this challenge can be seen as the new NFL Carolina Panthers play at Tiger Stadium in Clemson, South Carolina.

FUTURE TRENDS IN SPORT FUNDING

In his book *Megatrends 2000*, John Naisbitt predicts that "corporate sponsorship of sports will plateau while arts sponsorship continues to grow dramatically throughout the next decade." He further asserts that statistical proof will accumulate showing that consumers spend more time and money on the arts than sport.

If his prediction is true, this is good news for advertisers who are increasingly in search of upscale arts audiences for their products and services. Naisbitt concludes by suggesting that the renaissance of the arts in advertising and the media may lead to a Monday Night at the Opera instead of football or a Super Symphony rather than bowl.

The evidence of the demographic profile showing that the arts attract upscale audiences is firm. However, the expanding audience for sport events such as the women's figure skating competition during the Winter Olympics in Lillehammer, Norway, is also growing proof that an upscale audience continues to watch sport event advertising. While the controversy between skaters Tonya Harding and Nancy Kerrigan certainly piqued interest in this sport to an all-time high, ticket sales for professional and amateur figure skating events were on the rise even prior to the dramatic incident. Ticket sales for gymnastic competitions are also on the rise.

The interest in sport events, like that of other areas of consumer tastes, goes in and out of fashion. Dynamic tennis stars like Andre Agassi and Martina Navratilova create instant appeal. This appeal will be repeated in the future in other sports, which in turn will attract upscale audiences to sponsors' doors.

FINAL FUNDING FOCUS

Sport event managers and marketers are often ill-prepared to ask for funds because they have not focused on the intent, both short- and long-term, of the sport event. To sharpen your focus, make certain you have identified your market niche, communicate passionately and accurately the benefits and features of your sport event, and persistently explored every possibility for funding.

The buzzword in sport event marketing is *packaging*. World Cup Soccer tested this concept by incorporating television advertising time into its corporate sponsors package. As more and more large-scale events seek sponsorship, smaller properties will need to make alliances with other sport properties. Summer properties will perhaps need to acquire a winter property so that you can go to a sponsor with an integrated package in the same way as the NFL or the International Olympic Committee. To be successful in supporting a sport event in the future, Ukman advises you to first find a media and a supermarket sponsor; then you have the guaranteed reach and trade commitment that make selling cash sponsorships much easier. Unfortunately, the first two anchor sponsors are always the most difficult to secure. Jeff Ruday of Streetball Partner says, "Securing and keeping sport event sponsors is a true challenge. Corporate objectives change all the time and no company absolutely needs to spend money on sport events."

There may not be a pot of gold at the end of every sport event funding rainbow but you can be sure that there will be ample reward for your efforts, and that will be the celebration of sport itself due to your diligence and endurance.

In addition to the funding sources previously discussed, an ever increasing revenue source is licensed merchandising. Chapter 10 will demonstrate how a well thought-out merchandising program can promote long-term fiscal success.

GAME HIGHLIGHTS

- To seek funding, create a business plan in which you meticulously list all of your procedures for capitalizing and producing the successful sport event in a profitable manner.
- Consider prosperous individuals, corporations, foundations, venture capitalists, and public entities as potential sources of funding.
- Seek sponsorships early and prepare an attractive sponsorship proposal that lists various levels and categories of investment and describes in detail the benefits the sponsor will enjoy.

PLAY BOOK

business plan The detailed plan that describes your business methods for capitalization, marketing, operations, and achieving profitability. It should also include testimonials from individuals familiar with your capabilities and a history of your experiences.

cause-related marketing A marketing technique in which corporations appear socially responsible by returning a portion of their proceeds to a specified cause or charity.

cross-promotions A marketing strategy in which two or more sponsors share in the promotion of an event and each other.

foundation A charitable organization that distributes monies to typically not-for-profit organizations that meet specific funding guidelines established by the foundation.

funding The grease that shifts the gears of sport event commerce. You cannot move forward or in reverse without funding. Instead you will remain in neutral.

multiyear A sponsorship agreement that is automatically renewed for a specified number of years and/or events.

outside funding Sources of funds available to you from exogenous entities that may wish to invest in your sport event.

venture capitalist A business entity whose sole purpose is to invest in business ventures and provide needed capital.

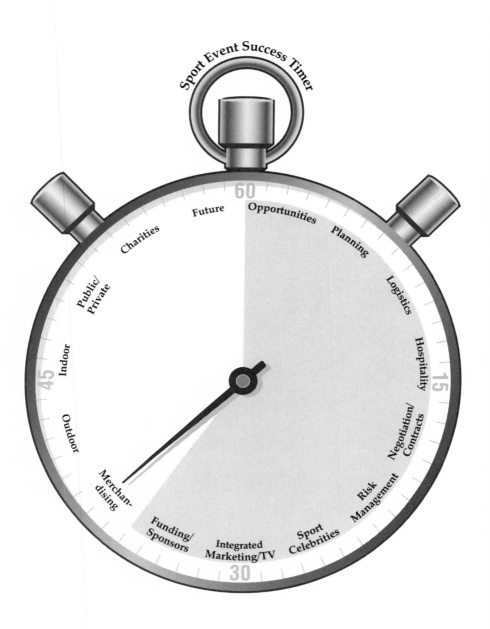

Chapter Ten

Merchandising:
The Magic Word for Long-Term Fiscal Success

"Be everywhere, do everything, and never fail to astonish the customer."

Macy's motto

H ow do you increase your passive income from sport events through merchandising and when and how do you implement this program?

"Always remember that the best way to sell your dream is to evangelize it effectively—not destroy your enemy's," advises Guy Kawasaki, former director of software product management for Apple Computer. Kawasaki defines evangelism as the process of selling a dream. Sport event merchandising requires rampant evangelism to guarantee success.

A few years ago, Joe Jeff Goldblatt was retained by the Sells Floto concession company (a division of Ringling Brothers & Barnum & Bailey Circus) to train the concession sales personnel who travel with the circus. Goldblatt promptly reported to a giant arena located on Long Island and introduced himself to the concession manager. The manager gruffly stated, "We've had five so-called consultants before, and none of them have been any good. My people only want to make money and make it fast. Most don't speak English. These are not career sales people. So, what are *you* gonna do?"

Goldblatt drew a breath and asked for further background on the sales people. He was told that many came from Bulgaria and

Russia and were cousins, brothers, and sisters of the circus performers. They traveled with the show to keep the family together and to earn extra money.

He then pressed further and asked the irritated concession manager whether his work was important to the overall profitability of the circus. The manager said, "Are you kidding? The major revenue and profits come from merchandise and food. My department pulls the whole operation."

At that point, Goldblatt was led from the manager's small office into the arena where 50 men and women had been assembled in seats close to the arena floor. They were talking loudly among themselves when the concession manager boomed, "Listen up. This fella Goldblatt is gonna show you how to sell better." With that eloquent and gracious introduction, Goldblatt was faced with 50 people who spoke little or no English and 30 minutes to turn them into super sales producers before the evening show.

Goldblatt quickly assessed the skill and language level of the group and determined that they were primarily profit driven. He asked the group, "When someone orders popcorn or cotton candy, how do you respond?" He asked them to demonstrate a typical example of selling these products in the stands and he watched as one of the sales people raised his index finger and another galloped up 30 steps to fill this single order.

"Tonight when someone signals that they want to buy, I want you to stop, shout 'how many' and wait for them to respond." The salespeople looked at him quizzically, but he now had their full attention.

"The customer will most likely hold up two or more fingers. Whatever number he displays, you are to shout it at the top of your lungs and then go into the stands to fill the order," Goldblatt continued. He then demonstrated this procedure several times, using members of the audience as buyers.

"The goal is multiple sales with less time and effort per sale. Each time I catch you doing this tonight and it results in a sale, I will reward you with an extra dollar. I'll be watching." In less than 30 minutes, he had taught them a simple skill that would increase the sales that evening by an amazing 43 percent.

What would a 43 percent sales increase mean to your sport event revenues this year?

Bob Brubaker, general manager of retail operations for Astrodome, USA in Houston, Texas, says attendance in 1993 was estimated at 3.76 million people. The per capita spending for merchandise sales was over $1.75. Although the Astrodome is one of the major sport venues in the United States, the figures illustrate the potential for a merchandising program for your sport event.

DETERMINING WHEN TO MERCHANDISE

The successful sport event manager and marketer will carefully analyze the benefits of introducing a merchandizing program before making this important investment (see Figure 10–1). At the same time, he or she will carefully analyze the potential risks involved. Additional considerations were provided in Chapter 5 under licensee contracts.

WILL YOU BE SUCCESSFUL?

This mysterious but all too apt question should be at the top of any marketer's list. While the answer will remain unknown until you receive the sales report, methods for analyzing your likelihood of success with a merchandising program are available.

In describing the attitude to which his team adheres, Nike founder and chairman Phil Knight says, "We take a chance and learn from it." Knight is saying that not every new idea is necessarily successful; however, it is critically important to Nike to continue to innovate and thereby increase the margin of success proportionately.

Every successful firm from Nike to Reebok, from Pepsi to Coca-Cola, carefully test-market their products to ensure success. Douglas Frechtling, associate professor of tourism studies at the George Washington University, cites a personal example.

> We sent out a survey to a random sample [of people] and the overwhelming response was positive. However, when we introduced the product very few responded with actual purchases. The gap between the intention to buy and the actual purchase is a large one. Every product and service should be test-marketed carefully to

FIGURE 10–1

Analyzing Merchandising Opportunities

Pre-Sport Event Development
- Have you conducted a market analysis to determine whether your target audience will purchase these products?
- Have you test-marketed similar products at events that attract the same demographic and psychographic concentrations as your event?
- Is there a licensed trademark agreement that may prohibit or increase merchandising opportunities?
- Can you identify a partner or coventurer who will assume all or part of the risk of the development and marketing of the products?

Existing Sport Event Considerations
- Is there a demand for the products? What do your spectator surveys report?
- Is there sufficient product development and testing time to introduce a new product?
- Are sufficient sales time and appropriate locations available for these sales at the sport event?
- What are the promotional possibilities for these products before, during, and following the sport event in off-site retail stores and by means of direct mail catalogs?
- Are there potential liabilities for potential injury from the products?
- Is your marketing team confident the product will sell?
- Will the merchandising program be handled internally or externally?
- Who is responsible for designing the merchandise and who will approve all final products?
- Do you have or can you recruit a qualified sales force to vend these products?
- What training will be required for these salespeople?
- Who will manufacture, stock, inventory, pull, and restock merchandise items?
- How can the merchandise be advertised before, during, and after the game?

determine consumer likes and dislikes, to set appropriate pricing, to finetune sales techniques, and to develop ideas for further product development.

Frechtling, whose specialization is statistical research in tourism, advocates extensive test marketing before making a major commitment to vend any product.

According to Phil Knight, "Nike is a marketing-oriented company and the product is our most important marketing tool." His analysis demonstrates the critical importance between product quality, value, and marketing momentum to achieve consumer investment.

To ensure your success, use the checklist in Figure 10–2 to monitor your merchandise product development and sales testing.

A focus group is usually comprised of 7 to 12 members with similar demographics and a trained facilitator. Depending on the diversity of your target audience more than one focus group may need to be convened. According to Professor Frechtling, this qualitative research is extremely useful in developing survey questions for further quantitative marketing research.

HOT MERCHANDISING IDEAS

The creation of the collector pin was perhaps the best merchandising idea in sport event history. What began as a simple advertising novelty has rapidly become, as described earlier, a tradition of the Olympic movement. In fact, Coca-Cola hopes through its support of the official 1996 Olympic Games Pin Society to expand the Olympic pin phenomenon to other sport events that the company sponsors (e.g., Super Bowl).

Relatively inexpensive to produce, corporate sponsors compete to see who can create the most popular pin design. They then barter or give them away. Sport event managers and marketers, however, design deluxe collectors' pin sets to chronicle their hallmark event and sell these at a premium price.

Stedman Graham says that T-shirts are by far the most popular merchandise item for all sport event sales. "A T-shirt allows wearers to show their allegiance and it also is considered a durable purchase, thereby offering more value."

Anthropologist Valene Smith states that T-shirts are the single most popular tourist merchandise item because not only are they functional but also they fulfill the desire of human beings to decorate themselves with a statement or design that proclaims their values.

Therefore, when developing wearable merchandise the message should match the values and pride quotient of the prospective purchaser. These relatively inexpensive items can also be sold at a premium price if the design is considered fine art or a collectible.

In the fabric category, hats are particularly popular with male fans and growing in popularity with females. Once again, they serve a

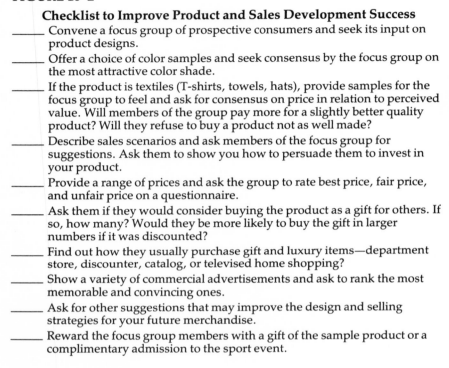

FIGURE 10–2

Checklist to Improve Product and Sales Development Success

_____ Convene a focus group of prospective consumers and seek its input on product designs.

_____ Offer a choice of color samples and seek consensus by the focus group on the most attractive color shade.

_____ If the product is textiles (T-shirts, towels, hats), provide samples for the focus group to feel and ask for consensus on price in relation to perceived value. Will members of the group pay more for a slightly better quality product? Will they refuse to buy a product not as well made?

_____ Describe sales scenarios and ask members of the focus group for suggestions. Ask them to show you how to persuade them to invest in your product.

_____ Provide a range of prices and ask the group to rate best price, fair price, and unfair price on a questionnaire.

_____ Ask them if they would consider buying the product as a gift for others. If so, how many? Would they be more likely to buy the gift in larger numbers if it was discounted?

_____ Find out how they usually purchase gift and luxury items—department store, discounter, catalog, or televised home shopping?

_____ Show a variety of commercial advertisements and ask to rank the most memorable and convincing ones.

_____ Ask for other suggestions that may improve the design and selling strategies for your future merchandise.

_____ Reward the focus group members with a gift of the sample product or a complimentary admission to the sport event.

functional purpose of protecting the head and face from the rays of the sun while allowing the wearer to proclaim his or her allegiance to a specific team, event, idea, value, or all of those. The demand for specially designed ties and socks is also on the increase.

Hallmark sport events such as the Olympic Games offer a whole new range of possibilities for merchandise development. Especially popular are crafts of the host nation. These can be reproduced in sufficient quantity at a reasonable price to allow the visitor to take home a historic collectible of this sport event.

Another hot item is an original poster of the hallmark event produced in a limited edition to increase its value. The poster can be sold either framed or unframed. Once again, purchasers have made an investment in visual art that will serve as a decorative item and a conversational piece when they return home.

Novelty merchandise such as light sticks that glow in the dark, team pennants, magnets, key chains, pens, and other low-end merchandise continues to remain popular, but its growth is not as rapid as that of textiles and original art-based products. The old maxim, "you get what you pay for," is more true than ever and today's savvy consumers are in search of greater value for every dollar invested. Value means quality, dependability, and historical significance. Successful products exemplify this winning formula.

THE CELEBRITY ATHLETE AS ENDORSER

An athlete will gladly endorse your product provided that the product has quality, is merchandised effectively, and can produce acceptable residual income for the athlete. When seeking an athlete to endorse your product, first determine which athlete the competition is using to avoid confusion among consumers. Next, make a formal presentation to the athlete's manager and describe the marketing approach, the athlete's responsibilities in marketing the product, the profit potential, and the auditing procedures. The agent-manager for the athlete may wish to have specific verification by an independent third party and may also desire separate compensation for the athlete for any commercial appearances on television, radio, or print in addition to live appearances. All of this is negotiable in the final agreement so you must carefully analyze how much you can afford to invest in the athlete, by weighing the potential return on your investment, before you begin your discussions.

SELLING EVERYWHERE

Stedman Graham says that "location is critical when selling merchandise at sport events." Although the fire marshal and the venue control the number of locations and placement, Graham advises the placement of as many spots (sales areas) as possible to saturate the venue.

In today's modern sport venue, you are likely to find a menu of merchandise items in your chair as soon as you are seated. From this menu, you can place an order with your vendor to purchase select items and pick them up on your way out of the arena. The simple use of a credit card number means that you don't even need to soil your hands with cash.

In the middle of the concourse of the venue, you are likely to find brightly colored kiosks vending T-shirts, posters, collectible pins, and a variety of other products. The kiosks are designed to stop traffic en route to rest rooms or fixed-position concession locations.

From the front gate where programs are sold, to the parking lot where grab bags of discontinued merchandise may be offered, the sport event venue of the 90s and certainly beyond has come to resemble a giant department store.

While some spectators have begun to complain, most probably like the convenience of the merchandise and find the concession kiosks a welcome distraction at a particularly slow game where little is happening on the field. Shopping certainly ranks a close second in popularity to sport event attendance among this increasingly upscale market.

When setting up your sport event merchandise locations, look at crowd flow as an indicator of where to position permanent or temporary selling areas. Also keep in mind the need to restock your inventory and the proximity of the location to the inventory. After all, you can't sell what is not on the shelf. Although the merchandise sales at the 1993 U.S. Olympic Festival in San Antonio concluded successfully, at one point no large T-shirts (the most popular size) were available anywhere.

Design your kiosks or stands with raised displays that can be easily seen over the heads of standing crowds. Tests show that lighted signs and three-dimensional displays are more effective in attracting consumers. Colors also play an important role in attracting customer response. Red and white attracts customers at close range while black and yellow is more visible from a distance. Also note that large amounts of merchandise are purchased during the come-in or arrival time as well as the blow-off or departure. Make sure you have peak staffing during these critical times.

Make sure that the sales area is visible to prospective buyers by lighting or elevation, and set up your displays so that the arriving public will see active buyers purchasing merchandise. Consumers follow the lead of people with a similar demographic and psy-chographic profile.

LICENSED MERCHANDISE

If managed correctly, sport event licensed merchandise can be one of your most lucrative revenue streams. The 1993 U.S. Golf Open grossed $5 million and the U.S. Olympic Festival - '94 in St. Louis grossed over $1.1 million from licensed merchandise. World Cup Soccer will gross approximately $1 billion worldwide on licensed merchandise.

One of the first decisions an event producer needs to make concerning licensed merchandise is whether to manage the licensing program in-house or hire an external organization such as the Time Warner Entertainment Group to coordinate the effort.

Whoever ends up with the job will be responsible for the following:

- Distribution and collection of license applications.
- Review and selection of licensees.
- Collection of minimum guarantees or bank guarantees.
- Development and dissemination of design handbook and marketing plan. How often will a new product line be intro-duced? How many designs should be allowed?
- Development and dissemination of approval process guide-lines.
- Review of all designs for quality and appropriateness.
- Accounting for all sales and royalties.
- Protection against counterfeit merchandise.

The number of licensees will depend on the exclusivity or nonex-clusivity of the license category. This decision is usually influenced by the philosophy of the management and market size as previously discussed in Chapter 5 (p. 103). There were 2,500 applications for 36 exclusive licenses for the 1994 Winter Olympic Games.

Applications are scrutinized in terms of the company's reputa-tion and knowledge of the retail business, financial status, and distribution channels.

DOES YOUR SPORT EVENT NEED MERCHANDISE?

Not every sport event will benefit from merchandising. As the manager of a corporate tennis tournament designed to attract new buyers or reward your vendors for loyal service, you will most likely give the merchandise away rather than sell it. However, if the merchandise is well designed don't be surprised if one of your guests inquires, "Where may I purchase this item?"

That is the magic in merchandising. Whether you are giving away an ad specialty pin or selling an upscale golf blazer, the classic adage reminds us that the customer is always right. Use your considerable creative talents to survey, test, develop, and sell what your sport event customers want and need, and you will discover a new profit stream that flows long and deep. And don't forget to ask, "How many?"

The number of sport events where merchandise can be distributed continues to grow, particularly outdoor events. On weekends, evenings, and holidays, millions of Americans can be found attending or participating in an outdoor sport event. In Chapter 11, you will discover how the biblical proverb, "There is no new thing under the sun," does not always apply to sport events. With outdoor events, you are limited only by your imagination.

GAME HIGHLIGHTS

- Incorporate sales training in your strategy.
- Always seek multiple sales.
- Use focus groups to recommend the best methods for effective merchandising.
- Test market the product to determine the projected level of sales.
- Select the location to sell the product based on traffic flow, visibility, and ability to restock quickly.

PLAY BOOK

blow-off The window of time for selling merchandise when the fans depart.

come-in The window of time for selling merchandise when the fans arrive.

concession manager An experienced full-time employee who manages vendors and is responsible for inventory control and financial accounting for all sales.

concessions Merchandise is often included in sales figures for concessions, but historically concessions refer to food and beverage sales.

merchandise Hard or soft items sold at live events.

plastic Merchandise such as souvenir mugs manufactured from plastic.

textiles Merchandise that includes T-shirts, pennants, hats, and other items manufactured from textiles.

vendor A temporary, part-time worker who sells merchandise either from a stand or in the seats.

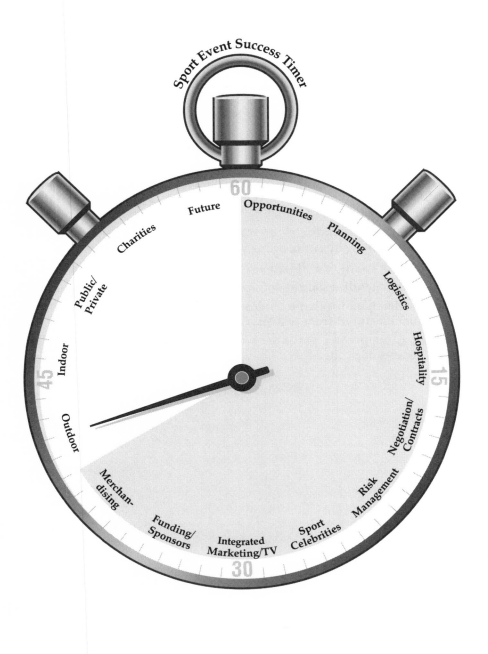

Chapter Eleven

Outdoor Sport Events

"I find baseball fascinating. It strikes me as a native American ballet—a totally different dance form. Nearly every move in baseball—the wind-up, the pitch, the motion of the infielders—is different from other games. Next to a triple play, baseball's double play is the most exciting and graceful thing in sports."

Alistair Cooke, journalist and broadcaster

What special tools and skills do you need and how do you apply them to produce successful outdoor events?

Despite 110 degrees temperature and 100 percent humidity, the runner climbs the next hill as part of an annual marathon. Through two feet of thick snow with wind gusts up to 50 knots, the downhill skier carefully navigates the slalom course at the World Cup in Aspen. Through it all, the sport event manager and marketer plans, measures, evaluates, and makes judgments that will ultimately determine the success or failure of the outdoor event.

When an event is held outdoors in the absence of four walls, a roof, a floor, controllable heating, air-conditioning, and a ventilation system, sport event managers and marketing professionals are forced to adapt and adopt freely to every change in atmospheric conditions. Topography, smooth and level indoors, may be uneven outdoors and require capital investment to allow for safe competition and efficient spectator ingress and egress.

Although outdoor conditions are often problematic, a well-prepared event coordinator should not only be able to produce successful outdoor events but also be able to benefit from the elements. For example, the Blue Angels, the U.S. Navy jet fighter exhibition squad, can fly only as an image in the Super Dome on the giant Jumbotron television, and the spectacle and heart-stopping site of the parachutists who brilliantly opened the Lille-hammer Winter Olympic Games by displaying the enormous flag of Norway could not be duplicated had the ceremony been held in the Viking Ship arena.

Chapter 3 described general logistical requirements for all sport events. This chapter will touch on a few additional sport-specific considerations but focus primarily on opportunities to turn a typical outdoor sport event into a special event. The technical rules and regulations for producing specific sport events are fairly standard and can be obtained through national sport governing bodies or affiliated sport federations. See Appendix II-E for ad-dresses.

CYCLING

The most common cycling event is the long-distance road race, with the most popular being the "Tour de France." Crossing great distances creates logistical challenges far greater than those of a sport event performed in a stationary venue. When asked what was the most difficult logistical aspect of the 1,000-mile Tour DuPont cycling race, Jim Birrell, technical director for the event produced by Medalist Sport, quickly answered, "the two-way communication system. Walkie-talkies are fine until your cyclists and management team are on two sides of a mountain. To combat such geographical elements, a fixed-wing airplane carrying three repeaters is hired to fly above the event allowing signals to be transmitted over the mountain." Another technical device used to help position both the television helicopter and the fixed-wing plane is the global positioning satellite (GPS). Since planes can normally fly only four hours and the event lasts six, at some time the plane must land and refuel. Once back in the air, pilots can immediately locate the cyclist by calling up GPS geographical coordinates. Birrell says, "Without a GPS, it takes pilots a long time to relocate the cyclists, wasting both time and money. Remember, from 2,000 feet in the air it isn't easy finding a pack of cyclists in the forest."

Another logistical challenge of the tour is that it crosses 150 different police jurisdictions, each with its own political bureaucracy. Birrell says that the best way to handle this is to "begin at the state level, followed by the county, then the city. This is especially important when traveling on state highways."

Cycling and running events share similar logistical considerations such as numbers, rest areas, and timing systems.

RUNNING RACES

More than 10,000 road races take place each year and each one requires an organization to make it successful and profitable. A number of logistical considerations will help you to produce a successful and profitable race.

Considerations for Races

1. Race application and permits. Organization begins with a race application that is sent to the racing organization with which you wish your race to be affiliated or sanctioned by. At this time, you should also submit the proper paperwork for what is usually called a "proposal for a parade permit," or permission to use the streets or parks on which your race will take place. This should be performed at least six months prior to the race date.

2. Budget. Obviously, the budget of a road race varies with the number of entrants, the length of the race, and the diversity of the course. "But," said Jim Vandak of 10K/Sport Productions in Arlington, Virginia, "there will always be some fixed costs if you have 500 people or 5,000." Both Vandak and Susan Kalish, head of the American Running and Fitness Association in Bethesda, Maryland, said the most expensive element is the purchase of T-shirts. The cost of contracting someone to organize the finish line is next.

Profits come from sponsors, or what Vandak calls "marketing the race." Vandak believes that signing up the sponsors is the most difficult part of organizing a race. "It takes a lot of time and a lot of work." Kalish believes that for this type of sport event, "your best bet for sponsors today are not the big companies but the small local businesses that are interested in promoting their name."

3. **Promotions.** To receive "more bang for your buck," place advertisements in newsletters and magazines in the local community and distribute brochures at other road races. The race should be promoted to a targeted audience with ample time for runners to train.

4. **Race equipment.** To set up the race, you need equipment including measuring devices, numbers, pins, time sheets, tempera (the water soluble, nontoxic paint used to line the course, costs about $1.40 per quart), stopwatches, finish-line clock, flags, banners, scaffolding, ladders, tools, typewriter and mimeograph machine or computer and printer, result board, awards, megaphone or public-address system, water, ice, cups, and some form of shade (trees, awnings, umbrellas). National magazines, such as *Running Times*, set up promotions in which they supply race organizers with numbers, pins, and "goody bags" in exchange for the distribution of discount subscription order forms to participants by the event organizer.

5. **Course monitors.** You must have volunteers or staff serving as monitors on the course to direct runners, watch for cars, and manage water stations. These individuals should wear bright colors and be briefed extensively about the course. Monitors should also be stationed where a crowd is expected to form in order to restrain the crowd from surging forward and interfering with the runners. A police escort is suggested for the first-place runner. Use the media to notify the public about roads that will be closed to avoid traffic problems.

6. **Medical attention and transport.** Every race must have a medical unit available. Although racers complete a waiver freeing race directors from prosecution for injuries, event organizers still have an unspoken responsibility to equip the race to handle running in-juries and emergencies. Many races actually assign a race medical director to be responsible for assisting in the choice

of the day, start time, evaluation of the course for potential hazards, and selection of the location for refreshments, shade, and medical stations.

7. Course measurement.   The worst way to measure a course is by using an automobile odometer. Many race associations will not accept race proposals that have measured the track this way. The best way to measure a course is with the calibrated bicycle method, which involves a wheel-revolution counter connected to the rear wheel of a bike. The number of revolutions are then compared with the measurement of the course by a steel tape. U.S.A. Track and Field Association (USATF), the national governing body of this sport, states that for a course to be certified, a USATF-certified individual must measure the course and give it a USATF number. This service costs approximately $200.

8. Brochure/entry form.   Brochures and forms should provide to the runner the following important information about the race:

- Race name
- Sponsors
- Time and date
- Location
- Cost
- Awards
- T-shirt information
- Entry form
- Mailing address
- Liability waiver
- Brief history
- Course map and distance

9. Registration.   An average race currently costs between $2 and $30 to enter. Fun-run courses are usually measured by odometers and rarely offer any awards or T-shirts. The registration fees for these events are therefore at the low end, $2 or $3, and the races are usually organized for the social aspect of racing. Many clubs organize fun-runs to solicit new members. The larger the expected race, the more you should charge for the entrance fee.

Decide whether to allow race-day registration or preregistration only. Runners registering on the race day are often charged an additional $5 to $10. Those who register prior to the race usually receive a break on the fee, and have the luxury of picking up their "race packet" a day or two before the race.

Sponsors of fund-raising events, such as the National Multiple Sclerosis Society, require entrants to collect pledges for eligibility, usually a minimum of $25.

10. Race packet. The race packet contains a course map, the entrant's race number, safety pins for the entrant's number, sponsor information and/or giveaways or coupons, and other information such as medical services, the awards ceremony, and so forth.

11. Split times. Larger races have mile-marker signs 10 feet high so that runners can see the mile they are approaching. Other races simply mark the mile on the road with paint. Either way, you know you are approaching a mile marker when you hear a volunteer, ideally dressed in common volunteer attire or a specific color, yelling out split times.

12. Finish line. Make the finish line noticeable by using flags, balloons, sponsor banners, race name banners, and cones. You must decide whether you want all finishers to cross into the same finish-line chute, or separate the male finishers from the female finishers.

Recording runners' times is another aspect of the finish line. At smaller races, two people complete this procedure. The caller, using a stopwatch, calls the time of each person as he or she crosses the finish line while the second person records the time. We suggest that you create a time sheet with preprinted numbers and times so the recorder has only to circle the times as they are being called. Most larger races, however, have automated this procedure. A small hand-held device about the size of a large calculator can be purchased or rented. You push a button on it each time a runner crosses the finish line, and the time is recorded and later printed out on a small sheet of paper. Even more sophisticated is the digital display timer that connects to the overhead timer as the runners cross the finish line.

The next responsibility is the placing of finishers. At small races, an index card with the place written on it is given to each finisher. After the runners have caught their breath, they walk to a table and complete the card with pertinent information. The cards are then combined with the information received by the timers in order to match places and names with the corresponding times. Another option is to purchase the numbers that come with a tear-off tab. Organizers apply the runner's information on this tab as each runner crosses the finish line. The tab is then torn off and placed in order of finish. This obviously expedites the greatly anticipated posting of results.

Organizing a road race, even one that expects only 500 runners, demands strict preparation and delegation of resources. Manage these tasks by breaking them down into committees. Even for smaller races, this relieves some of the burden placed on the race director, who is busy overseeing the entire race.

GOLF

Someone must have recognized many years ago that golf would become one of the most challenging and phenomenal games in sport event history. There are several types of golf events.

Corporate Outing

The corporate outing is probably the most popular type of golf event. Outings can range from a small group of corporate executives getting together on a specific day to play golf, each paying his or her own fees, to a major corporate outing like the "Crumby" sponsored by Sara Lee, where suppliers, celebrities, athletes, and corporate executives play golf for three days. The success of corporate golf outings relates to the amount of business that is conducted on the course. Where else can you spend four to six hours in conversation with someone over things in common and of course business and business opportunities? Molly O'Dea, district manager of a large photocopying company in Tampa, Florida, was quoted in the *Washington Post*: "In my career it's important that I work with customers, and important that I network. One of the best ways to do that, and one of the most effective ways, is through golf."

Anthony Triglione is president of Traffic Builders Unlimited, which specializes in innovative trade show marketing. His firm recognizes that many of the more than 25 million golfers in the United States attend trade shows. To build and attract traffic at trade shows, Triglione uses a giant video screen to project the 18th hole at Pebble Beach Golf Course in California and uses computer enhancements to provide a realistic playing atmosphere. Through this invention, novices and advanced golf customers use real clubs and balls to play this computer-designed ultimate indoor golf experience. Best of all, convention golf means business.

Charity Golf Outing

Another type of a golf tournament is the charity outing. This takes the name of the charity sponsor or is presented by a corporation such as the Junior Achievement Golf Classic sponsored by 3M Corporation. This type of golf outing is designed to be supported by members and friends of the charity who raise a certain amount of money of which net profits go to the charity. Some charity golf events obtain official 501(c)(3), not-for-profit tax status.

Celebrity Golf Outing

The celebrity golf outing usually benefits a charity. This event is typically designed around a popular celebrity who can bring in equally celebrated friends to attract sponsors who want to share in the limelight and glitz. Celebrity outings can be a lot of fun if they are run smoothly and the participants are not disappointed in the celebrities. The most popular ones are the Bob Hope Chrysler Classic, the AT&T Pebble Beach Pro Am, and Michael Jordan tournaments. This type of golf event also requires special accommodations, upscale hospitality, and attention to detail.

Professional Tour

The most exciting spectator golf tournament is the professional tour. This consists of the top professional golfers in the world who qualify to play for a predetermined money purse. Although there are different levels of tournaments that offer many prizes, the most popular are the PGA (Professional Golf Association), the Senior PGA, and the LPGA (Ladies Professional Golf Association) tours. These tournaments are sponsored by corporations and play in preannounced cities throughout the country.

Before planning any golf tournament, you need to identify the level of players who will be participating. Quoted in *The Official Meeting Planner's Guide to Great Golfing Destinations*, David Hancock, golf sales director at Marriott's Bay Point Resort in Florida, said "The level of players will affect your decision about what type of tournament to have and, if a resort has more than one course, which course to use."

Other data vital in the early planning stages are the number of people expected to play and the reason for the golf event (e.g., fund-raising, sales staff incentive, new product/service announcement, developing relationships with clients, announcing a new business strategy); and the intensity of the event—competitive, friendly, or educational.

This information helps determine the format of the tournament. The "shotgun start" is an excellent way to get everyone in the tournament energized. In the past, the golf pro would fire a shot gun, hence the name, to start the play. The teams arrive simultaneously, have refreshments, start their cart engines and drive to a preassigned individual tee, and tee off simultaneously at an agreed upon time.

For a team event, a "scramble format" enables the different levels of players to participate regardless of ability. Every person in the group tees off and then the ball closest to the hole is selected and played by the entire group until the hole is finished. The scramble is also the fastest tournament play.

When planning golf tournaments, remember the importance of involving women golfers. *Golf Magazine* reports that women now account for 22 percent of all golfers and 40 percent of all *new* golfers. There are currently over 5 million women golfers in the United

States. Among them are U.S. Supreme Court Justices Ruth Bader Ginsburg and Sandra Day O'Connor. Contrary to the stereotype, women who play golf frequently complete a round 10 minutes *faster* than men.

For first-time golf event planners, the golf professional at your selected course serves as a good point of reference. Sometimes, the golf course manager will run your event for you. The service charge is approximately $1–$3 per golfer in addition to the regular golf fee at the facility. The services that you or the professional must provide for a tournament include:

- Setting up score cards.
- Arranging the pairings based on handicaps.
- Assigning tee times.
- Making sure people get to their tees on time.
- Posting winners at the end of the tournament.
- Orchestrating hole contests and obtaining prizes.
- Arranging transportation.
- Preparing the award ceremonies or banquet
- Coordinating a silent auction in conjunction with the tournament to raise additional funds.

Most resorts and golf courses have checklists for those planning a golf outing or tournament. Gerald M. Plessner C.F.R.E., president of Fund Raisers, Inc., in Arcadia, California, and an expert in conducting successful golf tournaments, says "you need to begin planning at least six months prior to the golf event." He advises that the ideal location for a tournament site "is a private club that never allows tournaments, is the most exclusive in town, has excellent food service and banquet facilities for a first-class reception or dinner with dancing, and whose course is not too difficult to play but provides a challenge for the average player."

Plessner says that this formula is a winning one for charitable golf tournaments because it creates a demand mentality among players. This formula can easily be extended, however, to other sport events such as tennis or volleyball. The private beach that is opened only for an exclusive volleyball tournament could become in great demand and therefore a successful destination for players.

FIGURE 11-1
Golf Tournament Organizational Chart

Tournament Director		Chairman	
Assistant Director		Development Director	

Committee Vice Chairs or Managers		
Registration	Refreshments	Merchandise
First Aid	Financial	Celebrities
Corporate Hospitality	Marketing	Media
Public Relations	Equipment	Insurance Prizes
Gifts	Groundskeeping Facilities	Transportation
Accommodations	Entertainment	Scoring

Most charity or celebrity golf tournaments are planned through a tournament committee. The golf tournament organizational chart shown in Figure 11–1 is also adaptable to other outdoor sport events.

Note that the term "Groundskeeping Facilities" may be adapted to supervision of either a swimming pool or the running surface of a track, depending on the event. All facilities used by the athletic competitors should be assigned to one person to ensure compliance with competition standards as well as to provide security and safety for the athletes. Supervision of auxiliary facilities such as hospitality tents or merchandise and concession kiosks should be assigned to appropriate committee representatives.

The following checklist will help stimulate your thinking about the abundant possibilities available to you and your team to organize a successful golf event (see Figure 11–2).

Despite your best laid plans, you have no control over what Mother Nature has in store. Figure 11–3 offers ideas for what to do during inclement weather.

FIGURE 11–2
Tournament "Hole-in-One" Ideas

• Select a golf chairperson who is interested in and knowledgeable about the game.
• Include with the invitation or registration form a golf participant survey that requests the participant's handicap, rental equipment needs (shoe size if applicable), and the number of spouses or partners playing.
• Determine the number of attendees not participating in the tournament. This will help you plan alternative programs such as instructional clinics, putting tournaments, and tourist or shopping excursions.
• Remind players to clearly mark and identify all equipment and shoes before arriving at the course.
• Design and order personalized merchandise early.
• Decide what number of prizes will be needed (e.g. twosomes or foursomes), and the categories of winners (e.g. lowest score, highest score).
• Avoid changes in handicaps and last-minute changes in pairings.
• Meet with the golf operations coordinator to finalize all scheduling, group requirements, and special needs, including celebrity players. Provide a list of the pairings and rental needs at least one day before the tournament.
• Ask about tipping and gratuity policies at the course.
• Assign check-in people to greet players as they arrive to drop off their golf bags. Greeters should ask the players' names, inform them of the hole number at which they will start, and tag their bags with this number and place the bags on the corresponding cart. A receipt showing this hole number is a helpful reminder to golfers.
• Assign a parking attendant to direct all tournament traffic.
• Assign an individual or several individuals to pickup VIPs on tournament day to assure schedule is maintained properly.
• Publicize the availability of lockers, locker room facilities, and showers.
• Use beverage cart sponsors to provide refreshments to players on the green.
• Hole sponsors can offer prizes for the best score at each hole.
• Sponsors can offer special prizes for contests such as closest to the hole, longest drive, accurate drive, and so forth.
• The "hole-in-one contest" is a great idea to generate excitement and lots of advance free publicity. Try to get someone to donate a vacation trip or even a new automobile as the prize for this contest. To build excitement, park the automobile near the hole.

WORKING WHILE YOU PLAY

A celebrity golf pro appearance, clinic, or full-blown tournament provides an excellent opportunity for business networking. Chasing that little white ball can result in new sales leads, prospective customers, and—most important—lifelong friendships that started at your outdoor event on the green.

FIGURE 11-3

Making Sunshine on Rainy Days
• In case of inclement weather, be prepared to offer your golfers a suitable substitute that will at least provide entertainment until the weather clears.
• Ask the course golf pro to be prepared to offer a demonstration trick shot clinic or a special educational session. An even surer bet is to bring to the event your own golf pro, who can be ready to provide assistance on the course or in the clubhouse.
• Provide waterproof clothing, golf umbrellas, and golf club coverings for your guests who might like to continue playing in the rain.
• Ask audiovisual personnel to set up a television and video machine so that you can show instructional golf tapes or championship footage while golfers wait for the weather to improve.
• Research and secure cancellation insurance in your contracts. You also might consider a rain date.

FIGURE 11-4

Promoting Your Beach Volleyball Event
• Use a *tow plane* with a sign to promote the tournament. Have it fly past the beach a day or two in advance of the tournament to alert the sunbathers of your volleyball sport event.
• Hire a blimp to circle the tournament area and draw attention to the event.
• Use *colorful banners* showing the event and team names to create a festive atmosphere near the nets. Sponsors' names may be displayed in a similar manner.

BEACH VOLLEYBALL

Light the torches, build the bonfires, bring in the steel band and tropical refreshments! It's time to take to the beach for fun and healthy exercise. Beach volleyball is fast becoming one of the most popular participant and spectator sports. From the beaches of Delaware to California, thousands of amateur and professional athletes are participating in this sport while hundreds of thousands of spectators have become impassioned fans. Figure 11-4 suggests how to promote a beach volleyball event while Figure 11-5 indicates special considerations in producing it.

FIGURE 11–5

Special Considerations for Producing Beach Volleyball Events

• Erect temporary pop-up umbrellas and tents to shade athletes, judges, other officials, and the media. Make sure that you provide ample refreshments in this area.

• If the tournament is held at night, use a glow-in-the-dark dye to color the volleyballs and encourage the teams to wear clothing that glows in the dark. Sell glow in the dark jewelry and wands to the spectators to further illuminate the surroundings.

• At the end of the tournament, schedule a rock band to perform music from the 1960s for a blast from the past on the beach, or a steel or reggae band to create a tropical environment while you celebrate the team's victory in the moonlight.

FIGURE 11–6

Special Safety Considerations for Producing Water Sport Events

• Implement a counting system to keep track of the number of participants who enter the water and the number who return to shore.

• Use easily identified floatation devices to mark the competition course.

• Continually study the wind and water current patterns in order to begin the event when natural elements are at their weakest. Strong wind gusts and relentless ebb tides may force a delay or cancellation of the competition.

• Recruit volunteer boaters to stand by along the race course for rescue calls. At the Great Chesapeake Bay Swim, 65 boats from the Chesapeake Power Boat Association were on hand when nearly 600 swimmers raced 4.4 miles across the bay.

WATER SPORTS

Many of the promotional and logistical ideas presented for beach volleyball apply to water sport events such as surfing, sailing, and rough water swims. In addition, a number of important safety precautions inherent in these sports should be mentioned (see Figure 11–6).

BASEBALL

From Little League to the majors, baseball has fulfilled the Barnum of the Bushes mandate to never run out of ideas.

Master showman Bill Hall recalls that the Philadelphia Phillies saluted major-league home run champ Hank Aaron of the Atlanta

FIGURE 11–7

Baseball Event Ideas

- Plan a pregame fan party with autograph signing by players, live music, and sponsors' giveaways.
- Organize a photo day sponsored by a film manufacturer.
- Recruit a celebrity to sing "The Star-Spangled Banner."
- Use a parachutist to deliver the flag to the infield.
- Enlist a popular elected official to throw out the first ball.
- Conduct baseball trivia games during slow moments in the play.
- Invite Little Leaguers to warm up with the majors.
- Invite celebrities to play in pregame warm-up demonstrations against other celebrities.
- Don't forget the immense popularity of the "old-timers" game. Team up the Little Leaguers with the seniors for a terrific photo opportunity.

Braves with a massive in-stadium release of nearly 700 doves. Each dove (really small homing pigeons) represented a home run. The doves were recruited from homing pigeon fanciers in the Philadelphia area and all made a safe return to their home roosts.

In the U.S. bicentennial year of 1976, Hall and Phillies president Bill Giles created an opening day baseball promotion called "Revere to Rocket to Roberts." In this stunt, a rider costumed as Paul Revere left Boston's North Church carrying the opening game ball in a colonial lantern for a 16-day horseback ride to Philadelphia's Veterans Stadium. On opening day, the rider raced around the stadium before delivering the ball to Rocketman at third base. Rocketman then flew around the stadium and landed at a huge baseball on the pitcher's mound. The ball opened and out came retired Phillies pitcher and Hall of Famer Robin Roberts, who tossed the opening ball. Thus, "Revere to Rocket to Roberts!"

When planning baseball-related events, remember to incorporate some of the basic ideas shown in Figure 11–7.

A popular sport vacation trend is the baseball fantasy camp. You can create a camp for your corporate team members without investing in travel. Invite one of the minor league, college, or high school coaches to put your sales and marketing department through spring training. On the final day, have them play against

FIGURE 11–8

Equestrian Event Ideas

• Rodeo Fever! Take your group to the rodeo for barrel racing, bull riding, and other spine-tingling fun. Let your corporate managers chase a greased pig or try to remove a ribbon from a calf's tail.

• Derby Days! Celebrate the annual Run for the Roses at Churchill Downs in Louisville with video footage of previous races (contact the Kentucky Derby Museum gift shop for videos). Make sure you serve mint juleps (and have designated drivers)!

• Spring Horse Show! Watch the fillies and foals trot in the sunshine as your group sips iced tea under a tent.

• Wagons Ho! Circle the wagons and open the chuck wagon as you relive the days of the Wild West with this relaxed group activity.

---

members of the minor league team. Win or lose, they will long remember the experience in team building that can be used to win future sales for your firm.

EQUESTRIAN EVENTS

Equestrian events range from small one-day schooling shows to splashy five-day, A-rated events. The appeal of horses attracts an elite crowd and offers unique settings for corporate outings. Ron Thomas, chief executive of the Tennessee Walking Horse National Celebration in Shelbyville, Tennessee, recently opened the National Walking Horse Museum on the organization's grounds. Filled with a modern display of the history of the development of the walking horse breed and a salute to the past grand champions, this venue is ideal for corporations to host receptions before, during, and after the annual walking horse celebration or spring show.

Another innovation of Thomas's is the indoor Calsonic Show Arena. Located next door to the 20,000-seat outdoor national celebration arena, this arena offers a climate-controlled environment for year-round equestrian events. When planning equestrian events, you may wish to consider one of the fun activities shown in Figure 11–8.

FOOTBALL

The excitement of 10,000 parents and children rising in unison to cheer on the home team at the Saturday night high school football game is truly contagious. This scene is repeated every fall weekend in thousands of high school stadiums throughout the United States.

Gridiron Gold

High school homecoming games are by far the greatest fundraisers, but they also require extensive planning. Usually, you must write a letter to the state organization that controls interscholastic sport requesting an extension for the halftime show. The usual extension granted is 10 minutes, allowing for a 25-minute program, to keep within this time frame requires well-planned rehearsals.

Special considerations also need to be made for schools with all-weather tracks. For example, it may be appropriate for automobiles carrying homecoming honorees to drive on the track, but at no time should the cars be idle on the track. All materials from the halftime ceremony should be cleared immediately from the field. You need to be especially careful with dangerous items that may hurt or injure a player. Football officials do not particularly like extensions, so it is extremely important to keep on schedule. Other logistical matters to consider for football events are shown in Figure 11–9.

The homecoming game is a time to push school spirit as well as merchandise. Empty the school store inventory. Again, remember that more money is made at football homecoming games than at any other high school sport event.

Key components of this outdoor meeting of the gladiators is best exemplified in Figure 11-10.

No matter which aspect of the big game you devote the greatest attention to, you must carefully consider each one when planning effective events. Athletic organizations may have different rules about player involvement in your pregame and postgame events. It is important that you carefully coordinate your activities with the coaches to be in compliance with their regulations.

FIGURE 11–9

Football Logistics

- Can the football field lights be dimmed for the ceremonies?
- Is there enough electrical voltage for all the special effects (e.g., additional amps for music, stage microphone, additional popcorn and snow cone machines)?
- Are headsets or hand-to-hand radios available to give to important individuals running the event?
- For a homecoming game, the following individuals should be connected by radio: the student council advisor, the person in charge of the automobiles, the announcer in the press box, the athletic director or producer of the show, and the custodian or person designated as the troubleshooter (i.e., the person with the master set of keys or electrical fuses.)

FIGURE 11–10

Football Event Ideas

- Pep Rally Celebrations! Usually held the day before the big game, this event designed to increase school spirit features the band, cheerleaders, and an appearance by the mascot. Remember to introduce the coaches and the players!
- Pregame show! During this event, the drill team may dance; a local band, choir, or vocalist may perform; or a local dance studio or acrobatics troupe may entertain the arriving fans.
- Pregame hospitality! Why not supplement the traditional snack bar favorites with a bake sale to raise money for the local team?
- Tailgate parties are particularly prominent at the university level. This requires additional venue staff for security and clean-up.
- The National Anthem! "The Star-Spangled Banner" may be performed by way of audiotape or live by a vocalist or choir as Old Glory is hoisted up the flagpole. A spotlight is mandatory to illuminate the flag for after-dark games. Make sure that the players and other field personnel are positioned on the field facing the flag.
- Halftime! During this brief break in the athletic action, the excitement of the game action must continue with stirring performances by the marching band, enthusiastic dances by the drill team, sensational acrobatic feats by the cheerleaders, melodies sung by singers or a choir, and even variety acts by entertainers. Let your imagination soar, fill the field with entertainment, and whenever possible plan activities that require audience participation. Hill Carrow, then President and Executive Director of the 1987 US Olympic Festival in North Carolina, remembers the excitement generated at the opening ceremonies when 50,000 pairs of white socks were distributed to the audience who were instructed to put them on their hands and join in an aerobic-type dance led by the mascot. What a sight!
- Postgame celebration! Win or lose, now it's time to celebrate the achievements on the field. You may wish to engage a band to perform in front of the stadium or in the parking lot as the fans depart. This is an excellent opportunity to build additional team spirit by having the drill team greet the fans as they head for home. For championship and other major occasions, add aerial fireworks for a memorable effect.

Although famed football coach Vince Lombardi said, "Winning is everything," he also understood that the game is part of a much larger sport event. You, as the sport event planner and marketer, are the coach whose skills can turn even the most predictable game into an unexpected celebration of sport.

After your outdoor success, it is time to turn your sights inward and explore new opportunities. You will discover in Chapter 12 that although the terrain may be different, the creative possibilities are as infinite.

GAME HIGHLIGHTS

- Remember that outdoor events have many more logistical variables than indoor events. Allow for more planning time.
- Develop a rain contingency plan.
- Be sensitive to transportation variables including parking.
- Use free community resources to provide entertainment.
- Incorporate audience participation pregame, halftime, and postgame.
- Make sure that your halftime show is visible to fans from all seats including the top of the bleachers.

PLAY BOOK

corporate An organization that has stockholders and whose business goal is to make a profit.

charity An organization that has no stockholders and raises funds to distribute to approved beneficiaries.

professional One who earns his or her livelihood from an endeavor and is perceived by others as an expert.

tee times The assigned time players are to begin play.

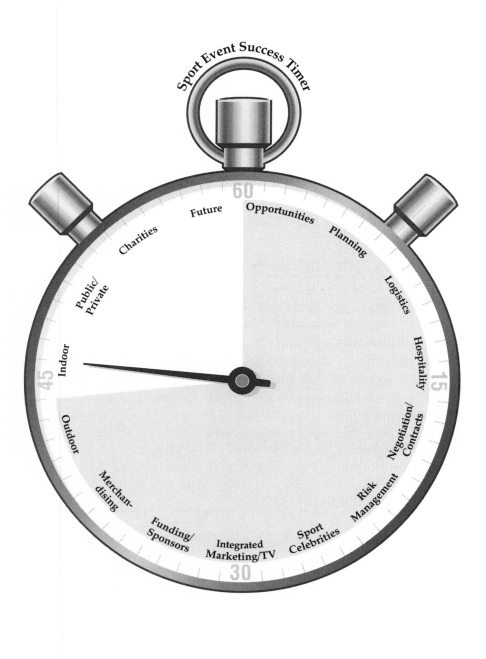

Sport Event Success Timer

60
Future
Opportunities
Planning
Charities
Logistics
Public/
Private
Hospitality
Indoor
15
45
Negotiation/
Contracts
Outdoor
Risk
Management
Merchan-
dising
Funding/
Sponsors
Integrated
Marketing/TV
Sport
Celebrities
30

Chapter Twelve

Indoor Sport Events

"Fortunately, in each championship game we were usually ahead enough right near the end so I could call a time-out in the last few minutes. During these time-outs, I reaffirmed to everyone that when the game was over we shouldn't act like fools. I told them it was a basketball game, and nothing more."

John Wooden, former UCLA basketball coach

Why is the indoor sport event achieving unprecedented interest among fans and how can you seize this opportunity to produce a championship season?

You have only to look at the growth of the National Basketball Association (NBA) to see why today's modern arenas have become major magnets for sport fans. True, the sport arenas must compete against traditional forms of indoor mass culture ranging from expositions to musicals and plays, but sport is consistently the best indoor entertainment seller for several reasons.

Despite recent concerns about security and safety, for the most part arenas are perceived by the general public as safe, comfortable environments in which to enjoy the game. The ease of access and many other comforts, such as an expanded food and beverage menu, are turning arenas into more upscale places of entertainment.

Remember that indoor sport events, particularly boxing matches, also take place in casino ballrooms such as the Trump Plaza in Atlantic City, New Jersey; convention center exhibition halls (e.g., Bass Masters annual fishing tournament celebration); and school and college gymnasiums. Regardless of the indoor site, the walls, roof, and level floor offer the infrastructure within which the sport event manager and marketer can plan successful events. The challenge is to make a festive atmosphere in the confines of the area.

An increasingly wide variety of sport events are being held indoors. Traditional indoor sport events such as ice hockey, gymnastics, and figure skating are being joined by soccer, football, tennis, and other formerly exclusively outdoor events.

BASKETBALL

Amusement Business, the weekly chronicle of the mass entertainment industry, reported that during the NBA All-Star weekend, "Coca-Cola Hoop City exceeded projections as basketball fans flocked to the entertainment center." This is but one example of how fans are hooping it up over this fast-growing sport. With the emergence of game superstars such as Magic Johnson, Michael Jordan, Charles Barkley, and Shaquille O'Neill, the sport has developed enormous fan loyalty from children through senior citizens.

Indoor basketball, however, is one of the most difficult sports for a high school athletic director to coordinate. Not only are there more games per season than football, but more taunting tends to take place between rival fans. "If the crowd is not constantly entertained, you are asking for trouble," says athletic director Monica Barrett. "Cheerleaders are fine for about five minutes, but do not rely on them for your total show. We often bring in the local YMCA "little guys" basketball for halftime fun. This is a basketball program for young children three to six years old."

Barrett finds herself constantly roaming the hallways, parking lot, and concession areas to make sure things are happening the way they should. The worst logistical nightmare in a basketball game is failure of the clock. Task lists for game events include: game management, ticket takers (usually staff or parents) supervision, announcers, cleanup, concessions, security, and emergency should be developed and continually updated as the school environment changes.

NCAA and NBA Influences on High School Tournaments

Tom Hilton is a 25-year coaching veteran and currently chairman of the Health, Physical Education, and CPR department at Good Counsel High School in Wheaton, Maryland. Hilton says:

The NCAA and NBA excitement prompted one of our alumni to organize a tournament in December at our school. This inaugural event attracted teams from many other states and hundreds of new fans. The event included a banquet saluting the players where a well known college coach spoke to our players. The major influence for the creation of this tournament was the popularity of the NCAA and NBA games.

3-on-3 = 7 Times the Fun*

Steve Schanwald was asked why he decided to start the Chicago Bulls 3-on-3 basketball tournament. He said:

> We get so much attention during our season—which is basically October through May, and sometimes, in a good year, through June—that we wanted to figure out a way to stay visible in the summer. We spend our advertising dollars to remain visible in the summer months since we receive all the advertising we need during the winter months through the newspapers. Starting the tournament was one thing that we could do, on top of our advertising, on top of the two to three million bumper stickers we distribute, on top of the billboards we buy, on top of the clinics we do throughout the area, on top of all Bob Love's appearances, and Benny the Bull's and Luv-a-Bull's appearances. This is something we could do to help us stay visible in the summer. We wanted to come up with a basketball festival, something that would be the equivalent of the Taste of Chicago (a major food and entertainment event attracting hundreds of thousands of guests). So we evolved to the point where I think the first year we had seven or eight hundred teams playing ball, and this year we expect twenty-five hundred teams. In the middle of Grant Park, we have ten thousand participants and hundreds of thousands of spectators coming down. It's really a great thing because last year we had people from all 50 states playing. It was a way for us to stay visible in the community and to promote not only the Chicago Bulls but the game of basketball itself. We expect that if we can promote the game of basketball, that is very good for the Chicago Bulls.

One of the most popular basketball events today is the 3-on-3 tournament. As described by Tom Swanson of the Championship

---

*3-on-3 tournaments are frequently held outdoors because of the number of participants.

FIGURE 12–1

3-on-3 Basketball Tournament Checklist

_____ Site selection
_____ Permits
_____ Advertise through leagues in the area
_____ Registration
_____ Sponsors
_____ Volunteers
_____ Game officials
_____ Insurance
_____ Medical, first aid
_____ Equipment (e.g., backboards, balls, scoreboards, whistles)
_____ Awards
_____ Booths for vendors
_____ Food and beverage concessions
_____ Sound equipment, staging

Group, a sport marketing firm based in Atlanta, Georgia, "3-on-3 basketball is a weekend street fair, a block party, an event born in the neighborhood, a family event, a media event, a charitable fundraiser, and a unique promotional opportunity." Companies not only sponsor one-day tournaments but a series across the United States and Europe. The Reebok Blacktop 3-on-3 tournament, for example, was produced in 12 markets. The series culminated in a televised national championship. According to Swanson, "3-on-3 works because it fits emerging lifestyle and consumer trends."

Today a number of different 3-on-3 tournaments are produced, with "Hoop-It-Up" being the most prominent. Tournaments like these are typically owned by one national company with on-site management subcontracted to a local project manager or firm. For example, Streetball Partner contracts with Global Sport to produce events in seven cities across the United States. Figure 12–1 has a checklist of things to do in producing a 3-on-3 basketball tournament.

Figure 12–2 provides you with ideas for activities that you may wish to incorporate in your basketball event.

TENNIS

Gerald M. Plessner, the golf fund-raising expert, says:

FIGURE 12–2

Basketball Event Ideas

- Pregame hoop-it-up celebration. Invite local celebrities to play a warm-up game prior to the start of the regulation game as they go one-on-one to entertain your fans.
- Pregame charity free-throw. Select fans from the audience by randomly calling out seat numbers and asking them to make a freethrow shot. For each "swoosh," the host organizer or sponsor donates a prescribed dollar amount to a favorite charity.
- Entrance of the players. Paint an eight-foot or taller basketball on white butcher paper. Score the paper so it tears easily and have the players make their entrance bursting through the giant ball. Special lighting such as strobes and spots add excitement to player introductions.
- Ask a local child to sing the national anthem and then have one of the players hoist the child to make the first basket.
- Use a blimp or low-flying aircraft to circle above the fans during the game. Contact Hystar Corporation in Vancouver, British Columbia, about its flying basketball aircraft and corporate sponsor program.
- Stage a series of stunts with the team mascot during the halftime and invite fans to pose for pictures.
- Have the band and cheerleaders prepare a brief, well-choreographed show to perform during halftime.
- Schedule a half court shooting contest. Promote a $1,000 or new car giveaway for the fan who makes the shot. Call this the "[Sponsor Name] Hot Shot Contest," or the "[Telecommunications Sponsor] Long-Distance Shot Contest." Be sure to have insurance!
- Following the game, have the mascot greet fans in the lobby and sign autographs.
- Create a "Dash for Cash" contest. Select a fan from the stands to try to pick up as much cash as possible from center court in 30 seconds. Of course, the denominations would be one-dollar bills and the participant would be allowed to use only one hand. They can however, stuff the money anywhere on their body!

The demographic figures for tennis are markedly different compared with those of other sport events. Although these figures are changing somewhat to include more mainstream sport fans, the tennis spectator is typically older, wealthier, and better educated than the average fan in other sports. Even organizers of golf tournaments report that their demographics are somewhat different from tennis fans and it is therefore unwise to combine a tennis tournament with a golf event the first year. It takes time to grow these events and generate widespread acceptance among different demographic groups.

FIGURE 12–3

Tennis Event Ideas

- Serve wine, wine coolers, sherry, international beers, international teas, or specialty coffees to your arriving fans.
- Provide a hospitality area near the arena and feature light jazz music or classical music performed by a harpist, violinist, or pianist before and after tournament play. Decorate this area with ficus trees with miniature lights, park benches, cocktail tables, and white ice-cream chairs placed on an astroturf flooring.
- Remember the famed Billy Jean King and Bobby Riggs battle of the sexes in 1973? More recently, Martina Navratilova played Jimmy Connors and the match was shown on pay-per-view television. Identify your own choice of an unusual pairs to compete in a doubles competition. An interesting warm-up match might place basketball giant Shaquille O'Neill and Emmanuel Lewis of *Webster* fame as partners paired against another equally unlikely matchup.
- Use flags of major international tennis championships such as Wimbledon and the US Open as decor.

Therefore, when designing events for tennis fans, remember their unique demographics and provide a series of experiences that will satisfy their needs.

Figure 12–3 demonstrates the various ways to produce a sophisticated event for your tennis fans.

Always plan and coordinate the tennis event with a sensitivity to the taste of the most sophisticated audience you are likely to attract. If you err, do so on the side of conservatism because this sport's traditions and customs are slower to change than football, basketball, and even baseball.

HOCKEY

The knights on the ice continue to grow in popularity not only in Canada but increasingly throughout the United States.

At the 1994 National Hockey League (NHL) All Star Weekend celebration in New York City, sport event producer Frank Supovitz was concerned with the tiniest detail that might affect the success of the game. "Should the ad panels be up when the announcer is talking about Coca-Cola?" Supovitz asks an assistant far away in the rafters of Madison Square Garden but connected by way of electronic headset. He receives immediate confirmation and the panels are revealed.

The next section takes you behind the scenes of the 1994 NHL All Star Weekend so that you can learn from seasoned professionals who have increased the popularity of this sport tremendously.

BEHIND THE SCENES AT THE NHL ALL STAR GAME REHEARSAL

2:00 P.M. Lisa Delpy and Joe Goldblatt arrive at the venue to observe the rehearsal. They are led through the media area, which is comprised of a curtained area with a small stage, head table, and backdrop for press conferences and 200 chairs. Immediately adjacent to this area is the media working area, which is cordoned off by pipe and drape and equipped with dozens of long tables, hundreds of chairs, and electronic hookups for computers, telephones, and other communications requirements. Immediately adjacent to this area is the canteen, which provides coffee, drinks, and food for the media and event staff. The press conference area, media work stations, and canteens are located less than 100 feet from the arena floor, which may be reached by direct access. Guarding this critical entrance is private security hired by the National Hockey League. The security forces are trained to recognize key individuals and interpret all credentials.

2:05 P.M. The event producer, Frank Supovitz, greets Delpy and Goldblatt and escorts them into the arena where he explains, "We are holding segment rehearsals throughout the afternoon. This way we are able to rehearse each group of people at a convenient time. We are doing this with full technical support with the exception of follow spots as this will save us nearly $2,000."

2:07 P.M. Delpy and Goldblatt are led into the penalty box, a space 8 feet deep and 30 feet long. Its size is reduced dramatically due to the mass of electronic equipment and number of tables from which Supovitz and his producers will coordinate the event. Supovitz explains:

> We use three sets of clear coms (communication headsets) to communicate with the various line producers. One is for the preshow producer, the other is for the skills competition coordinator, and the third is for the

television truck for the broadcast feed. Using individual clear coms reduces confusion for me because I know exactly what group of individuals I am connected to when I pick up the set.

Goldblatt inquires about the 30 lighting effects that sweep the ice arena floor and the 18,000 seat arena. Supovitz responds, "Those Intellibeam spotlights are terrific. They allow us to project the team logos as well as atmospheric projections of flags and other symbols to instantly change the mood of the show. During the laser show they really get a workout."

2:12 P.M. A second voice-over is given by the live announcer as he welcomes the invisible audience. Supovitz quickly stops the segment to fix a light cue that appears to be late. As soon as this problem is fixed, the preshow producer shouts to him, "Let's talk about the carpet for the anthem—color? length?"

Supovitz quickly responds, "I think for the anthem we use a regular white carpet."

Turning to Goldblatt he adds, "Bobby Goldwater, the executive producer of the Garden is terrific. The Garden is not the least expensive venue but in terms of professionalism it is hard to beat. They do over 400 events here annually so there is little ego among the staff. The goal is to satisfy the customer and this weekend that's the NHL."

2:20 P.M. Speaking to the lighting director over his headset Supovitz says, "That's a nice look, Bill" referring to the dazzling intellibeam patterns reflecting off the gleaming white ice surface. The U.S. gobos are then suddenly projected on the floor and he exclaims, "They read my mind!"

2:21 P.M. Almost simultaneous with the appearance of the U.S. designs, 52 youngsters appear on the ice carrying flags and skating in formations. They were recruited from an arena in Connecticut and will perform in the event. To ensure that they appear professional, the NHL has hired an experienced ice choreographer to work with them. She can be seen in the shadows giving cues. The addition of lighting helps correct any obvious flaws. The overall look is graceful and forceful as the flags snap as they catch the rink's cool breeze.

2:23 P.M. The Heroes of Hockey are the old-timers. There will be no rehearsal for them, Supovitz explains, because they know exactly what is expected. "We assign their entrance order based upon their player number with the captain at the end of each group. This provides us with a system that eliminates any disagreements over who's on first."

2:38 P.M. Supovitz begins to give an order to a subordinate but his line producer for the preshow steps in and quietly says, "Frank, please?" Supovitz responds, "You produce the show." An experienced veteran of Radio City Music Hall events such as the Super Bowl half-time show and bicentennial of the U.S. Constitution, Supovitz knows there can be only one producer.

2:31 P.M. "Why are you using a live announcer when most televised events now use a prerecorded voice," Goldblatt inquires. Supovitz answers directly, "A hockey game is totally unpredictable. Having a live voice allows me to have flexibility. If we have to dump a segment, I can cover with the live announce." Goldblatt says, "Frank, you have the latest technology combined with old-fashioned values like the Boy Scouts. Be prepared." Supovitz laughs.

2:42 P.M. While waiting for the next rehearsal segment, Supovitz recalled his responsibilities for the New York Skates program, an entire week of pre-All-Star activities, including shoot-out at Rockefeller Center, a Hockey Hall of Fame exhibit at Grand Central Station, clinics, and more. It was associated with, but separate from All-Star weekend. Supovitz also explained how the entire week got the name New York Skates. "We wanted something that would capture the feeling of the entire city and also be flexible enough so that when we move the event next year, we can keep the word 'skates' and add the new destination's name."

2:46 P.M. His explanation is interrupted by a commercial appearing on the giant television screen. "Damn! I told them no commercials. That's not the video I saw. The video I saw earlier did not include that chase. I don't want to offend our biggest sponsor," Supovitz says to his staff over the electronic four-lane highway attached to his right ear.

2:47 P.M. His line producer inquires, "Would you prefer Bob or Bobby on the live announce? The prerecorded video says one thing and the live script still another." Supovitz, ever the diplomat, responds jovially, "Ask Bobby."

3:00 P.M. Supovitz calmly and firmly tells his crew to clear the ice for the laser rehearsals. The argon laser beams have begun to project throughout the arena and he is concerned for the safety of young people still lingering on the ice.

3:01 P.M. A voice-over is played and laser beams appear from the top of the arena to cast a sharp blue-green image onto the ice. Next, all of the team gobos appear simultaneously on the ice. Fog is used to give the laser beams greater definition; Supovitz explains that two laser projectors are being used for this show, "one for the graphic image projection and one for the aerial beams."

3:11 P.M. "Are all the extraction fans on?" Supovitz asks Bob Goldwater, who confirms that the engineers are checking to verify this.

3:12 P.M. "I want to see how long it takes to clear the arena of fog, otherwise the television people will go ballistic," Supovitz mutters as he strides onto the ice to inspect the extraction process.

3:14 P.M. Returning to the penalty box, he picks up the headset and tells the laser technician, "Kill the lasers before we bring the kids back onto the ice." Always concerned about safety and security, he is usually one step ahead of his crew in these observations. This is generally the rule because the producer of the sport event has an overall view of the entire proceedings whereas each manager is concerned only with his or her individual discipline.

3:15 P.M. Following the laser show rehearsal, Supovitz invites your authors to join him for an inspection of the postgame party at the Paramount Theater, which is also located in the Madison Square Garden complex. With the theme, "A Night at the Paramount," the party will salute the top officials of the NHL and entertain more than 3,500 people in a proscenium theater with fixed seating. To transform a theater into a party site, several hundred seats were draped with white fabric and NHL gobos will project on them throughout the party. On this − 10 degree evening, his event coordinator, Ann Devney, has arranged for coat check staff to receive coats in one area and return them in another. To accomplish this with a minimum of confusion, signs will be posted and notes will given to the patrons, who will also be verbally instructed on where to retrieve their garments. The entire Paramount Theater complex will be used for the party, including the bar/restaurant, VIP dining room, and public function spaces.

3:25 P.M. "Our special events operation at the NHL works well because of our organizational system," Supovitz continues. "I am fortunate that my staff bring strong but different skills to each of their management positions. I have six managers working with me and together we produce 40 events annually including those that travel."

3:35 P.M. Leaving the party site, Supovitz makes his way through the seemingly endless tunnel in the Garden and stops in the tiny operations office that the NHL special events department has established. The office is approximately 15 feet by 10 feet and is occupied by six people including the ice choreographer, computers, a copier, a printer, and several telephones. "My biggest concern is making sure all the participants get to their locations," he explains to one of his producers. He then advises the staff to "check the script to make sure the player roster matches."

4:00 P.M. We return to the arena in time to listen to the rehearsal of the "O Canada" anthem by a strikingly beautiful woman who is one of Canada's most popular vocalists. She briskly walks over the white carpet carrying her wireless hand-held microphone. She begins to sing a cappella, but we can hardly hear her strong voice even though we are located only a few feet away. An embarrassed stage manager mutters, "Turn the switch on." A simple switch is thrown and a glorious coloratura sopranic voice fills the great arena.

Following this rehearsal, we adjourn to the canteen for a bite to eat before the evening event. During dinner, Goldblatt talks to one of Supovitz's producers, a veteran director in Canadian television, Jack Budgell, who explains:

> What makes Frank so unique is his ability to remain calm because he knows exactly what he's doing. He has a firm handle on the concept, of the end product. He can actually visualize the end product and communicate that to his team. He strikes the proper compromise between entertaining the live audience and the television one. He always has an answer and offers this or that option. Most importantly, he exhibits strong leadership.

6:56 P.M. Delpy and Goldblatt rejoin Supovitz in the crowded penalty box. The cool sensation of the ice does little to ease the tension about to be played out before 18,000 live fans and millions more on television.

7:12 P.M. The Canadian national anthem is sung flawlessly. Corrected in rehearsal, the switch is on and the adrenalin is flowing.

7:14 P.M. The U.S. national anthem is sung a cappella by an African-American group.

7:20 P.M. The Heroes of Hockey (aka the old-timers) are introduced by prerecorded videotape and live announcements.

7:39 P.M. Once they have all assembled, one of the referees skates over to Supovitz and asks incredulously, "Where's the pucks?" The pucks, which are being frozen for play, are located and quickly brought to the ice.

7:45 P.M. An Alka Seltzer commercial rolls on the big screen and Supovitz waves wildly to the referee, "Armstrong, blow the whistle!"

7:55 P.M. Another commercial rolls and the technical crew assembled in the penalty box draws a collective breath of relief.

7:58 P.M. The rink lights are extinguished and the mascots entertain the crowds, mingling among them in their seats. The line producer asks Supovitz, "You want to start the game early?" Simultaneously, the referee skates up and asks "Can we say we checked the replay and the puck crossed the line?" Supovitz replies, "Yes, yes, yes!" He then asks his producer "Still looking at 8:36 P.M. for laser?" The producer responds affirmatively, "Whenever it is, we'll be ready. We're looking at 8:36 P.M. back to TV."

8:29 P.M. Two Zamboni machines bedecked in Coca-Cola logo designs make their appearance on the ice. "This is unusual to use two machines but we do so for this event to save time," Supovitz remarks.

8:39 P.M. It's show time once again. At 8:52 P.M., the NHL All-Star teams introductions have been completed and Supovitz is talking into the headphones while holding a clipboard in his hands. Several sheets of loose paper are wedged between his knees. Despite this awkward appearance, he is calm and collected as he explains, "This is not supposed to be on Garden vision, go past it."

9:10 P.M. The television announcer who is broadcasting live from immediately in front of the penalty box is having trouble giving out the latest scores. He turns angrily to no one in particular and shouts, "We gotta get that right!"

9:22 P.M. Another event segment is set up on the ice. The announcer turns to Supovitz for verification of the information he is about to announce. Supovitz tells his crew that someone should be feeding the announcer numbers.

9:45 P.M. At the end of the skills competition, Supovitz pays a compliment to one of the line producers: "Doing great, it's nice and tight." Bobby Goldwater of the Garden alerts Supovitz that there is a medical emergency. "Can we do a page?" Frank asks. Goldwater says it can wait. Supovitz immediately says, "If it is life threatening do it now." Both Goldblatt and Delpy are impressed with Supovitz's clear directions when critical judgment is required. When asked later, Supovitz says "There's nothing more important than someone's life."

9:59 P.M. The event concludes with the All Stars presenting their sticks to the youngsters who appeared earlier. As the music swells and lights sweep the arena, cheers erupt in the penalty box as the producers led by Frank Supovitz celebrate the conclusion of several weeks of successful preparation. Their sport event has been well received by the fans. But before Supovitz can enjoy the many accolades, he is off to check on the party at the Paramount before starting preparations for tomorrow's events.

This illustration shows you the importance of timing, preparation, and judgment throughout the sport event. Murphy's law certainly was in force, but because of Supovitz's experience and talent, old Murphy didn't stand a chance. The indoor sport event, although conducted in a more controlled environment than the outdoor examples, requires many of the same logistical considerations. The outdoor sport event manager is concerned about the threat of rain. In contrast, the indoor sport event manager must remember to alert the venue's fire representatives that a fog effect will be used or the fire sprinklers might produce rain indoors.

The manager of both indoor and outdoor events must be alert to the physical constraints and opportunities provided by the space where the event is held. Once these opportunities and limitations are identified, creative sport event management and marketing planning may commence. A comprehensive planning approach will ensure that the sport event you are planning has sunny days both indoors and out and that your game will be a title holder that will be talked about for many years to come.

The many things in common between indoor and outdoor sport events are a perfect prelude to our next chapter. In Chapter 13, you will see how the intrinsic relationship between public and private sport events create opportunities for everyone.

GAME HIGHLIGHTS

- Create event task and equipment lists and designate responsibilities.
- Create fan participation contests pregame, halftime, and postgame.
- Be sensitive to specific tastes when providing hospitality for different sport events (e.g., tennis fans may require more sophisticated entertainment or hospitality).
- Work with the engineer at the venue to understand the HVAC and other specific systems.
- Always make safety a priority.

PLAY BOOK

aerial beams Laser light beams 100 feet or longer that are projected, using an argon light source with mirrors to create patterns.

clear coms A wired or wireless communications systems consisting of a headset (earpiece and microphone).

extraction machines Reverse fans used to remove smoke, fog, and odors from an indoor site.

gobos A metal template used in an ellipsoidal spot or intellibeam to project a graphic image.

intellibeam spotlights A spotlight that tilts, pans, and performs other moves with its beam.

Zamboli machines A machine, named for the inventor, used to resurface ice.

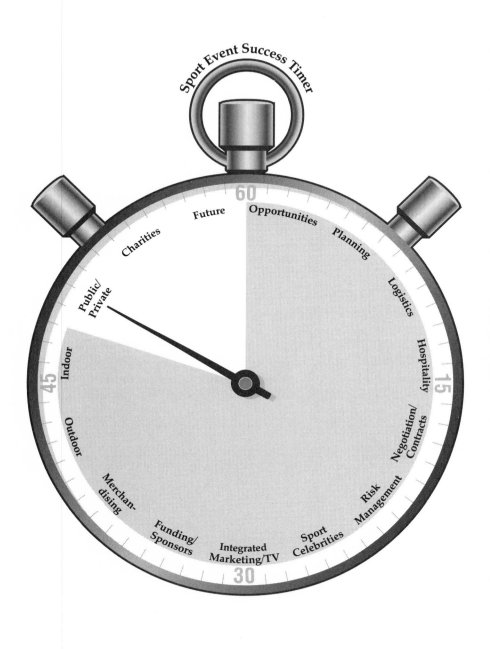

Chapter Thirteen

Public and Private Sport Events

"The ultimate goal should be doing your best and enjoying it."

—Peggy Fleming, Olympic Gold Medalist

How can a public and private sport event partnership benefit both parties and accelerate economic development?

According to Dave Jensen, Washington, D.C., venue executive director for World Cup USA, Inc., the estimated national economic impact for United States hosting the World Cup soccer tournament was $4 billion, $330 million to the Washington, D.C., area economy alone. Although final figures are not yet available, the Sheraton Hotel in Crystal City, Virginia (near Washington, D.C.), reported the best June in their history and the third best month ever. Dallas, Texas, headquarters for the World Cup International Broadcast Center, reported an increase in sales tax by 15% and in hotel tax receipts by 31%. In Chicago, general retail sales were up 20-30% during the World Cup period and hotel occupancy was up 9.2%. Of course, not all venue locations or sport events can produce such tangible benefits, but in general sport events provide a popular revenue generating opportunity.

SPORT COMMISSIONS AND PUBLIC INVESTMENT

Throughout the United States, the development of municipal, regional, and even state sport commissions has been accelerating at an Olympian pace. Public investment in the business of sport is one of the most remarkable developments in the sport event field over the past century.

"City sport commissions like ours are cropping up all over the country," explains Diane Hovencamp, president of the Orlando Area Sport Commission and chair of the National Association of Sport Commissions (NASC). "The economic impact that major sporting events can create has spurred many cities into the sports marketing arena." Today there are over 75 sport commissions marketing their communities as a host for sport events.

Numerous reasons explain the increased interest in sport and subsequent public support. Elected officials and their constituents realize that sport events can generate attention, television exposure, and economic benefits to a community. Athletic events are more than entertainment; they augment tourism and provide employment and business opportunities. A typical Super Bowl city will invest approximately $2 million in hosting the event. The return on investment, however, is a staggering $100 million or more. The economic impact of the 1984 Los Angeles Olympic Games included gross expenditures of approximately $1.4 billion and approximately 75,000 temporary jobs. Initial estimates of the economic impact of the 1996 Atlanta Olympic Games are $3.5 billion of primary and secondary expenditures in the Georgia economy and the creation of some 83,000 jobs.

High-profile sport events are not the only economically beneficial ones. National championships for youth sports illustrate how low-profile events also can generate a significant economic impact relative to the funds expended. These events attract athletes, coaches, officials, and their families, and fans who pay their own way, stay in hotel rooms, eat in restaurants, and spend money on other essentials. The Amateur Athletic Union (AAU) national championships, for example, attracts approximately 5,000 athletes not counting their entourages. Chris Green, a youth volleyball coach who frequently travels with her team exclaims:

the biggest problem with youth volleyball tournaments is that event organizers do not communicate with the host community. We often play in small towns and when 20-40 teams of 10 players each, not counting significant others, ascend on local restaurants they typically are not ready for the crowd and run out of food.

FIGURE 13–1

Economic Benefits of Sport Events

Direct income: Sales tax, occupancy/room tax, alcoholic beverage tax, tobacco tax, gasoline tax, admission tax, licenses, and municipal fees.

Indirect income: Income tax from increased employment opportunities, construction expenditures, business-related (supplies) income.

Induced effects: Regional multiplier effects from the recycling of income in the local community.

Intangible benefits: Quality of life, community exposure, local development, business expansion, and civic pride.

Tangible benefits: Increase in car rentals, public transportation, food, beverage and entertainment, general retail sales, employment opportunities, new construction.

The idea of commercial sport benefiting the community extends beyond the borders of the United States. In Vigevano, a town 30 minutes from Milan, Italy, journalist Gianni Merlo explained how the expenditure of $400,000 on a new track at an old stadium benefited the town. Not only did the town recoup its investment through organized track and field competitions but made sport a centerpiece in the life of its citizens.

Figure 13–1 lists overall economic benefits a community might receive from hosting a major sport event.

The creation of the sport commission, while a relatively new occurrence, provides a foundation or central body through which events can be solicited, private funds raised and public support directed. The proliferation of sport commissions in the United States, led to the formation of the NASC to provide community leaders with the opportunity to share information and to benefit from one another's experiences. Whether independent or associated with the convention and visitors bureau or chamber of commerce, the sport commissions are primarily responsible for coordinating a number of services (see Figure 13–2).

This public and private partnership may evolve from the decision to hold a sport event in a host city or from a bid process in which a league or other sport organization seeks a city to host the sport event. Regardless of the starting point of this process, the sport commission is often the bridge between the idea and the reality.

FIGURE 13–2

Role and Scope of Sport Commissions

- Promote a geographic area, usually a city, to sport organizations and event producers.
- Attract sport events through well-prepared bid proposals and tactful political lobbying.
- Host and organize sport programs from grass root to professional events.
- Serve as a liaison between the community and private sport promoters or event managers interested in staging a competition in your area.
- Raise funds to support the work of the sport commission, particularly for bidding campaigns.

The 100th anniversary celebration of the International Olympic Committee (IOC) held in Paris, France, in the summer of 1994* is an example of how four entities worked together to fund a sport event. Of the reported $16 million budgeted for this congress, corporate sponsors offered $600,000, the IOC provided $6 million, and $9.4 million were supplied by the Parisian and French governments.

Perhaps you are the manager of a recurring sport event or your corporation is interested in using part of its marketing budget to sponsor and produce a major sport event. When seeking a qualified host city, the first step is to research your options.

The checklist (see Figure 13–3) will assist you in developing a request for bid proposal (RFP) that can be sent to qualified cities. The United States Olympic Committee (USOC) has produced a comprehensive bid questionnaire for cities interested in hosting the U.S. Olympic Festival. This document is available through the USOC in Colorado Springs, Colorado, and is an excellent tool for developing your RFP. This bid proposal will ultimately become the prototype of formal bid presentations made by cities interested in hosting a specific sport event.

The proliferation of organizations whose mission is to attract sport events dramatically increases the competitiveness for sport event acquisition. A study commissioned by the Greater San Diego Sports Association on what makes certain cities successful in competitive bidding for major national or international sport events

---

*Although the first IOC session was held in 1894 in Paris, the first Summer Olympic Games were held in 1896. Thus, Atlanta will host the centennial Olympics in 1996

FIGURE 13–3

Components of a Request for Bid Proposal

Introduction and History

_____ What is the background of the sport event?

_____ What year did the event begin?

_____ Who founded it?

_____ What cities have previously hosted the event?

_____ When, if ever, was the event first televised?

_____ What is the total number of television impressions?

_____ Who sponsors the event?

_____ Other relevant historical information.

Site and Logistical Specifications

What are the physical requirements for the venue(s) where the sport activities will take place?

_____ Facility size and location

_____ Electrical power

_____ Heating

_____ Air-conditioning

_____ Ventilation

_____ Loading-door entry sizes

_____ Floor weight

_____ Hanging points in ceiling

_____ Permanent, temporary, and box seating capacity

_____ Parking facilities

_____ Handicapped (Americans with Disabilities Act) provisions

_____ Venue dimensions

_____ Fire safety standards

_____ Meeting/storage rooms

_____ Locker rooms

_____ Telecommunications capabilities

_____ Satellite downlink/uplink capability

_____ Lighting

_____ Food service

_____ On-site training rooms

_____ Press seating

Financial

What are the financial responsibilities that the host city will need to assume?

_____ Capital improvements

_____ Marketing

_____ Advertising

continued

FIGURE 13–3 concluded
_____ Public relations
_____ Ticket services
_____ Special events and promotions
_____ Public safety
_____ Transportation and parking
_____ Venues
_____ Participant services (housing, food, laundry, gifts)
_____ Employment of local performers for entertainment segments
_____ General administration

Other
List any other responsibilities the host city may expect to accept as a privilege of hosting the event.

Benefits
What are the economic, social, and public relations benefits of hosting this event? Provide descriptions or documentation.
_____ Financial history for last three years.
_____ Samples of positive public relations.
_____ Spectator survey comments about the event.
_____ Testimonials from athletes, participants, spectators, elected leaders.

suggests that a city serious about capturing its share of major events must be focused; that is, it must have its objectives clearly defined and disseminated to everyone assisting in the bidding process. To accomplish this, the key bidding organization must have a good understanding of the sports event(s) that it wants to attract, and its own capabilities and limitations concerning facilities, infrastructure, public and private support, and venues. A city also should convey a friendly image and provide the information shown in Figure 13–4.

All this information will help to sway tournament directors or site selection committees who are closely comparing your city with others.

Frank W. King described in his book, *It's How You Play the Game*, the steps that he and his colleagues took to win the 1988 Winter Olympic Games bid for Calgary, Canada. As chairman of the Calgary Olympic Development Corporation, King was responsible for securing the games for Calgary. As a former coach, he understood how to tap the Olympic spirit.

King estimated that it would take well over $2 million to prepare an effective bid, but he also understood that the decision would

FIGURE 13-4

Attracting Sport Events to Your Community

- Describe in detail the successful history of other major sport events held in your community.
- Describe available sport facilities suitable for the event.
- Describe the availability of food and housing within the area proposed for the event.
- Identify medical facilities.
- Include testimonials from team owners, tournament directors, sponsors, political figures, and other important players.
- List the economic benefits of holding a sport event in your community.
- Describe tax advantages, reductions in rent, free parking, and other economic considerations that will reflect positively upon your community.
- Stress convenience of transportation systems including air and railroad hub systems and other advantages of your location.
- Provide an estimated budget.
- Provide information on the number of people who live in a two-hour driving radius of your community? Describe the demography and psychographics of the population.
- Provide information on the media market.
- Describe the characteristic attitudes of your citizens. Will they be supportive of this sport event and why? How does your business community feel about sport events of this type?
- Describe historical and significant tourist points of interest.

be made ultimately by the IOC and that decision would be based on the confidence it had in the organizers. Therefore, King and his colleagues traveled over two million kilometers to meet with every IOC member and express the magic words, "We need your help." King would then add, "You are the trustees of Olympic ideals. Please help us understand every detail of what the games should be."

When preparing your sport event bid presentation, follow Frank King's lead and tell the decision makers: "We need your help." Your candor and openness will go a lot further, as King and his colleagues demonstrated by winning their bid, than other strategies. After losing a U.S. Olympic Festival bid, the San Antonio Sport Council asked selection committee members why they were unsuccessful. They followed through on all the recommendations and achieved success on the next round.

Marilyn Carlson Nelson of Phoenix, Arizona, was chair of Super Bowl Task Force XXVI. Nelson says she rallied a team of leading business people which, in various configurations, spent five years courting the National Football League. Five years and five rejections later, the NFL gave Phoenix the green flag. Remember, persistence is omnipotent.

Master sport event managers and marketers such as the Los Angeles Olympic Game's Peter Ueberroth recognize the importance of relationships and persistence as a foundation for future success. Both Ueberroth and King worked hard at forging sincere, open relationships with their partners, the IOC members. This partnership led to success in both Los Angeles and Calgary. This strategy also worked well for the Atlanta Olympic bid committee, whose members poured on Southern hospitality and engaged in close personal relationships with IOC members.

NAVIGATING THE LEGAL HURDLES

Because public money is frequently used to fund sport councils, there is often strict regulatory control over what can and cannot be funded. This has led to controversy in some instances. In Tennessee, the Greater Nashville Convention and Visitors Bureau, a division of the Nashville Chamber of Commerce, responded to a request for a bid proposal to attract the Gay Games to its city.

Like most convention and visitor agencies, the bureau receives partial funding from the hotel taxes collected in Nashville. Therefore, newspapers reported that this quasi-public agency was using city money to attract what some council members described as the wrong element to Nashville.

Although the Gay Games would generate more than $500,000 in income for hotels, restaurants, transportation, and retailers plus tax income, the outspoken council members continued to hammer away at the bureau's vice president who explained that it was the business of the bureau to provide any potential group with information about the viability of holding a sport event in Nashville. It remains to be seen whether the Gay Games will ever be held in Nashville, but the case has been made that when forging a public-private partnership, both entities must walk very carefully along an often fine line.

If the sport event attracted to your city offers little opportunity for local people to attend, it is most important for the organizers to offer an entertainment alternative. Local citizens may otherwise feel as though someone were having a party in their backyard and using their barbecue and swimming pool, but forgot to invite them. Such dismay in the long term may hurt future bid campaigns if public support is low. In the case of the Super Bowl, where tickets are expensive and in great demand, the NFL fortunately created a unique football theme park called the "NFL Experience" that brings the sights, sounds, and feel of the NFL closer to all fans and local citizens unable to attend the real game. Alternatives like this should always be considered to serve the general public during sport events.

HIDDEN IMPACTS

Many times sport events begin as one individual's dream and build into a national or international event. The *Des Moines* (Iowa) *Register* newspaper's Annual Great Bicycle Ride Across Iowa (Ragbrai) is but one example. This event was first planned in 1971 by a cycling enthusiast employed by the *Des Moines Register*. In 22 years, the number of participants has increased consistently from 6 to 13,000 (of the 13,000 riders only 8,000 paid entry fees and are considered sanctioned participants) with an additional 300 support staff and volunteers per overnight city stop.

Large sport events such as the Tour DuPont, Tour de France, and the Ragbrai can bring favorable publicity to and have an enormous economic impact on a region. In 1993, the economic impact of Ragbrai on the Sioux City area was $900,000. Because of the high visibility and interest in being a host city along the tours, a competitive bid process is implemented. The organizers of each of these cycling events provide prospective cities with a bid manual outlining all the needs of the committee and responsibilities of hosting the start, finish, or overnight stop. A committee reviews each proposal based on established criteria and special circumstances that may enhance the event (e.g., the 100th anniversary of a city or special festival). Dennis Gann states that

> The Ragbrai route is often planned for a specific reason and that an attitude of a city is very important in the selection process. It's amazing how many towns of two to three thousand want to host an event

consisting of 13,000 participants. Surprisingly, it is these small towns that tend to do a better job.

Registration fees of $75 for Ragbrai are paid directly to the State of Iowa. Each host city is then reimbursed (e.g., Sioux City received $6,000 to offset some costs). Additional funds are raised through concessions. During the Ragbrai, 10×10 concession booths are rented at a flat fee ($250-$350) and the organizers take 10 percent of the gross sales. When looking at most sport events purely from a bottom-line perspective, typically not much profit is shown. The intangible and trickle-down economic impact, however, is what makes sport events worth the effort.

THE LEGAL PROCESS IN PUBLIC-PRIVATE SPORT PARTNERSHIPS

Not all sport events require a legal document outlining the relationship between the public and private parties. However, with increased worry about cost overruns, such contracts are becoming more common. A perfect example is the relationship that the Atlanta Committee for the Olympic Games (ACOG), a private, nonprofit corporation, has with the Metropolitan Atlanta Olympic Games Authority (MAOGA). MAOGA is a public authority responsible for the review of ACOG construction contracts, financial statements, and budgets; approval of venue changes; and construction of the Olympic Stadium. Its main purpose is to ensure that the City of Atlanta will not be left with a huge deficit following the Olympic Games. To structure such a relationship follow the guidelines shown in Figure 13-5.

MEASURING THE OUTCOMES OF THESE RELATIONSHIPS

Like corporate sponsorship agreements, the private sport event firm has a required reporting responsibility to its public partner. Once the final whistle has blown, it is time to count the yards run, total the completed passes, and, more importantly, count the money earned through the economic impact of the event.

Ideally, the original bid should contain estimates of economic benefits and the resources necessary to conduct an economic

each year as your sport event reduces its overhead through long-term investment.

Local banks and other financial institutions will also be helpful in securing this long-term agreement because you are more than likely to bank locally. The multiplier effect will provide substantial benefit for the entire community. Approach these financial institutions early for a letter of support and keep them posted on your progress.

When creating a strategy to secure a multiyear, long-term commitment from your public partner, follow the checklist illustrated in Figure 13–6.

Long-term agreements have both positive and negative possibilities for the development of your sport event. On the positive side, there is the opportunity to forge long-term and trusting relationships with your public partners. It may take a year or more to learn the labyrinth of civic offices with which you must do business, so having a long-term agreement means you are banking on this investment of time for future benefit. On the negative side, there is the problem of a constraining, outdated agreement that may provide less return each year. You must weigh the advantages and disadvantages before deciding to pursue or enter into a long-term agreement.

The Gay Games 1994 success in New York City as well as numerous examples can be cited as successful sport event partnerships with sport commissions and other government and quasi-government partners. It is important to recognize that whether you are a corporate meeting planner organizing a major golf tournament to benefit a charity or a private sport event promoter staging a national tournament, the potential for government support is great.

Start your search for a potential partner by making a telephone call to either the convention and visitors bureau or sports commission, or perhaps both in the city where your event takes place. If neither is receptive, phone the mayor, governor, or the member of Congress for the district. Someone will not only want to throw out the first ball but will also recognize the huge advantage to be gained by getting in the game early.

This public and private partnership ultimately will enable you to understand the fundamental role sport events can play in bringing about positive social change. Chapter 14 offers a preview of the

FIGURE 13–6

Developing Long-Term Support

_____ Put out feelers early to determine if support is a possibility.

_____ Establish a timetable for decision making and appoint a negotiating team from both sides.

_____ Identify common objectives and goals.

_____ List reasonable and attainable financial objectives.

_____ Describe important community and lifestyle benefits that will accrue as a result of this partnership.

_____ Describe a process for settling disputes.

_____ Identify a cancellation clause and include a due notice statement.

_____ List a series of benchmark dates when you will review the success of the agreement. Determine who will conduct this review and what methodology will be used.

_____ Include a renewal clause should both parties wish to renew the agreement under new terms.

great power you and your sport event have to share with a charitable organization.

GAME HIGHLIGHTS

- Contact local convention and visitors bureaus or sport commissions to determine whether they are interested in your sport event.

- Prepare a detailed request for bid proposal and distribute it to qualified sport commissions or government sponsorship organizations.

- Use legal counsel to help you prepare a final agreement and make sure the agreement identifies the various taxing authorities, decision makers, policy makers, and other critical entities.

- Appoint a measurement and evaluation team from both entities.

- Determine whether a long-term agreement is desirable and develop a strategy and timetable for formulating the necessary instruments to solidify this relationship.

PLAY BOOK

convention and visitors bureau An organization with roots in late 19th-century Detroit which is responsible for attracting convention business primarily and tourists secondarily to a community.

direct impact The amount of new money that is injected in the local economy strictly as a result of the sport event and related activities.

public Any organization whose complete funding is derived from government funds.

quasi-public Any organization that receives partial funding from government funds. Often the organization is a private enterprise that receives government funds; therefore, it has certain auditing and reporting responsibilities incumbent upon a public organization.

regional multiplier A weighted average of the multipliers for each industry that is economically stimulated by the sport event (e.g., hotel industry, construction industry, etc.). Such industry multipliers are compiled by the Bureau of Economic Analysis in Washington, D.C. The use of such a multiplier is necessary because a dollar that directly enters into the local economy is recycled within the local economy (e.g., money paid to local construction workers will find its way into local restaurants).

sport commission An organization that promotes and attracts appropriate sport activities in its geographical region.

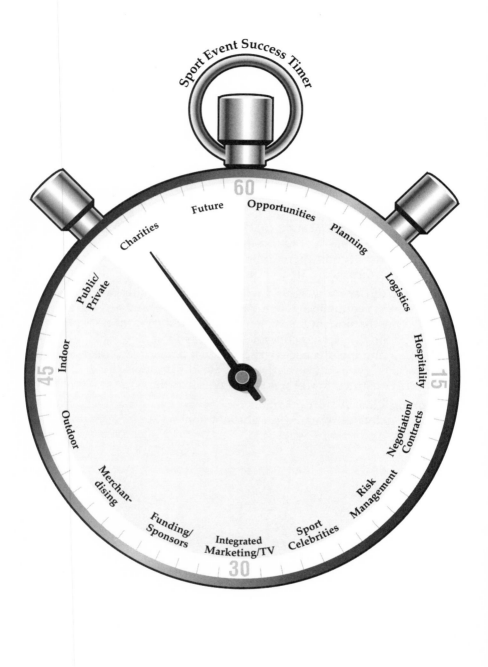

Chapter Fourteen

Charitable Events

"No matter how far you look and no matter how far you go, the greatest athletes in this world are the special athletes."

The late Lyle Alzado, Denver Broncos defensive lineman, on the Special Olympics.

W hy do charities align themselves with sport events and what are the benefits for each?

In 1993, former world heavyweight champion Riddick Bowe donated thousands of dollars to charity as a reward for individuals who turned in their guns to District of Columbia police officials. The timing and unique concept brought Bowe widespread and uniformly favorable publicity.

The Race for the Cure, the March of Dimes Walk-a-thon, the Barbara Mandrell Celebrity Softball Game, and the Dinah Shore Golf Tournament are familiar events because of the annual publicity they receive through television, radio, and newspapers. Each of these highly popular sport events also provides an opportunity to help others through sport.

In a charitable sport event, the proceeds—loosely defined as the funds remaining after all expenses have been paid—are donated to a worthwhile cause such as AIDS research. Each year thousands of sport events benefiting charities take place throughout the United States and around the world.

Why the popular connection between sport and fund-raising? One reason is the enormous universal popularity of sport events. Whether you are selling tickets to a benefit basketball game where a local radio station's personalities are battling the Harlem Globetrotters or creating your own fun-run to benefit cancer research, you will find widespread support for your sport event program.

Another reason is that charitable sport events are spectator-friendly. The fans do not need to wear an evening gown or a black tie and tailcoat. Casual dress allows them to relax. Some individuals view the participation in the activity (e.g., bicycling, running) as added value for their charitable donation.

Perhaps the most important reason for this linkage is that sport represents health and many charities are concerned with illnesses that have no known cure. An excellent example is the Susan B. Komen Race for the Cure. Starting in Dallas, Texas, this sport event has spread to numerous cities from Washington, D.C., to Los Angeles. The event is a run to benefit breast cancer research. The event received national publicity in 1990 when Marilyn Quayle, wife of the former Vice President of the United States, chaired the Washington race and recruited many major name celebrities to join her in the sport event.

WHO BENEFITS?

The charity ultimately benefits from the proceeds of the sport event, but the linkage with a charity might also bring about greater fan interest in the sport. In the best of worlds, three interrelated groups will also benefit.

1. The charitable organization will benefit from new monies to aid its cause and from greater visibility for the organization. Because sport events are highly public spectacles, the charitable organization has an opportunity to obtain a wider public through a well-planned public relations campaign tied to the sport event.

2. The participants benefit not only from the knowledge that their entry fees and even concession dollars are benefiting a worthwhile cause, but also because they are attending a healthy activity in cycling, bowling, golf, or tennis.

3. The greater business community will benefit from the residual revenues that may be brought in as a result of the sport event. As discussed earlier, hotels, restaurants, retailers, and parking lot operators will benefit from this activity.

FINDING THE RIGHT CHARITABLE ORGANIZATION

One of the most difficult tasks for a sport event professional is to identify a well-organized and reputable charitable organization to participate in a sport event. This task may be made easier by following the simple instructions in Figure 14–1.

One key element to consider is how the charity's mission will appeal to your target audience. Some sport events attract primarily a male audience; therefore, a charity such as ovarian cancer research may have limited appeal to this audience. However, you can possibly broaden the appeal of the charity by introducing a famous soap opera actor or actress who will attract the wives and significant others of the primarily male audience.

Once you have identified your target audience, the next essential step is to begin discussions with the charity whose constituents will support your sport event. Find an opportunity for the charity's leadership to witness one of your sport events. Invite leaders of the organization to the arena, park, or bowling alley to see your sport event in action. It will be easier to enlist their support and full participation following this positive experience.

Organize the important planning meeting with the charity well in advance. Speak with the executive director of the charity and get his or her agreement on the agenda. This planning meeting is critical to your overall success and therefore it must be well organized. Figure 14–2 suggests a sample agenda for this meeting.

WHAT DOES THE CHARITY BRING TO THE SPORT EVENT

Athletes Against Drugs, the Chicago-based charity, provides a detailed proposal to event organizers and asks that sport promoters do the same. "Once, during a golf tournament, we discovered that the promoter was unscrupulous. Had we done our homework, we could have avoided this awkward and potentially embarrassing situation," says Stedman Graham, its executive director.

FIGURE 14–1

How to Find a Charity That Works

1. Ask the National Society of Fund Raising Executives to recommend names of reputable charitable organizations in your community.
2. Determine the type of charity that is a complementary match for your sport event. Drag car racing is probably an inappropriate match for Mothers Against Drunk Driving (MADD) while tennis, golf, or basketball might be fine.
3. Interview the charity's executive director and find out what his or her strategic plan is. How does your sport event activity fit in?
4. Ask what the charity's leadership will contribute in terms of mailing lists, volunteers, and other contributions in exchange for being designated the official beneficiary of your event.

FIGURE 14–2

Sample Agenda: Planning the Charitable Sport Event

1. Welcome and introduction of committee members.
2. History of sport event and charity.
3. Goals and objectives of sport event and charity.
4. Strategies for achieving goals and objectives.
5. Public relations, marketing, and advertising.
6. Financial goals.
7. Role and scope of individual responsibilities.
8. Discussion.
9. Establish next meeting date.
10. Adjournment.

The charity may possess numerous resources that will contribute to the success of the sport event. Figure 14–3 indicates the range of resource possibilities although you will not necessarily require all of them.

These are only a few of the resources that most major charities can bring to your event. The best organized charities such as United Way will have a detailed planning guide for staging your live event that will make the implementation of these resources easier to accomplish.

FIGURE 14–3

Possible Charitable Resources

- Volunteers for:
  - Mailings
  - Telemarketing of tickets
  - Staffing the event such as ushers, ticket takers, and officials
- Concession suppliers and operators for:
  - Programs
  - Food and beverage
  - Athletes' commissary
  - Merchandise
- Transportation for:
  - VIPs
  - Entertainers
  - Athletes
  - Game officials
  - Spectator parking shuttles
  - Media
- Entertainment for:
  - Pregame
  - Halftime
  - Postgame
  - Private hospitality tents
  - Contacts with major-name stars supporting the charity
- Guest and mailing lists for:
  - Major donors
  - Corporate donors to purchase skyboxes
  - General admission sales
  - Participants
- Name identity (charity's official name) for:
  - Credibility
  - Merchandising
  - Publicity
  - Recognition
- Prospective sponsors for:
  - Corporate in-kind support such as food, beverage, seats
  - Directed giving such as underwriting the cost of tents
- Nonprofit postage rate for:
  - Direct mail
  - Invitations

LEGAL CONSIDERATIONS

Nonprofit organizations are required by federal, state, and local law to report their activities on a regular basis. As a fund-raising activity, your sport event may be required to document its activities. Therefore, good financial records are essential. In setting up your ledger, seek the advice of an accountant who specializes in not-for-profit organizations. You are not allowed to show a profit but must re-invest in the charity's operations and distribute profits to those who benefit such as the elderly or children.

During your first meeting with the charity's leadership, identify the financial goals for the event and establish your fees for planning and managing it. A standard rule of thumb for planners and managers of charitable sport events is to charge fixed and direct expenses plus a management fee. This limits the earning potential for the sport event management organization, but it also establishes a secure margin of potential retained earnings for the charity. The donors will want to know prior to their investment how much of their financial gift will be received by the beneficiaries and how much will be used for overhead. Figure 14–4 demonstrates a simple way to state the donation so that charitable donors understand and accept your invitation to contribute.

The actual percentage which the charity receives as a result of the sport event may vary according to your agreement. Some charities may require a minimum guaranteed donation in the contract. Some event owners may include a maximum cap on earnings to be awarded to a beneficiary. Take, for instance, a successful 3-on-3 basketball tournament in which the Multiple Sclerosis Society of Washington, D.C., provided volunteers, assisted with mailings, and recruited teams. The event organizer specified that the charitable contribution will be calculated solely on the entrance fees with a minimum guarantee of $300 and a maximum $2 per registered team. At this point, the charity must calculate its potential income to see whether participation in this event is worthwhile.

One standard used in measuring the validity of charitable events is that less than 20 percent of gross revenues should be allocated for fixed and direct expenses. The remainder should be used for direct support of charitable services. This standard may be difficult

FIGURE 14-4

Sample Donor Language Describing Charitable Gifts

According to the National Society of Fund Raising Executives, the Federal Omnibus Budget Reconciliation Act of 1993 requires that charitable organizations soliciting for events where the cost to the purchaser/donor is $75 or greater must disclose in writing to the purchaser/donor the actual monies that are directly benefitting the charity and are therefore deductible by law. The amount that is not deductible is the fair market value of the goods or services used to produce the event. Sample lanaguage to notify donors might state: "$50 of your $75 is tax deductible as a charitable donation."

---

to achieve when staging a sport event because of the large up-front costs, but it can be achieved through sponsorship.

Another legal consideration is the Unrelated Business Income Tax (UBIT) law that the Internal Revenue Service has recently been enforcing. This law spells out the difference between a purely corporate donation to a charity and a corporation giving money to a not-for-profit organization for specific purposes such as advertising (e.g., sponsorship contracts for college bowl games).

In order to guarantee a return on their investment, corporations have included specific requirements that a bowl committee must provide a sponsor X minutes of TV exposure, X number of signs, and X number of mentions. The IRS considers this to be a taxable service contract between the sponsor and the nonprofit bowl committee acting as an advertising agency, not simply a charitable contribution between a sponsor and an educational arm of a university, which would not be taxed. After numerous hearings, the ruling now stands that such agreements are acceptable under the tax-exempt clause as long as there is no direct endorsement of the product by the organizing committee (e.g., "The Orange Bowl encourages you to drink Coke") and no language in the contract requiring that such services be rendered in order to keep the donation.

Two examples of successful sport events that benefit charities are golf tournaments and various "athons," (e.g., walk, ride, swim). Half of all proceeds from major golf tournaments are usually designated to a charity. In addition, a Pro-Am golf tournament typically precedes the event which generates additional revenue for the charity. Pro-Am tournaments provide an opportunity for local residents to play golf with professional golfers and other celebrities for a specified charitable contribution.

The most common sport-related fund-raiser among charities is the walk-a-thon or bike-a-thon where participants pay an entrance fee and solicit sponsors for a certain amount of money per mile completed. Barry Glassman, formerly program director for the Muscular Dystrophy Association, created the "Tour de Bud" event, which is basically a glorified bike-a-thon.

Why an "athon" versus a race? Glassman explains that "it all comes down to the bottom line." By staging a "tour," you can avoid the expense of a timing system (approximately $6,000) and the hassle of officials, awards, and so forth. The target audience also consists of fund-raisers versus competitors. You want to attract individuals who will bring in a minimum of $65 worth of pledges, not those interested in becoming Olympic medalists.

SEEKING SPONSORS

Through their networks, charitable organization can be very helpful in steering you toward prospective corporate donors. The leaders of not-for-profit boards are often successful business professionals with extensive contacts in the world of commerce. See Chapter 9 for more information on seeking sponsors.

THE CHARITY SPOKESPERSON

At some point, a check may be presented to the charity that benefited from the sport event. Therefore, it is important to designate a spokesperson. Many charities have official national or, in the case of UNICEF, international ambassadors who promote their cause.

During your exploratory meetings with the charity, find out whether it has an official spokesperson and if this person is a celebrity. If the spokesperson is a well-known celebrity, determine if the "star" will appear in a public service announcement (PSA) to promote the event. A televised or radio PSA is extremely effective in generating excitement about the forthcoming sport event. You may also wish to invite the celebrity to appear at the sport event to throw out the first ball, fire the starting pistol, or make brief remarks. Be sure that the celebrity's role and fees (if any) are spelled out clearly in writing when you develop your agreement with the charity (see Chapter 7 on sport celebrities).

POTENTIAL LIABILITIES

In any relationship, there is always the potential for liabilities caused by either or both parties. Figure 14–5 lists some threats you should recognize early in your planning and monitor throughout the development of the sport event.

MEASURING YOUR SUCCESS

Long-Term Success

Charitable golf tournaments, especially in states with warmer climates, walk-a-thons, and bike-a-thons have successfully provided a source of funds to nonprofit organizations and will continue to do so. The key to long-term success is to keep your sponsors and charitable committees and board members happy.

Despite the founder's death, the Dinah Shore Golf Tournament continues to benefit charities. This 20-year-old tournament prospers not only because of the commitment of its organizers and charitable beneficiaries but, most importantly, because it has been organized to achieve long-term success.

To establish your own long-term success, consider planning not merely in terms of years but of eras. Planning in five- or ten-year blocks will help you focus your sights on a long-term future for the development of your sport event. Granted, things change. You may decide to award the proceeds to a new charity, the location may shift, or other significant changes may take place, but with proper planning this recurring event will endure.

One major advantage of long-term planning is your ability to attract sponsors who wish to amortize the cost of their event over

FIGURE 14–5

Charity Threats

- Lack of organization by the charity's permanent staff.
- Inability of the charity's staff and volunteers to focus on your event until late in the planning.
- Limited or no commitment from the charity's volunteers.
- Too many legal problems in establishing the relationship.
- Inability of the charity to market the event effectively to its constituents.
- Lack of sponsorship prospects on the part of the charity.
- Inability to focus on the sport event because of other responsibilities.
- Limitations of staff that can be dedicated to this sport event.

---

several years. Whether you are negotiating long-term deals with bottlers or other brand-name products, the marketing decision makers will appreciate and possibly support your long-term vision. In golf, for example, the baby boomers are expected to flood the fairways in the next decade. Therefore, it is a smart move for a sponsor or city to get in on the action early and enjoy the ride as interest in the sport accelerates.

How to Measure Your Success

The charity will measure its success primarily in one way: the total net proceeds that benefit its constituents. Additional measurement scales include positive public relations, new volunteer involvement, expanded mailing lists, and opportunities to reward and recognize volunteer leaders.

You, as the sport event planner and marketer, will measure success by your ability to recover your investment, earn a fair profit (although this will be less than if the sport event were a strictly commercial venture), develop new fans for your sport event, and generate new business.

These goals and objectives are not mutually exclusive. In fact, they are quite similar. When both the sport event management and marketing executive and the charitable organization's executive director mutually respect these common goals, a win-win scenario is developed. You could say that a win-win-win opportunity exists!

A wise fund-raiser once was invited to lunch. He declined. When his host asked why he had declined, he responded, "There is only one good reason to go to lunch. One reason is for me to help you, two is for you to help me. The best reason is for the two of us to help someone else."

Opportunities are infinite to help the greater community through planning, managing, and marketing a successful charitable sport event. The next time you are presented with the opportunity to develop a sport event, why not ask your team, "Who might we help, together?"

As we enter the final turn or approach the 18th hole, we refuse to end this game of learning and instead choose to go into overtime with some additional advice. Remember Yogi Berra's remark, "It's not over until it's over"? Yogi was right and it's just the beginning as you will see in the pages that follow.

GAME HIGHLIGHTS

- Determine if a charity tie-in is appropriate for your sport event.
- Contact the National Association of Fund Raising Executives for sources of reputable charitable organizations.
- Organize a planning meeting between your organization and the charity's leadership.
- Develop mutually acceptable goals and objectives, especially financial.
- Establish what resources the charity can bring to your event.
- Create a measurement and evaluation program to identify areas for improvement.

PLAY BOOK

charity An organization whose funds are used to help a cause or people in need.

fund-raising executive or fund-raiser An individual who is responsible for the financial development of a not-for-profit organization.

not-for-profit (or nonprofit) A tax definition used to identify those organizations whose purpose is not to distribute profits to shareholders but to use retained earnings for improving the lives of the stakeholder.

sponsor An organization (usually a corporate entity) that purchases the right to a specific product or category of service for an event.

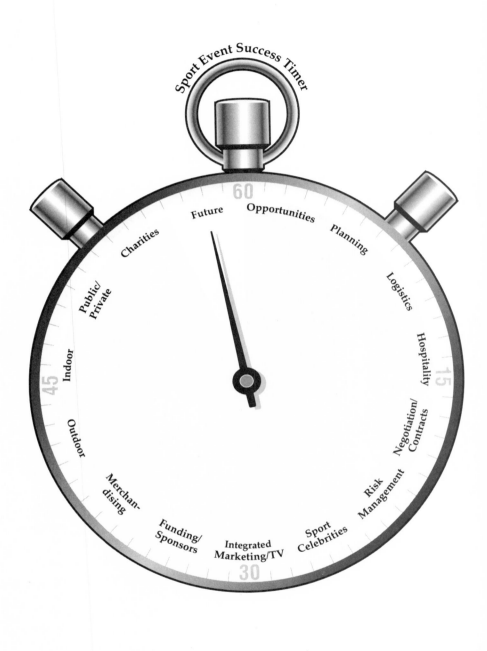

Chapter Fifteen

Closing Ceremonies:
Advice to New Sport Event Management and Marketing Professionals

"I don't get my kicks from flirting with death. I flirt with life. It's not that I enjoy the risks, the dangers, and the challenge of the race. I enjoy the life it gives me. When I finish a race, the sky looks bluer, the grass looks greener, the air feels fresher. It's so much better to be alive"

Jackie Stewart, race car driver

GET UP AT DAWN: THE FUTURE IS YOURS

Golfer Ben Hogan was famous for having a brusk manner. A young golfer called him one morning and asked for some free advice.

Hogan answered crisply, "Got an alarm clock?"

"Yes", the young golfer answered in a shy and somewhat confused voice.

He started to ask why when Hogan interrupted, "Tonight, before you go to bed set it for dawn and go out on the green tomorrow and start hitting until dark. Do that every day for a year and I'll be asking you for pointers." With that, Hogan hung up!

We don't know what happened to that young golfer. If statistics can be trusted, he probably failed to heed "professor" Hogan's advice, as do many students. A professor of writing once told his class of budding authors, "You signed up for a class on How to Write a Book but what most of you really want to learn is how to 'sell' a book.'' The embarrassed adults in the classroom nodded affirmatively.

Succeeding in the competitive world of sport event management and marketing requires a combination of talent, hard work, training, and persistence. The champions whose names appear in the acknowledgments made it to the top of their profession because they were prepared to do something they loved so much that they would have done it for nothing. Through training and experience, they mastered their craft and are now financially rewarded for it.

When asked what he liked most about his job, Chicago Bulls executive Steve Schanwald replied:

> Knowing that you have given the fans a good show and good value for their entertainment dollar. That is really what we are here to do. We are here to provide a diversion from the drudgery of everyday life, a little bit of an escape, a minivacation for the people who come to the games. If we accomplish that, then we can feel good about ourselves. But also you get a lot of satisfaction out of seeing the growth of the individuals within the company—seeing them grow as people and professionals. I think for the most part, people get into it because they enjoy it, even though they can make more money doing other things.

Tanisha Howard is a graduate student majoring in sport and event management and marketing at The George Washington University. She also manages the baseball team at the university and is part of the new generation of sport managers and marketers. She eloquently describes her aspirations:

> As an African-American and a female, I thought my options were somewhat limited with regard to this field. I have come to appreciate the wide scope of opportunities in this growing industry and have decided to pursue it as my career.

When asked why sport and special event management? Howard said:

> Since my first athletic experience, I always wanted to be an insider. I wanted to work with others to achieve a common goal. When you produce a sport event, this is exactly what happens and you experience a certain pride in your accomplishment.

Her mentor and supervisor, Jeff Fried, says that "the best way for anyone to learn the sport event business is to jump right into the middle of it and that is what Tanisha has done. She is practical enough to realize what she doesn't know and is not afraid to ask questions."

Today, Howard is preparing to earn her master's degree in this emerging field while serving as special assistant to the attorney of former world heavyweight boxing champion Riddick Bowe. As a member of the socioeconomic group demographers refer to as Generation X, it would be easy for Howard to fall into the disappointment and depression of some of her peers who bemoan the ever shrinking job market. Instead, Howard has set her sights on unlimited success in this emerging field. To achieve personal and professional success, she is committed to networking with those individuals who can provide her with the contacts, mentoring, and skills to steady her climb.

Lisa Delpy, assistant professor of sport and event management at The George Washington University, advises her students to "see and be seen." Delpy, who regularly attends major sport events such as the Super Bowl, the Olympic Games, and other hallmark events, says:

> I am constantly making contacts that will increase my students' chances for landing an important job. Knowing the major sport executives on a first-name basis is essential for networking. I feel as though I am building a network for the students not unlike a series of bridges that they may elect to cross as they move from academia into industry.

Delpy realizes, however, that for her students to take full advantage of these contacts they must understand the sport business and possess the necessary skills for achievement in the field.

Susan Roane, author of *How to Work a Room*, recommends that job seekers develop a brief introduction of themselves that can be given easily during social encounters such as a reception. She also advocates collecting as many business cards as possible and following up later with a brief written thank you note with your business card enclosed. This technique allows you to collect contact cards for later reference and to send your own card directly to the offices of people you met. In this way, the chances of their misplacing your card are much less likely. More important, the personal written note reminds them of the meeting; you have begun to weave your net to include them in your contact group (see Figure 15–1 on networking tips).

No matter how the introduction is made, relationships require care and feeding. You must extend a hand, take advice, and put it to good use. Do not waste their time or yours. It is also wise to select a variety of mentors from different professional and political backgrounds. Avoid being pigeonholed into any social circle early in your career.

REACHING OUT

Active participation in the sport event management process will enable you to identify opportunities to succeed. As the game of sport event management and marketing continues to change, more challenges will present themselves. The solutions will often be found through the creation of new ways of thinking. A major way to do this is to take a fresh look at how to promote the best and the brightest in the field. Through creativity, we strengthen our offense by including everyone in the increasingly competitive world of sport event management and marketing.

READY, SET, GO!

Set your alarm clock for dawn. Go out on the green on cloudy as well as sunny days. You are now ready to aim and fire your first shot. But don't stop there. As golf legend Ben Hogan advised, stay later, practice longer, and one day you will not only be producing award-winning sport events but also the next generation of pros will seek *you* out for advice. When they ask, be generous with your knowledge because there is so much to learn. You are helping to sculpt a new profession. Use your talents to create a masterpiece of design that will be a tribute to the champions who brought you this rich opportunity that you now recognize as sport event management and marketing.

FIGURE 15—1

Networking Tips

- If possible, have someone else introduce you to a key person you wish to meet. It is always better to have a referral than to make a cold call.
- Always find out the dress code for any function that you attend. Dress conservatively but memorably. Develop a personal style that sets you apart from the other contenders. When in doubt, overdress slightly.
- When introduced to someone say, "It is a pleasure meeting you." Then flatter them in a straightforward manner. For example, "Joan says that you are enjoying great success this season with your new radio promotion strategy. Tell me about it."
- Encourage others to talk about themselves and listen intently. Showing keen interest in others will create interest in you.
- Before you end the brief encounter, ask the contact for help. Briefly explain what you are trying to accomplish and then ask for suggestions. At this point, it is extremely important that you take a deep breath and listen carefully because your contact is likely to open up and share some golden information with you.
- At the conclusion of all encounters, thank the contacts for their time, tell them it was a great pleasure to meet them, and ask for their card. When they ask for your card, tell them you do not have cards with you but will mail one to them.
- Always follow up promptly. Within 72 hours, write a personal note and enclose your business card. Refer in your note to particular comments made by the contacts and thank them again for their suggestions.

A FINAL WORD

"Like you, I am a student of this emerging profession of sport event management and marketing. It is my hope that you will use your talents to research, plan, manage, and measure sport events in a way others never dreamed.

"Your talent is needed in this field but even more crucial to the field's continued growth is your commitment to raise the level of professionalism to one of consistent quality. As you pursue your dreams in this exciting field, don't let small defeats prevent you from winning your game.

"In sport, as in politics, it only takes one point to emerge victorious. Put in the extra effort that will help you score the extra point, not only for yourself but for the entire profession of sport event management and marketing."

—Stedman Graham

"That little white ball won't move until you hit it, and there's nothing you can do after it has gone."

Babe Didrickson Zaharias,
multitalented athlete credited with opening the door to the
male-dominated domain of sports

P A R T

II

PHOTO FINISH

2.1 The millions of dollars that are invested in sport event sponsorships require strategic management and marketing to ensure the growth of your event.

Source: Photograph courtesy of Lisa Delpy

2.2 Women's sport events are rapidly growing in popularity and offer new opportunities for sport event managers and marketers.

Source: Photograph courtesy of Tom Hilton

2.3 High schools are a major showcase for numerous sport events. They require many of the same critical planning skills used in major professional events.

Source: Photograph courtesy of Tom Hilton

2.4 Sport event sponsors use novel approaches to convey their message to the widest possible audience in order to increase sales of their product or service. This colorful train transported spectators in Lillehammer, Norway, to the 1994 Winter Olympic Competition venues and promoted Coke to thousands of onlookers and millions of television viewers at the same time.

Source: Photograph courtesy of Kristin Kruhm-Walter

2.5 As shown in this retail store window in Monte-Carlo, Monaco, the integration of trade-marks, logos, and licensed merchandise helps sport event sponsors to increase consumer awareness, enhance corporate image, and boost sales.

Source: Photograph courtesy of Lisa Delpy

2.6 Indoor sport venues offer many opportunities, including fast-growing events such as the gymnastic competition shown here, for management and marketing professionals.

Source: Photograph courtesy of Lisa Delpy

2.7 One of the major goals of a successful sport event is to engage the fans in the excitement of the competition.

Source: Photograph courtesy of Kemper Lesnik

2.8 Sport event managers may be responsible for organizing thousands of volunteers with limited preparation and rehearsal time, which makes advance planning critical as shown at the 1992 Barcelona Olympic Games parade of athletes.

Source: Photograph courtesy of Lisa Delpy

2.9 Even during the traditional victory lap, the credentialed media is ever present to capture the final moments and demonstrate the infinite power of the modern sport event.

Source: Photograph courtesy of Lisa Delpy

2.10 Regardless of the outcome, sport event activities such as cheerleading keep the fans entertained.

Source: Photograph by David Hathcox, courtesy of The George Washington University, Sport Information Department

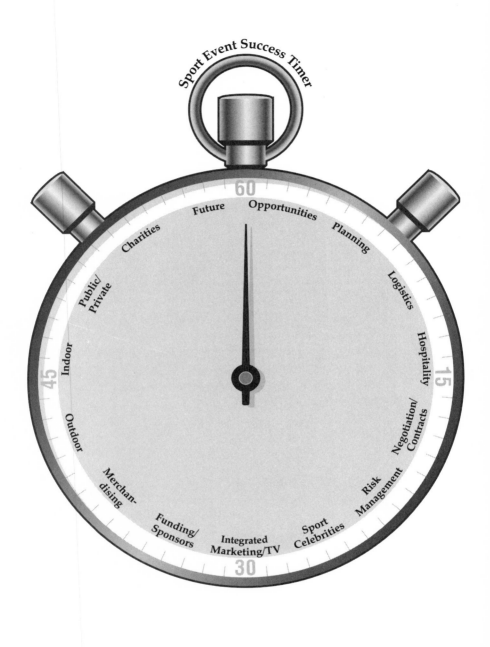

P A R T

III

APPENDIXES

Appendix One

Sample Agreements

A. INDEPENDENT CONTRACTOR AGREEMENT

INDEPENDENT CONTRACTOR AGREEMENT

This Independent Contractor Agreement ("Agreement") is entered into this _____ day of _____, _____ by and between [Company Name and State Corporate Status if applicable], ("Company"), and [Contractor Name], ("Contractor").

RECITALS

A. The Company is engaged in the business of, among other things, sport event management and sport event marketing.

B. Contractor represents that he/she is experienced in the areas of public relations, event management, TV production, or sports and entertainment marketing.

C. The Company desires to engage Contractor to provide his/her services to the Company, and the Contractor desires to provide such services, all on the terms, and subject to the conditions, contained in this Agreement.

AGREEMENTS

NOW, THEREFORE, the parties hereto agree as follows:

1. *Term of Engagement.* Subject to the terms and conditions set forth herein, the Company will engage Contractor, and Contractor will provide services for the Company, as a Contractor of the Company, for a period commencing on the date hereof and, unless terminated sooner as provided herein, terminating upon thirty (30) days advance written notice by either party (the "Term of Engagement"). Also, the parties agree to renegotiate the Agreement if the Company desires Contractor to become an employee of the Company.

2. *Duties.* During the term of Engagement, as a Contractor, Contractor will have the duties and responsibilities as determined by, and at the direction and control of, the President of the Company. Contractor is being contracted to do the work associated with the job title of [Job Title of Contractor]. A job description is attached to this document. Contractor will, during the Term of Engagement, serve the Company faithfully, diligently, competently, and to the best of his/her ability. Contractor will devote his/her full business time during the hours of [Beginning Time] to [Ending Time], Monday through Friday and at other times and at such places as designated by the Company and give his/her best efforts and skill, to perform the duties with respect to the business, affairs, and operations of the Company.

3. *Independent Contractor.* Contractor and Company hereby acknowledge that (i) Contractor shall be solely responsible for and shall pay all taxes in respect of Contractor's income and engagements hereunder, (ii) Contractor has requested that the Company not withhold taxes and other amounts from any payments of compensation to Contractor hereunder, and (iii) Contractor shall be solely responsible for his/her retirement and disability protection, subject to paragraph 5 below, and all other so-called "fringe benefits" and the Company shall not in any way be responsible therefore. Nothing in this Agreement shall be construed as giving Contractor any rights as a partner in or owner of the business of the Company or entitling Contractor to control in any manner the conduct of the Company's business.

4. *Compensation.* During Contractor's engagement, he/she shall be paid $_____ per month. Of this $_____, $_____ shall be paid on the 1st day and $_____ on the 15th day of each month. Contractor shall be entitled to _____ percent of the net profits from any project that is designated the "Contractor's Project" by the Company. These projects will be named in writing by the Company, will be signed and dated by both parties, and will include the payment terms of the percentage of net profits. This document will become an addendum to this agreement.

5. *Expenses and Other Benefits.* Reasonable business expenses incident to the rendering of services by Contractor hereunder will be paid or reimbursed by the Company, subject to the approval of the Company in advance, and the submission of appropriate vouchers and receipts in accordance with the Company's policy from to time in effect.

6. *Death or Disability.* This Agreement shall be terminated by the death of the Contractor. If Contractor becomes permanently disabled during the Term of Engagement, this Agreement shall terminate as of the date such permanent disability is determined. Contractor's right to his/her compensation, if any, provided for under Section 4 shall cease upon his/her death or permanent disability, it being understood that Contractor shall be entitled to his/her compensation, if any, for services performed as of the date of termination of this Agreement.

7. *Disclosure of Information.* Contractor will promptly disclose to the Company all processes, concepts, techniques, inventions, methods, designs, developments, improvements, discoveries, and other ideas and information that may be of benefit to the Company, whether or not patentable (collectively, the "Developments"), conceived, developed, or acquired by him/her alone or with others during the Term of Engagement, or within six (6) months after termination of his/her engagement, or during his/her earlier engagement by the Company or any of its predecessors whether or not during regular working hours wherever such Developments relate to, would be useful in, or arise out of any part of the business of the Company or incorporate or make use of information relating to the Company's business which he/she shall have acquired during any past or present period of engagement with the Company or which were developed using materials or facilities of the Company. All such Developments made within the scope of engagement shall automatically be the sole and exclusive property of the

Company. In the event the Company does not request such an assignment of rights in any such Developments, the Company shall have a nonexclusive right to use such Developments and make and sell items embodying the Developments, without obligation to make any payment for such usage. At the Company's request, whether during or after the Term of Engagement, Contractor (or in the event of Contractor's death, his/her personal representative) shall, at the expense of the Company execute and deliver to the Company such assignments and other documents, including without limitation all drawings, sketches, models, and other data and records relating to such Developments, and perform or cause to be performed such other lawful acts, and give such testimony, as the Company deems necessary or desirable to obtain patents on, or otherwise perfect its ownership interest in, any Developments. The Company shall automatically own as a "work for hire" within the meaning of the U.S. Copyright Act, all copyrights in any drawings, reports, software, notes, customer lists, work papers, correspondence, and other tangible things, including but not limited to any which embody a Development, which Contractor creates, in whole or in part, within the scope of his/her engagement.

8. *Certain Definitions.*

(a) for the purpose of this Section 8:

(i) "Competing Business" means any person or entity which is engaged or making plans to engage, in whole or in part, in public relations, TV production, event management and/or sports and entertainment marketing, design, development, manufacture and/or offering of any product(s) or service(s) that compete with any product(s) or service(s) which the Company is then marketing or preparing to market in any market of the Company.

(ii) "Confidential Information" means all information, and all documents and other tangible things which record it, relating to or useful in connection with the Company's businesses, which at the time or times concerned is protectable as a trade secret under applicable law, and which has been or is from time to time disclosed to or developed by Contractor as a result of his/her engagement with the Company or any of its predecessors in interest. Confidential Information includes, but is not limited to, the following especially sensitive types of information: (*a*) the Company's product development and marketing plans and strategies; (*b*) the Company's unpublished drawings, manuals, know-how, laboratory books, production techniques, proprietary formulas, research in progress, and the like; (*c*) the Company's finances; (*d*) the identity, purchase and payment patterns of, and special relations with, the Company's customers; (*e*) the identity, net prices and credit terms of, and special relations with, the Company's suppliers; (*f*) the Company's proprietary software and business records; (*g*) the Developments, and (*h*) any other information or documents which Contractor is told or reasonably ought to know the Company regards as confidential. Confidential Information does not, however, include general business knowledge acquired from published sources or experience in dealing with the public; nor does it include information which Contractor establishes as of the time concerned is available from published sources, was known to him/her prior to his/her first engagement by the Company or any of its predecessors in interest, or was publicly disclosed by the Company.

(b) *Restrictive Covenants.* Contractor agrees that for so long as he/she is engaged by the Company, he/she will faithfully and to the best of his/her ability perform and render such services and duties for the Company as the Company directs. He/she shall not:

(i) While so engaged, engage in any other business activity (except passive personal investments and real estate holdings in a non-Competing Business), whether or not such business activity is pursued for gain, profit or other pecuniary advantage, unless the Company gives its prior written consent, understanding such written consent will not be unreasonably withheld; or

(ii) While so engaged, and for a period of one (1) year after the termination of such engagement, with or without cause, directly or indirectly, own any interest in any Competing Business, or be employed by or be associated in any way with any of the Company's past or active clients at the time of termination or potential clients who are in negotiation with the Company at the time of termination.

(c) *Confidentiality.* Contractor shall hold Confidential Information in the strictest confidence, as a fiduciary. Without limiting this obligation, he/she shall comply with all of the Company's instructions (whether oral or written) for preserving the confidentiality of Confidential Information, and shall use Confidential Information only at places designated by the Company, in furtherance of the Company's businesses, and pursuant to the Company's directions. In addition, he/she shall not, except as the Company otherwise directs

(i) Copy Confidential Information;

(ii) Directly or indirectly sell, give, loan, or otherwise transfer any copy of Confidential Information to any person who is not an employee or a signed independent Contractor of the Company;

(iii) Publish, lecture on, display, or otherwise disclose Confidential Information to any third party; or

(iv) Use Confidential Information for his/her personal benefit or the benefit of any third party. The obligations of Contractor as set forth in this Section 8(c) shall survive termination of this Agreement and remain in effect with respect to particular information for so long as that information continues to fall within the definition of Confidential Information or until the fifth anniversary of the termination of this Agreement, whichever shall occur first.

(d) *Return of Documents.* Promptly on the termination of his/her engagement with the Company for any reason, Contractor (or, in the event of his/her death, his/her personal representative) shall surrender to the Company without retaining copies, all tangible things that are or contain Confidential Information. Such person shall also surrender all computer print-outs, laboratory books, floppy disks, and other media for storing software and information, work papers, files, client lists, telephone and/or address books, Rolodex cards, internal memoranda, appointment books, calendars, keys, and other tangible things entrusted to him/her by the Company, or authored in whole or in part by him/her within the scope of his/her engagement by the Company, even if such things do not contain Confidential Information. Contractor acknowledges that he/she does not have, nor can he/she acquire, any property rights or claims to any of such materials or the underlying data.

(e) Contractor acknowledges that the restrictions contained in the Agreement are reasonable and necessary to protect the company's interest and that the compensation being paid to Contractor reflects additional consideration for these restrictions.

(f) During the term of this Agreement and for a period of one year thereafter, Contractor agrees not to solicit, or encourage any other person, firm, or entity to solicit, the customers of the Company. For the purpose of this Agreement, "Customer" means any person or entity to which Company provided services to prior to the date of this Agreement and such Customer which Company is responsible for bringing to the Company during the term of this Agreement.

9. *Remedies.* Contractor acknowledges that irreparable damage would result to the Company if the provisions of Sections 7 and 8 were breached by Contractor, and the Company would not have an adequate remedy by law for such a breach or threatened breach. In the event of such a breach or threatened breach, Contractor agrees that the Company may, notwithstanding anything to the contrary herein contained, and in addition to the other remedies which may be available to it, enjoin Contractor, together with all those persons associated with him/her, from the breach or threatened breach of such covenants.

10. *Termination for Cause.* Contractor's engagement with the Company may be terminated immediately by the President for cause which shall include (i) Contractor's conviction for, or plea of nolo contendere to, a felony or crime involving moral turpitude, (ii) Contractor's commission of an act of personal dishonesty or fraud involving personal profit in connection with Contractor's engagement by the Company, (iii) Contractor's commission of an act which the President of the Company shall have found to have involved willful misconduct or gross negligence on the part of the Contractor in the conduct of his/her duties hereunder, (iv) habitual absenteeism, chronic alcoholism, or any other form of addiction on the part of the Contractor, (v) Contractor's material and continued failure, after reasonable notice and opportunity to cure, to satisfactorily perform his/her duties hereunder as determined by the President of the Company, or (vi) Contractor's breach of any material provision of this Independent Contractor Agreement including without limitation, Sections 7 and 8 hereof. In the event of termination under this Section 10, the Company's obligations under this Agreement shall cease and Contractor shall forfeit all right to receive any future compensation under this Agreement except that Contractor shall be entitled to his/her compensation for services already performed as of the date of termination of this Agreement.

11. *Waiver of Breach.* Any waiver or any breach of this Agreement shall not be construed to be a continuing waiver or consent to any subsequent breach on the part of either Contractor or the Company.

12. *Assignment.* Neither party hereto may assign his/her/its rights or delegate his/her/its duties under this Agreement without the prior written consent of the other party; *provided, however,* that this Agreement shall inure to the benefit of and be binding upon the successors and assigns of the Company.

13. *Severability.* In the event that any provision of this Agreement, including any territorial or time limitation, shall be held to be unreasonable, invalid, or unenforceable for any reason whatsoever, the Company and Contractor agree that (i) such invalidity or unenforceability shall not affect any other provisions and provisions hereof shall remain in full force and effect and (ii) any court of competent jurisdiction may so modify the objectionable provision as to make it valid, reasonable, and enforceable and that such provision as so modified, shall be valid and binding as though the invalid, unreasonable, or unenforceable portion thereof had not been included therein.

14. *Notices.* All notices required or permitted to be given hereunder shall be in writing and shall be deemed given when delivered in person, or two (2) business days after being deposited in the United States mail, postage prepaid, registered or certified mail address to the Contractor's last known address:

[Contractor Address]

and if to the Company:

[Company Address]

and/or to such other respective addresses and/or addressees as may be designated by notice given with the provisions of this Section 14.

15. *General.* The terms and provisions of this Agreement shall be construed and enforced in accordance with the laws of the State of [Company State Name], and any disputes regarding this Agreement shall be settled in the Circuit Court of [Company County Name]. This Agreement shall constitute the entire agreement by the Company and Contractor with respect to the subject matter hereof, and shall supersede any and all prior agreements or understanding between Contractor and Company, whether written or oral. This Agreement may be amended or modified only by a written instrument executed by Contractor and the Company.

IN WITNESS WHEREOF, the parties have executed this Agreement as of the day and year first above written.

CONTRACTOR   [Company Name]

_____ BY:_____

                                                    PRESIDENT

B. SPONSORSHIP AGREEMENT

SAMPLE EXCLUSIVE SPONSORSHIP AGREEMENT

The following will confirm the agreement between [Name] ("Company") and XYZ Productions ("Contractor") for the services of the [Name] ("Attraction") in connection with Company's products all collectively referred to herein as "Company's Products".

1. Company shall be the exclusive sponsor of the Attraction tentatively scheduled for [dates]. Without limiting the generality of the foregoing, no other party may be listed or mentioned as a sponsor or presenter of the Attraction.

2. As full compensation for the rights and services granted herein, Company shall pay Contractor the sum of [amount] payable in three (3) equal installments: [specify dates].

3. In connection with said Attraction, Company will receive seventy-five (75) free tickets at each performance. Such tickets shall be for favorable seats in the highest price range locations. In addition, Company shall have the right to purchase, at the face value ticket price, up to ten percent (10%) of tickets at each venue, said tickets to be favorable seats in the highest price range locations and to be made available to Company at the earliest date(s) possible.

4. (a) An official logo and identification phraseology shall be developed for the Attraction by Contractor which shall be subject to the approval of Company and which shall refer to Company (in first position), Attraction and XYZ Productions (e.g., COMPANY presents an XYZ production"). Said logo and/or identification phraseology, as applicable, shall be prominently included in all promotional and advertising references that relate to the Attraction and are disseminated throughout any media (e.g., print, radio, television, and point of sale) by Company or Contractor announcing the Attraction. Nothing herein contained shall constitute an obligation on Company's part to advertise or promote the Attraction, it being understood that Company may do so at its option or may refrain therefrom.

5. (a) Company's sponsorship of the Attraction shall be prominently featured and/or displayed in connection with the Attraction and all aspects thereof, including but not limited to, references on tickets, passes, handbills, inflatables (if any), indoor and outdoor venue signage (if any), venue marquee, stationery (if any), press releases, the stage (and curtain, if any) and a sponsor reference on the front cover of the Official Program. The form of such sponsorship references shall be subject to the mutual approval of Company and Contractor. Company shall also receive a full-page advertisement in the Official Program on the inside back cover. Company shall be responsible for providing: banners with its name and/or logos of Company's Products and/or references to its sponsorship of the Attraction to be prominently displayed in the venues, graphic layouts, and any other materials deemed necessary or desirable by both shall appear on the backside of all T-shirts and on all of the clothing items sold (the manner and location of such sponsorship reference on such other clothing to be determined by Contractor and approved by Company); provided, however if Contractor feels it advisable, up to twenty-five percent (25%) of such T-shirts and up to twenty-five

percent (25%) of such other clothing items offered for sale need not include such sponsorship reference. Company sponsorship reference on T-shirts and clothing shall be at least one inch in diameter and comparable in size to any reference to XYZ Productions references, and Contractor will use its best efforts to satisfy Company's reasonable requirements with respect to such sponsorship reference. All such Company sponsorship reference shall refer to XYZ Productions in a manner mutually agreeable to Contractor and Company. The official logo and/or identification phraseology shall be included on the posters offered for sale by or under the auspices of Contractor or Attraction or their respective agents or licensees.

(b) Company's Products will be the only such products provided in the backstage area and none of the products of Company's competitors shall be publicly consumed at the venue or otherwise during the term hereof.

6. Contractor shall use its best efforts to provide Company with exclusive venue signage and to permit Company to sell or distribute its Products at all venues; subject, however, to each venue's rules, regulations, and contractual obligations.

7. Contractor shall hold a Press Conference regarding the Attraction on or about [date], and, unless Company otherwise agrees, the only reference to Company shall be Company's sponsorship of the Attraction.

8. Company shall have the right to offer a single poster, T-shirts, and other items as premium merchandise for sale to the public, which features the identification of one or more of Company's Products and Attraction's name and/or likeness; provided such items shall be subject to Contractor's prior approval of quality, design, appropriateness, and consumer value. Company recognizes that Contractor and Attraction shall be exploiting merchandising rights in connection with the Attraction and that the Company's premium items shall in some manner differ in design from those offered in connection with Contractor's exploitation of its merchandise rights so as to minimize direct competition between Company's and Contractor's respective items. The poster and other items shall be offered on a free or self-liquidating basis.

9. Company shall use its best efforts to promote to the public Contractor's licensed merchandise during the term of this Agreement, provided such material is acceptable to the Company with respect to quality, appropriateness, design, and consumer value. Company will use its best efforts to assist Contractor to develop licensed merchandise items that meet Company's reasonable criteria as provided herein. Contractor shall indemnify Company for any liability in connection with its licensed merchandise. Company shall similarly indemnify Contractor and Attraction for any liability from Company's premium merchandise offer, exclusive of product liability relating to the materials provided by Contractor.

10. Attraction grants the Company the right to use the Attraction's name and likeness for advertising and promotional materials during the term of this Agreement in connection with Company's Products on the following terms and conditions:

(a) Attraction shall be available and shall cooperate in pre-production consultation. Attraction shall provide Company with five (5) consecutive full days of its services, tentatively scheduled for the first week in [month], to produce and record such advertising and promotional materials. All such workdays shall otherwise be at mutually agreeable times.

(b) From the results of the services rendered pursuant to subparagraph (a) above, the Company may produce two (2) television commercials with two (2) local TV tag formats, two (2) radio commercials, with two (2) local radio tag formats, two (2) print advertising designs, two (2) outdoor billboard advertising designs, and one (1) point-of-sale design, all for use from January 1, [year] through December 31, [year] to promote Company's products separately and/or in connection with the Attraction. Print advertising, outdoor billboards, and the point-of-sale pieces can be appropriately modified as to size and other minor modifications, provided such modifications do not change the basic concept.

(c) The commercial materials produced hereunder may be used throughout the United States, Canada, and Mexico from January 1, [year] until December 31, [year]

(d) Attraction shall neither endorse nor render any promotion, publicity, or advertising services for any other product or service during the term of this Agreement, nor grant any other licenses for name or likeness in connection therewith.

11. The term of this Agreement shall commence with the execution hereof by Contractor, Attraction, and Company and shall continue until [Date].

12. Company shall be given the right of first negotiation and first refusal with respect to the comparable television material, whether on free, pay, or cable television, prominently featuring Attraction, which is substantially filmed, taped, and/or produced during the negotiation and refusal shall not apply to materials substantially produced, taped, or filmed prior to the effective date of this Agreement.

13. All trademarks, photos, transparencies, and similar production materials produced hereunder shall be the exclusive property of the Attraction and shall be returned promptly after expiration of this Agreement, provided that any underlying music and lyrics provided by Company shall be owned by Company. Further, following expiration or termination of this Agreement, no further uses whatsoever may be made of official logo by Company, Contractor, or Attraction, but the official logo may be used by Contractor or Attraction without a reference to Company or Company's Product.

14. Contractor and Attraction shall secure and maintain throughout the term of this Agreement all insurance customarily secured for events of this stature and size, subject to mutual approval of the type of insurance and amount of coverage, which policies may, at Company's option, name Company as an additional named insured. If Company is so named, Company will bear a proportional cost of the premium.

15. If Contractor is prevented from fully performing this Agreement due to a Force Majeure as customarily defined in the entertainment industry, Contractor and/or Company may suspend and/or terminate this Agreement in accordance with standard industry provisions for such occurrences, provided in no event

shall Contractor be obligated to return sums advanced, loaned, or paid hereunder. The parties will attempt in good faith to negotiate a more detailed Force Majeure clause as provided below.

16. Company, Contractor, and Attraction agree that the terms and conditions of this Agreement are confidential and cannot be disclosed to any third party except as expressly provided herein.

17. Company shall have no liability whatsoever with respect to any commissions due agents of Contractor in connection with the securing of this Agreement, all of which obligations shall be Contractor's sole liability, and Company shall likewise be solely responsible for any commissions due its agents.

18. Company shall have the right to hold receptions and other social affairs in association with the Attraction for the purpose of entertaining clients, retailers, contest winners, etc. Attraction shall have the obligation to participate in these receptions.

19. Attraction, Contractor, and Company warrant and represent they have the right and authority to enter into this Agreement and their performance hereunder shall not conflict with rights granted any other party. Contractor and Attraction agree to be jointly and severally liable for the performance of their obligations under this Agreement.

This Agreement is intended to be fully binding on the parties hereunder provided this Agreement shall not become effective until formally approved by Attraction, which approval must occur within seven (7) business days from the date hereto and executed by all other parties listed. It is contemplated that this Agreement shall be supplemented by a more detailed Agreement between parties containing additional terms and conditions customarily contained in agreements of this type (e.g., rights to secure life insurance, indemnities, conduct clause, protection of trademark, reasonable notice and cure provisions, where appropriate, etc.), all of which shall be negotiated in good faith. Provided, however, that until such more detailed Agreement is executed, this Agreement will remain in full force and effect after approval of Attraction.

Agreed to this date as evidenced by the signatures below.

_____   _____
Contractor   Date

_____   _____
Attraction   Date

Source: Courtesy Ron Bergin, *Sponsorship Principles and Practices*.

C. LICENSING AGREEMENT

STANDARD LICENSE AGREEMENT

This agreement, effective this _____ day of _____, 19____, is made by and between (organization), having offices at _____ (hereinafter referred to as "LICENSOR"), and _____ having its principal place of business at _____ (hereinafter referred to as "LI-CENSEE").

RECITALS

WHEREAS, LICENSOR has established and desires to preserve, protect, enhance, and promote the national and international reputation and prestige of the (organization), as a (state nature of organization), and LICENSEE acknowledges and recognizes this reputation and prestige; and whereas, the (organization) is the exclusive owner of various trademarks, trade names, logos, initials and other symbols/devices associated with the (organization); and

WHEREAS, LICENSOR possesses valid Federal and/or State Registrations for TRADEMARKS, and (if applicable) State/Local Law provides further protection under Statute/Code, etc., and

WHEREAS, LICENSEE desires a License to use certain of LICENSOR's TRADEMARKS on and in connection with the products and in the geographic areas specified below, and LICENSOR is willing, subject to certain conditions, to grant such a license;

NOW, THEREFORE, for and in consideration of the mutual covenants and undertakings hereinafter set forth, and other good and valuable consideration hereby acknowledged, it is agreed as follows:

1. DEFINITIONS

1.1 The term "LICENSED MARKS" shall mean the LICENSOR's TRADE-MARKS and any other trademark, service mark, mark, logo, insignia, seal, design, or other symbol/device used by the LICENSOR and associated with or referring to the (organization) or any of its facilities, and such LICENSED MARKS are shown in Exhibit A, attached hereto and made a part hereof.

1.2 The term "LICENSED PRODUCTS" shall mean any product or part thereof bearing a LICENSED MARK and listed in the attached Exhibit B, attached hereto and made a part hereof.

1.3 The term "TERRITORY" shall mean the United States of America and its territories.

1.4 The term "PARTIES" and/or "PARTY" shall mean LICENSOR and/or LICENSEE.

1.5 The term "NET SALES PRICE" shall mean the final selling price of the LICENSED PRODUCTS to any and all customers by LICENSEE, after deducting any credits for returns actually made or allowed. In computing NET SALES PRICE, no direct or indirect expenses incurred in manufacturing, selling, distributing, or advertising (including cooperative and other advertising and promotion allowances) the LICENSED PRODUCTS shall be deducted, nor shall any deduction be made for uncollectible accounts. NET SALES PRICE must include the royalty amount. Any taxes actually paid and any universally offered published discount actually applied may be deducted. Sales to any party directly or indirectly related to or affiliated with LICENSEE shall be computed based on the NET SALES PRICE.

1.6 The term "NET SALES" shall refer to the total of all sales by LICENSEE of LICENSED PRODUCTS at NET SALES PRICE.

1.7 The term "AGREEMENT" shall mean this License Agreement between LICENSOR and LICENSEE.

2. GRANTS

2.1 Subject to the terms of the AGREEMENT and to the extent permitted by law, LICENSOR hereby grants LICENSEE a non-exclusive License to use the LICENSED TRADEMARKS on the LICENSED PRODUCTS in the TERRITORY.

2.2 LICENSEE may not export LICENSED PRODUCTS from the TERRITORY or otherwise use LICENSED TRADEMARKS outside the TERRITORY, and any such right is expressly withheld from this AGREEMENT.

2.3 LICENSEE may not assign its rights or sublicense the use of the LICENSED MARKS to third parties, and any such right is expressly withheld from this AGREEMENT. LICENSEE may use a sub-contractor to manufacture LICENSED PRODUCTS but must require said third party to be bound to the same terms and conditions as is LICENSOR relating to this AGREEMENT.

3. QUALITY ASSURANCE

3.1 LICENSEE agrees to submit samples of all LICENSED PRODUCTS to LICENSOR at no cost for review and approval prior to any use, sale, or other distribution to the public. LICENSEE agrees not to distribute any LICENSED PRODUCTS until such approvals of final samples are received in writing from LICENSOR. LICENSEE further agrees to submit all examples of LICENSED MARK use on LICENSED PRODUCTS to LICENSOR prior to any use, sale, or other distribution.

3.2 LICENSEE agrees the LICENSED PRODUCTS it manufactures and sells meet or exceed the quality and specifications of the final samples approved by LICENSOR. LICENSEE agrees to remove from public sale or distribution any previously approved LICENSED PRODUCT to which LICENSOR rescinds approval.

3.3 LICENSEE agrees that any proposed change to LICENSED PRODUCT, involving the graphic or any change in the use of LICENSED MARKS, or any alteration in the product structure, design, or quality of the LICENSED PRODUCT shall be submitted to LICENSOR for approval prior to any use, sale, or other distribution of the LICENSED PRODUCT.

3.4 LICENSEE agrees to maintain such reasonable manufacturing, servicing, and quality standards as may, from time to time, be requested by LICENSOR.

3.5 LICENSEE agrees that LICENSOR, or its duly authorized representatives, may inspect the manufacturing premises and LICENSED PRODUCTS of LICENSEE during all reasonable hours of operation upon reasonable notice during the term of this AGREEMENT to assure that LICENSED PRODUCTS are being produced in accordance with this AGREEMENT.

4. TRADEMARK USE AND OWNERSHIP

4.1 LICENSEE agrees to use the LICENSED MARKS only in the form and manner with appropriate legends as prescribed from time to time by LICENSOR, and not to use any other trademark in combination with any of said LICENSED MARKS without the prior written approval of LICENSOR. LICENSEE agrees it will not alter, modify, dilute, or otherwise misuse the LICENSED MARKS.

4.2 LICENSEE agrees that upon request it shall cause to appear on or within each LICENSED PRODUCT by means of a tag, label, imprint, or other appropriate device, such copyright, trademark, or service mark notices as LICENSOR may from time to time, upon reasonable notice, designate. LICENSEE agrees that all LICENSED PRODUCTS will bear an "Official Licensed Product" label or identification on the product or packaging in a form and manner that LICENSOR may from time to time, upon reasonable notice, designate.

4.3 LICENSEE agrees to submit to LICENSOR for approval samples of all tags, labels, and packaging to be used in connection with any LICENSED PRODUCT, and to remove therefrom or add thereto any element LICENSOR may from time to time, upon reasonable notice, designate.

4.4 LICENSEE agrees to submit to LICENSOR copies of any advertisement or promotional materials containing LICENSED MARKS for LICENSOR's approval prior to any use thereof, and to remove therefrom either any reference to LICENSED MARKS or any element which LICENSOR may from time to time, upon reasonable notice, designate.

4.5 LICENSEE acknowledges the ownership of LICENSED MARKS in LICENSOR, and LICENSEE agrees that it will do nothing inconsistent with such ownership, and that use of the LICENSED MARKS by LICENSEE shall inure to the benefit of LICENSOR. LICENSEE agrees that it shall not apply for registration or seek to obtain ownership of any (organization) TRADEMARK in any nation.

4.6 LICENSEE agrees that it will not state or imply, either directly or indirectly, that the LICENSEE or the LICENSEE's activities, other than those permitted by this AGREEMENT, are supported, endorsed, or sponsored by LICENSOR and upon the direction of LICENSOR, shall issue express disclaimers to that effect. LICENSEE agrees not to use the name of (organization) in business or affairs except for the use of the LICENSED MARKS as authorized herein or as may be incidental to its financial and internal reports.

4.7 LICENSEE agrees it will use the LICENSED MARKS only in a fashion authorized by the AGREEMENT and will comply with all appropriate local and national laws in the United States.

4.8 LICENSEE recognizes the goodwill associated with the LICENSED MARKS and acknowledges that said goodwill belongs to the LICENSOR.

5. ROYALTIES

5.1 LICENSEE agrees to pay LICENSOR a royalty of _____ percent (%) of NET SALES of all LICENSED PRODUCTS sold by LICENSEE at NET SALES PRICE during the term of this AGREEMENT. LICENSED PRODUCTS shall be deemed to have been sold when invoiced, or if not invoiced, then when delivered, shipped, or paid for, whichever occurs first.

5.2 Royalty payment shall be made in April, July, October, and January for the preceding calendar quarter's sales, and no later than thirty (30) days following the end of each quarter.

5.3 (If exemptions permitted) LICENSEE shall not include any amount for royalties in the NET SALES PRICE for sales of LICENSED PRODUCTS to the _____ (e.g., university book store), or for sales of LICENSED PRODUCTS to any department or organization of the LICENSOR when said purchaser states the sale is for their own consumption and not for resale. But if LICENSEE does charge royalties for such sales, the royalties are also owed to LICENSOR.

5.4 LICENSEE shall pay LICENSOR an annual minimum payment of $_____ ($_____) for each calendar year in which this AGREEMENT is in effect. Upon signing the AGREEMENT, LICENSEE shall pay as an advance a prorated share of the annual minimum guarantee due for the first year of the License. LICENSEE may then credit quarterly royalties owed in the first year to that advance. In succeeding years, no advance will be required but LICENSEE will be expected to meet the annual minimum requirement within the Calendar/Fiscal Year. Failure to meet the annual minimum guarantee is cause for cancellation of the AGREEMENT. Upon termination of this AGREEMENT, the annual minimum royalty payable shall also be prorated for the period of the year in which the license was in effect.

5.5 In the event the royalty payment is not received by LICENSOR when due, LICENSEE agrees to pay LICENSOR interest charges at an annual rate of either (a) ten percent (10%), or (b) five percent (5%) plus the rate of interest that was charged by the (location) Federal Reserve Bank to member banks twenty-five (25) days prior to the date the payment was due, whichever is greater. Such interest shall be calculated from the date payment was due until actually received by LICENSOR.

6. ACCOUNTING AND REPORTING

6.1 LICENSEE shall submit to LICENSOR quarterly reports of its NET SALES of LICENSED PRODUCTS. Said reports shall be prepared in a format agreeable to LICENSOR and shall itemize all sales of LICENSED PRODUCTS by product category, style, units, dollars, and customer numbers. Reports of sales made in each calendar quarter shall be submitted within thirty (30) days following the end of each quarter, in April, July, October, and January. Each quarterly report shall be accompanied by a statement from a chief financial officer of LICENSEE acceptable to LICENSOR certifying that the report is correct and complete and prepared in accordance and in compliance with this AGREEMENT. If no sales or other use of the LICENSED PRODUCTS are made during any reporting period, a statement to that effect shall be provided to LICENSOR.

6.2 LICENSEE shall keep account books, records, and duplicates of all invoices to customers showing the manufacture, sales, and other distribution of LICENSED PRODUCTS. These books, records, and invoices shall be maintained for a period of at least three (3) years after the payment of the corresponding royalty. Such records shall be available for inspection and copying by duly authorized representatives of LICENSOR during regular business hours upon reasonable prior notice. LICENSEE shall cooperate fully with LICENSOR in making the inspection.

6.3 Once during each calendar year in which this AGREEMENT is in effect, and once after expiration or termination of this AGREEMENT, LICENSOR shall be entitled to an independent audit of LICENSEE's account books, records, invoices, and other pertinent data by a certified public accountant or qualified auditor to be designated by LICENSOR, to determine LICENSEE's sales of LICENSED PRODUCTS. The audit shall be limited to the determination of LICENSEE's sales of LICENSED PRODUCTS, and shall be conducted during normal business hours at LICENSEE's home office. The costs of the audit shall be paid by LICENSOR unless the audit shows the LICENSEE understated sales of LICENSED PRODUCTS by more than ten percent (10%), in which case the LICENSEE shall pay all of the LICENSOR's costs of the audit.

7. LIFE OF THE AGREEMENT

7.1 This AGREEMENT shall be in full force and effect from the date first herein written and shall remain in effect for [number of years] (_____) years unless terminated by operation of law or by the acts of the PARTIES in accordance with the terms of this AGREEMENT.

8. INFRINGEMENT

8.1 LICENSEE agrees to notify LICENSOR promptly of any known use of LICENSED MARKS by others not duly authorized by LICENSOR. Notification of such infringement shall include all details known by LICENSEE that would enable or aid LICENSOR to investigate such infringement.

8.2 Upon learning of any infringement, LICENSOR shall at its sole discretion take all such action as may be necessary or appropriate to enforce its rights or suppress or eliminate such infringement. LICENSEE agrees to fully cooperate with LICENSOR in the prosecution of any action against an infringer but LICENSEE shall not be liable for any legal fees or other expenses unless agreed upon in advance.

9. TERMINATION BY LICENSEE

9.1 LICENSEE shall have the right to terminate this AGREEMENT at any time upon ninety (90) days' written notice to LICENSOR provided, however, that such termination shall not impair or affect any accrued rights of LICENSOR.

10. TERMINATION BY LICENSOR

10.1 LICENSOR shall have the right to terminate this AGREEMENT at any time upon ninety (90) days' written notice to LICENSEE provided, however, that such termination shall not impair or affect any accrued rights of LICENSOR.

10.2 It is expressly agreed that, notwithstanding the provisions of paragraph 5.5 herein concerning late payments, if LICENSEE should fail to materially perform any act required by this AGREEMENT, or otherwise breach any covenant or agreement herein, LICENSOR shall give written notice of default to LICENSEE. If LICENSEE should fail to repair such default within thirty (30) days, LICENSOR shall have the right to terminate this AGREEMENT by sending to LICENSEE a notice of termination. This AGREEMENT shall automatically terminate on the date indicated in the notice. However, such termination shall not impair or affect any accrued rights to LICENSOR. Any of the following may be considered curable defaults by LICENSEE; (1) fails to commence production of LICENSED PRODUCTS with one hundred twenty (120) days from the effective

date of this AGREEMENT; or (2) fails to commence selling LICENSED PROD-
UCTS in commercial reasonably quantities within one hundred eighty (180) days
from the effective date of this AGREEMENT; or (3) after having commenced sale,
fails to continuously sell LICENSED PRODUCTS for three (3) consecutive
quarters. (4) fails to maintain required quality of product. (5) fails to obtain or
maintain insurance of the amount and type required by this AGREEMENT. (6)
is more than fifteen (15) days late in making its royalty payments or providing
sales and royalty reports more than once in any calendar year; (7) fails to file a
sales and royalty report for two consecutive quarters; or (8) fails to apply
appropriate trademark designations, or fails to use proper licensed markings.

10.3 LICENSOR shall have the right to immediatley terminate this AGREE-
MENT by giving written notice to LICENSEE if LICENSSE does any of the
following:

(1) files a petition of bankruptcy or is adjudicated as bankrupt or insolvent, or
makes an assignment for the benefit of creditors, or an arrangement pursuant to
any bankruptcy law, or if the LICENSEE discontinues its business or a receiver
is appointed for the LICENSEE for the LICENSEE's business and such receiver
is not discharged within sixty (60) days; or (2) if the LICENSED PRODUCTS
become the subject of a recall by the Consumer Product Safety Commission or
any corresponding state or federal agency and LICENSEE fails to take immediate
action to recall such products; or (3) ceases to operate as a business; or (4)
undergoes a change of more than fifty percent (50%) of its ownership or sells or
disposes of more than fifty percent (50%) of its stock.

10.4 In no event shall LICENSOR's termination or this AGREEMENT for any
of the reasons recited above relieve LICENSEE of its obligations to pay royalties
for the actual sales of the LICENSED PRODUCTS.

10.5 LICENSEE acknowledges that money damages alone are inadequate to
compensate LICENSOR for any breach by LICENSEE of any provision of this
AGREEMENT. Therefore, in the event of a breach or threatened breach of any
provision of this AGREEMENT by LICENSEE, LICENSOR may, in addition to all
other remedies, immediately obtain and enforce injunctive relief prohibiting the
breach or compelling specific performance.

11. EFFECT OF TERMINATION

11.1 Upon termination of this AGREEMENT, LICENSEE agrees to: (1) immediately discontinue the manufacture of all LICENSED PRODUCTS and the use
of all LICENSED MARKS. (2) immediately destroy all dies, molds and screens
used to apply the LICENSED TRADEMARKS to the LICENSED PRODUCTS, or
their packaging or advertising, and to certify their destruction to LICENSOR
specifying the type and number of each destroyed. These items may also be
returned to LICENSOR. (3) immediatley return to LICENSOR at LICENSEE's cost
all materials relating to the LICENSED TRADEMARK including, but not limited
to, all artwork, color separations, prototypes and the like. (4) within thirty (30)
days LICENSEE shall provide LICENSOR with a written inventory of all
LICENSED PRODUCTS currently in its stock at the time of termination or
expiration.

11.2 Notwithstanding the provisions of 11.1 above, LICENSEE shall have the privilege of disposing of all approved LICENSED PRODUCTS within said stock at its normal wholesale price within three (3) months after said termination or expiration; provided that such disposal is not allowed where the basis for termination is LICENSEE's failure to comply with the quality requirements of Section 3, and/or the Trademark Use requirements of Section 4.

11.3 All such disposition shall be subject to the terms of this AGREEMENT, including the requirement to pay royalty. After the three-month (3) period, LICENSEE agrees to destroy all remaining unsold LICENSED PRODUCTS and to report to LICENSOR the number of each destroyed.

11.4 In no event shall LICENSEE sell such inventory to wholesalers, diverters, jobbers, or any other entity which does not sell exclusively at wholesale.

11.5 LICENSEE agrees that all legal rights and goodwill associated with the (organization) TRADEMARKS shall remain the property of the LICENSOR and LICENSEE shall make no claim to them.

12. INDEMNIFICATION

12.1 LICENSEE shall defend, indemnify, and hold harmless LICENSOR, its officers, employees, and agents from and against any losses and expenses (including attorneys' fees), claims, suits, or other liability, including product liability, resulting from injury to or death of any person, or damage to property arising out of or in any way connected with the exercise of the license granted by this AGREEMENT, provided such injuries to persons or damage to property are due to the acts of commissions or omissions of LICENSEE, its officers, employees, or agents, or the products manufactured or sold by them.

13. INSURANCE

13.1 During the term of this AGREEMENT, LICENSEE shall maintain in effect insurance for both bodily injury and property damage liability, including product liability, in per occurrence limits of not less than One Million U.S. Dollars (US $1,000,000) for personal injury and not less than One Million U.S. Dollars (US $1,000,000) for property damage. The policy(ies) shall include an endorsement naming LICENSOR as an additional insured insofar as this AGREEMENT is concerned and provide that notice shall be given to LICENSOR at least thirty (30) days prior to cancellation or material change in the form of such policy(ies). LICENSEE shall furnish LICENSOR, prior to commencing any performance hereunder, certificates of insurance with the endorsements required herein. LICENSOR shall have the right to inspect the original policies of such insurance.

14. SEVERABILITY

14.1 Should any provision of this AGREEMENT be held unenforceable or in conflict with the law of any jurisdiction, then the validity of the remaining provisions shall be affected by such a holding.

15. NEGATION OF AGENCY

15.1 LICENSEE is an independent contractor. Nothing contained herein shall be deemed to create an agency, joint venture, franchise, or partnership relation between the PARTIES, and neither PARTY shall so hold itself out. LICENSEE shall have no right to obligate or bind LICENSOR in any manner whatsoever, and nothing contained in this AGREEMENT shall give or is intended to give any rights of any kind to third persons.

16. MODIFICATION AND WAIVER

16.1 The PARTIES agree that *Exhibits A* and *B* of this AGREEMENT may be modified from time to time in a writing signed by both PARTIES for the purpose of adding or deleting items therefrom.

16.2 It is agreed that no waiver by either PARTY hereto of any breach or default of any of the provisions herein set forth shall be deemed a waiver as to any subsequent and/or similar breach or default.

17. LICENSE RESTRICTIONS

17.1 It is agreed that the rights and privileges granted to LICENSEE are each and all expressly conditioned upon the faithful performance on the part of LICENSEE of every requirement herein contained, and that each of such conditions and requirements may be and the same are specific license restrictions.

18. LIMITED WARRANTY

18.1 LICENSOR warrants it has the lawful capacity to execute this AGREEMENT, but does not warrant and shall not be held to have warranted the validity or scope of all TRADEMARKS licensed under this AGREEMENT.

18.2 LICENSOR makes no warranty, express or implied, that LICENSED PRODUCTS will be commercially successful.

18.3 LICENSOR makes no representations or warranties with respect to the products manufactured or sold by LICENSEE and disclaims any liability arising out of the sale of LICENSED PRODUCTS sold or service rendered under the LICENSED MARKS.

18.4 LICENSEE warrants that the products manufactured or sold by LICENSEE under this AGREEMENT will be suitable for the purpose for which they are intended to be used.

19. ASSIGNABILITY

19.1 This AGREEMENT shall inure to the benefit of LICENSOR, its successors and assigns, but will be personal to LICENSEE and shall be assignable by LICENSEE only with the prior written consent of LICENSOR, except to a wholly owned subsidiary or as a result of a sales, consolidation, reorganization, or other transfer involving substantially all of the LICENSEE's business and assets.

20. GOVERNING LAW

20.1 This AGREEMENT shall be construed in accordance with and all disputes hereunder shall be governed by the laws of the State of _____. The PARTIES hereto consent to the jurisdiction of the courts of competent jurisdiction, federal or state, situated in the State of _____ for the bringing of any and all actions hereunder.

21. HEADINGS

21.1 The headings herein are for reference purposes only and shall not constitute a part hereof or be deemed to limit or expand the scope of any provision of this AGREEMENT.

22. NOTICES AND PAYMENTS

22.1 Any notice required by this AGREEMENT shall be deemed to have been properly received when delivered in person or when mailed by registered first-class mail, return receipt requested, to the address as given herein, or such addresses as may be designated from time to time during the term of this AGREEMENT.

To Licensee: To Licensor:

_____   _____
_____   _____
_____   _____

23. COMPLETE AGREEMENT

23.1 It is understood and agreed between the PARTIES that this AGREEMENT constitutes the entire agreement between them, both oral and written, and that all prior agreements or representations respecting the subject matter hereof, whether written or oral, expressed or implied, shall be abrogated, cancelled, and are null and void and are of no effect.

IN WITNESS WHEREOF, the PARTIES have caused this AGREEMENT to be executed by their duly authorized representatives and to become effective as of the day and year first above written.

_____   _____
LICENSEE   Date   LICENSOR   Date

_____   _____
_____   _____

EXHIBIT A

LICENSED MARKS

1. _____   6. _____
2. _____   7. _____
3. _____   8. _____
4. _____   9. _____
5. _____ 10. _____

EXHIBIT B

LICENSED PRODUCTS

1. _____   6. _____
2. _____   7. _____
3. _____   8. _____
4. _____   9. _____
5. _____ 10. _____

Source: Revoyr, J. *A Primer on Licensing* (1994) GB Press: Stamford, Connecticut.

In addition to the sample agreements and resources contained in this appendix, the following additional agreements and resources are available for purchase from the Forum for Sport and Event Management at The George Washington University in Washington, DC. Please write or fax your request to:

The Forum for Sport and Event Marketing
The GWU
2020 K Street NW
Suite B-100
Washington, DC 20052

(202) 293-2650 (Facsimile)

Available resources

1. Arena Lease Agreement: A sample of the legal terminology exhibited in a traditional lease agreement used by sport event management.

2. Endorsement Agreement: The agreement used by sport event marketers to identify endorsement policies and procedures.

3. Insurance Application: A sample of a typical application for comprehensive general liability insurance in regular use in the sport event field.

4. Celebrity Speakers: A listing of popular speakers, their topics, and other information relative to sport event programs.

Appendix Two

Useful Resources

A. CAREER OPPORTUNITIES IN SPORT EVENT MANAGEMENT AND MARKETING

1. *Not-for-profit charitable organizations* produce walks, runs, cycling, and other fund-raising, sport-related activities (e.g. Special Olympics, multiple sclerosis, muscular dystrophy).
2. *Secondary and collegiate sport programs* require special event coordination for promotions, fund-raisers, halftime shows, media- and marketing-related activities, and tournaments. For example, the importance of events in sports led The George Washington University to hire a promotions manager to assist the marketing and sport information directors.
3. *Corporate or association special event management* with a focus on developing sports-related events such as golf tournaments. One example is the *New York Times* sports marketing division; another is Xerox Corporation's Olympic Games team.
4. *National sport organizations* responsible for producing events such as national olympic festivals, state games, Olympic trials, and others that require experienced special event managers to coordinate production companies and handle hospitality, catering, transportation, media, cultural, and other highly detailed tasks (e.g. United States Olympic Committee, United States Track and Field governing body).
5. *Professional minor league sports organizations* that rely on promotions often driven by special events to boost attendance.
6. *Professional major league sports organizations* that often have an entire special events department, which may produce hundreds of events annually especially for marketing and public relations purposes.
7. *International and hallmark events* such as the Olympic Games and the Goodwill Games, which require highly experienced special event management personnel to design and organize these visible and increasingly complex activities.
8. *Independent or freelance consulting opportunities* are increasing because more and more corporations, including sports organizations, are relying on project managers rather than full-time employees in order to reduce costs.
9. *High-level consulting with corporate executives* to produce feasibility studies and other data to determine the viability of staging a corporate sport special event. Management expertise might be provided if the project is given a green light.

More and more opportunities are generated as companies downsize and hire consultants to work on a contract basis.

10. *Entrepreneurial opportunities* abound. Dozens of new sport management and marketing firms are launched each year. If you identify the right market for your services, you may find a lucrative way to use your talents.

11. *Sport manufacturers and retail stores* such as Nike, Adidas, Wilson, and Footlocker offer marketing and management opportunities. Consider how you would guide thousands of qualified buyers through the aisles straight to your booth at The Super Show, the fourth largest trade show in the United States. In addition to buyer previews, ad packages, and fashion shows, some exhibitors spend over $1 million annually to have celebrity athletes appear at their booths.

12. *Representation and management* is another major field to consider. The development of athletes as full-fledged superstar sports celebrities is a major field dominated by three firms: International Management Group (IMG), ProServ, and Advantage International. In 1992, IMG had annual earnings in excess of $700 million. With 1,500 full-time employees, IMG dominates the field and makes entry difficult to all but the best funded and most aggressive of competitors.

13. *New opportunities in Europe, the Pacific Rim, and the rest of the world.* Individuals with a specific interest in other cultures and international business, and who have a strong second or even third language ability, may wish to consider international marketing through sport and special event management. This field is literally wide open, especially in Eastern Europe and the Pacific Rim. The National Basketball Association (NBA) raised $12.9 million through exhibition games in 1992 and is looking beyond the possible 250 million U.S. NBA fans to 5 billion international fans.

14. *Sport museums, halls of fame, and venues* are staging special events, primarily in response to increased financial pressures. Owners now use sports arenas and stadia for events such as tractor pulls, rodeos, concerts, trade shows, flea markets, and professional wrestling exhibitions to provide new revenue streams.

B. TYPES OF SPORT EVENTS

Acrobatics	Ballooning	Boating
Aerobics	Bandy	Bobsledding
Aikido	Baseball	Bocce
Air hockey	Basketball	Bodyboarding
Air sports	Beach volleyball	Bodybuilding
Archery	Beach soccer	Bowling
Arm wrestling	Biathlon	Boxing
Auto sports	Bicycling	Bridge
Badminton	Billiards	Canoeing
Backgammon	Boardsailing	Chess

Climbing
Cricket
Crew
Croquet
Curling
Cycling
Darts
Diving
Dog racing
Equestrian events
Exercise/fitness
Fastball
Fencing
Field hockey
Figure skating
Fishing
Flag football
Foosball
Football
Frisbee/ultimate
Golf
Greyhound racing
Gymnastics
Handball
Hang gliding
Hockey
Horse racing
Horseshoes
Hunting
Hydroplaning
Ice hockey
Ice racing
Ice skating
In-line skating
Jai alai

Jousting
Judo
Karate
Kayaking
Kiting
Korfball
Lacrosse
Lawn bowling
Lifesaving
Luge
Martial arts
Military sports
Motorboating
Motorcycling
Motorsports
Netball
Orienteering
Paddle sports
Paddle Tennis
Parachuting
Pentathlon
Platform tennis
Polo
Power lifting
Racquetball
Rodeo
Roller hockey
Roller skating
Rowing/crew
Rugby
Running
Sailing
Scuba diving
Shooting
Shuffleboard

Skateboarding
Skeet shooting
Skiing
Skimboarding
Skydiving
Sled dog racing
Snowboarding
Snowmobiling
Snowshoeing
Soaring
Soccer
Softball
Speed skating
Squash
Stickball
Street hockey
Surfing
Swimming
Synchronized
  swimming
Table tennis
Taekwondo
Team handball
Tennis
Track-and-field
Trampoline
Triathlon
Tug-of-war
Underwater hockey
Volleyball
Water Polo
Waterskiing
Weight lifting
Wrestling
Yachting

C. SELECT SPORT EVENT MANAGEMENT AND MARKETING ORGANIZATIONS*

Advantage International
1025 Thomas Jefferson St., NW
Washington, DC 20007

The Championship Group, Inc.
3690 N. Peachtree Rd.
Atlanta, GA 30341

D & F Group
5301 Wisconsin Ave., NW
Washington, DC 20015

Del Wilber & Associates
1410 Springhill Rd., Ste. 450
McLean, VA 22102

Faulk Associates (FAME)
5335 Wisconsin Ave., NW
Washington, DC 20015

Global Sports
15 E. Ridge Pike, Ste. 405
Conshohocken, PA 19428

International Management
  Group/IMG
22 E. 71st St.
New York, NY 10021

International Sports & Entertainment
  Strategies
230 Park Ave. S
New York, NY 10003

ISL Marketing AG
Zentralstrasse 1
6003 Lucerne
PO Box 3339
CH–6003 Lucerne
SWITZERLAND

Medalist Sports, Inc.
3228 W. Cary St., Ste. D
Richmond, VA 23221

ProServ, Inc.
1101 Wilson Blvd.
Arlington, VA 22209

RSB Ventures
1320 18th St., NW
Ste. 100
Washington, DC 20036

Sports Marketing Group
4243 Windhaven Lane
Dallas, TX 75287

Sports Media Group
629 N. Barry Ave.
Mamaroneck, NY 10543

Streetball Partners
4006 Belt Line Rd., Ste. 230
Dallas, TX 75244

Traffic Builders Unlimited and
  Convention Golf Associates
50 Rowley Rd.
Boxford, MA 01921–9901

21st Century Marketing Group, Inc.
80 Field Point Rd.
Greenwich, CT 06830

---

*For a more comprehensive listing refer to *The Sport Market Place*.

D. SELECT CORPORATE SPORT SPONSORS*

Adidas America
541 NE 20th St., Ste. 207
Portland, OR 97232

American Express Company
American Express Tower
200 Vesey St.
New York, NY 10285

American Telephone & Telegraph
    Company/AT&T
1301 Ave. of the Americas
New York, NY 10019

Anheuser-Busch Companies, Inc.
One Busch Place
St. Louis, MO 63118

Avis
900 Old Country Rd.
Garden City, NY 11530

Bausch & Lomb
1400 N. Goodman St.
PO Box 450
Rochester, NY 14692–0450

Blockbuster Entertainment Corp.
1 Blockbuster Plaza
Ft. Lauderdale, FL 33301–1860

Burger King Corporation
Subsidiary of Grand Metropolitan
    PLC
17777 Old Cutler Rd.
Miami, FL 33157

Campbell Soup Company
Campbell Place
Camden, NJ 08103

Champion Spark Plug Company
900 Lipton Ave.
Toledo, OH 43607

Coca-Cola Company
One Coca-Cola Plaza, NW
Atlanta, GA 30301

Coors Brewing Company
Subsidiary of Adolph Coors
    Company
311–10th St.
Golden, CO 80401–1295

Delta Airlines
Dept. 790, Adm. Bldg.
Hartsfield Atlanta Intl. Airport
Atlanta, GA 30320

Dr. Pepper Company
Subsidiary of Dr. Pepper/Seven-Up
    Companies, Inc.
8144 Walnut Hill Ln.
Dallas, TX 75231

Duracell, Inc.
Berkshire Industrial Park
Bethel, CT 06801

Eastman Kodak Company
343 State St.
Rochester, NY 14650

Evian
500 W. Putnam Ave.
Greenwich, CT 06830

Federal Express Corporation
2005 Corporate Ave.
Memphis, TN 38132

Ford
300 Renaissance Center
PO Box 433320
Detroit, MI 43320

Foot Locker
Subsidiary of Kinney Shoe Corp.
233 Broadway
New York, NY 10279

Frito-Lay, Inc.
Subsidiary of Pepsico, Inc.
7701 Legacy Dr.
Plano, TX 75024

*For a more comprehensive listing refer to *The Sport Market Place* and *The Sport Sponsors Factbook*.

Fuji Photo Film U.S.A., Inc
Subsidiary of Fuji Photo
   Film Co., Ltd.
555 Taxter Rd.
Elmsford, NY 10523

Gatorade
PO Box 049001
Chicago, IL 60604

Gillette Company/Personal Care,
Shaving Division
One Gillette Park
Boston, MA 02127

Home Depot, Inc.
2727 Paces Ferry Rd.
Atlanta, GA 30339

International Business Machines
   Corporation/IBM
Old Orchard Rd.
Armonk, NY 10504

JC Penney Company
6501 Legacy Dr.
Plano, TX 75024

John Hancock
PO Box 111
Boston, MA 02117

K Mart Corporation
3100 W. Big Beaver Rd.
Troy, MI 48084–3163

Kraft General Foods, Inc.
One Kraft Ct.
Glenview, IL 60025

L'Eggs Products, Inc.
Operating Unit of Sara Lee Hosiery
5660 University Pkwy.
Winston-Salem, NC 27105

M&M/Mars
High St.
Hackettstown, NJ 07840

Mastercard International, Inc.
888 Seventh Ave.
New York, NY 10106

McDonald's Corporation
One McDonald's Plaza
Oak Brook, IL 60521

MCI Communications Corp.
1801 Pennsylvania Ave., NW
Washington, DC 20006

Metropolitan Life Insurance
One Madison Ave.
New York, NY 10010

Miller Brewing Company
Subsidiary of Philip Morris
   Companies, Inc.
3939 W. Highland Blvd.
Milwaukee, WI 53208

Mobil Corporation
3225 Gallows Rd.
Fairfax, VA 22037–0001

Molson Breweries
175 Bloor St. E
2nd Fl., N. Tower
Toronto, Ont. M4W 3S4
Canada

NATIONSBANK Corporation
600 Peachtree St.
Atlanta, GA 30308

Nike, Inc.
One Bowerman Dr.
Beaverton, OR 97005

Olive Garden
6100 Lake Ellenor Dr.
Orlando, FL 32809

Panasonic
One Panasonic Way
Secaucus, NJ 07094

Pepsi-Cola Company
Subsidiary of Pepsico, Inc.
One Pepsi Way
Somers, NY 10589

Philip Morris U.S.A./Marlboro,
   Virginia Slims Brands
120 Park Ave.
New York, NY 10017

Proctor & Gamble Company
One Procter & Gamble Plaza
Cincinnati, OH 45202

Reebok International
100 Technology Center Dr.
Stoughton, MA 02072

Sears Roebuck & Company/
  Craftsman Tools, Diehard Battery
  Brands
3333 Beverly Rd.
Hoffman Estates, IL 60179

Sony Corporation of America
Subsidiary of Sony Corporation,
  Tokyo Japan
Sony Dr.
Park Ridge, NJ 07656

Sprint
8140 Wark Pkwy.
Kansas City, MO 64114

Swatch Watch
35 E. 21st St., 9th Floor
New York, NY 10010

Time Warner Inc./Sports Illustrated
1271 Ave. of the Americas
New York, NY 10020

Timex Corporation
PO Box 310
Middlebury, CT 06762

USAir
Crystal Park Four
2345 Crystal Dr.
Arlington, VA 22227

Visa U.S.A., Inc.
3155 Clearview Way
San Mateo, CA 94402–3798

Xerox Corporation
800 Long Ridge Rd.
Stanford, CT 06904

Upper Deck
5909 Sea Otter Pl.
Carlsbad, CA 92008

E. SELECT SPORT EVENT LEAGUES AND ORGANIZATIONS*

Air Sports
Balloon Federation of America
112 E. Salem
Indianola, IA 50125

U.S. Hang Gliding Association, Inc.
559 E. Pikes Peak
Ste. 101
Colorado Springs, CO 80933

Archery
National Archery Association of the
  United States
One Olympic Plaza
Colorado Springs, CO 80909

Arm Wrestling
American Arm Wrestling Association
PO Box 132
Scranton, PA 18504

Auto Sports
National Association for Stock Car
  Auto Racing/NASCAR
1801 W. International
  Speedway Blvd.
Daytona Beach, FL 32114

National Hot Rod Association
  (NHRA)
2035 Financial Way
Glendora, CA 91740–0750

Sports Car Club of America/SCCA
9033 E. Easter Pl.
Englewood, CO 80112

Badminton
U.S. Badminton Association
One Olympic Plaza
Colorado Springs, CO 80809

*For a more comprehensive listing refer to *The Sport Market Place*.

Baseball
American Women's Baseball
    Association, Inc./AWBA
PO Box 651
Glenview, IL 60025

Little League Baseball Incorporated
PO Box 3485
Williamsport, PA 17701

Major League Baseball
350 Park Ave.
New York, NY 10022

U.S. Baseball Federation
    (USA Baseball)
2160 Greenwood Ave.
Trenton, NJ 08609

Basketball
National Basketball Association
645 Fifth Ave.
New York, NY 10022

USA Basketball
One Olympic Plaza
Colorado Springs, CO 80909

Billiards
U.S. Billiards Association
757 Highland Grove Dr.
Buffalo Grove, IL 60089

Boardsailing
United States Professional
    Windsurfing Association
Bayview Business Park #10
Gilford, NH 03246

Boating
American Power Boat Association
17640 E. Nine Mile Rd.
Eastpointe, MI 48021

Bowling
National Bowling Association
377 Park Ave. S
7th Fl.
New York, NY 10016

Professional Bowlers Association
    of America/PBA
1720 Merriman Rd.
Akron, OH 44313

Boxing
Golden Gloves Association
    of America, Inc.
8801 Princess Jeanne NE
Albuquerque, NM 87112

United States Amateur Boxing, Inc./
    USA Boxing
One Olympic Plaza
Colorado Springs, CO 80909

Canoeing/Kayaking
U.S. Canoe and Kayak Team
Pan American Plaza, Ste. 470
201 S. Capitol Ave.
Indianapolis, IN 46225

Climbing
American Sport Climbers Federation
125 W. 96th St. #1D
New York, NY 10025

Cycling
American Bicycle Association
6501 W. Frye Rd.
Chandler, AZ 85226

U.S. Cycling Federation (USCF)
One Olympic Plaza
Colorado Springs, CO 80909

Equestrian Events
American Horse Council, Inc.
1700 K Street, NW
Ste. 300
Washington, DC 20006–3805

Exercise/Fitness
The International Association of
    Fitness Professionals (IDEA)
6190 Cornerstone Ct. E
Ste. 204
San Diego, CA 92121

Fencing
U.S. Fencing Association
One Olympic Plaza
Colorado Springs, CO 80909

Field Hockey
United States Field Hockey
  Association
One Olympic Plaza
Colorado Springs, CO 80909

Fishing
B.A.S.S., Inc.
5845 Carmichael Rd.
Montgomery, AL 36117

Football
National Football League
410 Park Ave.
New York, NY 10022

Frisbee/Ultimate
Ultimate Players Association
3595 E. Fountain Blvd. Ste. J2
Colorado Springs, CO 80910

Golf
Ladies' Professional Golf Association/
  LPGA
2570 Volusia Ave., Ste. B
Daytona Beach, FL 32114

Professional Golfers' Association
  of America
100 Ave. of the Americas
PO Box 109601
Palm Beach Gardens, FL 33410

Gymnastics
USA Gymnastics
Pan American Plaza
201 S. Capitol Ave.
Ste. 300
Indianapolis, IN 46225

Hockey
National Hockey League
650 Fifth Ave., 33rd Fl.
New York, NY 10019

USA Hockey
4965 N. 30th St.
Colorado Springs, CO 80919

Multisport Organizations
Atlanta Committee for the Olympic
  Games/ACOG
250 Williams, Ste. 600
Atlanta, GA 30303

The General Association of
  International Sports Federations
  (GAISF)
Villa Henri
7, Blvd de Suisse
Monte Carlo, Monaco

Goodwill Games
1 CNN Center
PO Box 105366
Atlanta, GA 30348

International Association of Sports
  Museums and Halls of Fame
101 W. Sutton Place
Wilmington, DE 19801–4115

International Olympic Committee
Chateau de Vidy
CH-1007 Lausanne
Switzerland

International Sport Show Producers
  Association
PO Box 480084
Denver, CO 80248–0084

International Sports Marketing
  Association
1080 Holcomb Bridge Rd., Bldg. 100,
Ste. 300
Roswell, GA 30076

National Association of Sport
  Commissions
1520 Sugar Bowl Dr.
New Orleans, LA 70112

National Collegiate Athletic
  Association/NCAA
6201 College Blvd.
Overland Park, KS 66211

National Federation of State High
  School Associations
11724 NW Plaza Circle
Kansas City, MO 64195–0626

National Handicapped Sports
451 Hungerford Dr., Ste. 100
Rockville, MD 20890

Special Olympics
1350 New York Ave. NW, Ste. 500
Washington, DC 20005–4709

United States Olympic Committee
One Olympic Plaza
Colorado Springs, CO 80909

U.S. National Senior Sport
  Organization
14323 S. Outer 40 Rd., Ste. N–300
Chesterfield, MO 63017

U.S. Armed Forces Sports
Hoffman Bldg. #1, Rm. 1465
2461 Eisenhower Ave.
Alexandria, VA 22331–0522

Running
American Running and Fitness
  Association
4405 E. West Highway
Ste. 405
Bethesda, MD 20814

Road Runners Club of America
1150 S. Washington St., Ste. 250
Alexandria, VA 22314–4493

Soccer
American Professional Soccer League
4300 Fairlakes Ct.
Ste. 300-B
Fairfax, VA 22033

U.S. Soccer Federation
U.S. Soccer House
1801–1811 S. Prairie Ave.
Chicago, IL 60616

Softball
Amateur Softball Association
2801 N.E. 50th St.
Oklahoma City, OK 73111

Swimming
U.S. Swimming, Inc.
One Olympic Plaza
Colorado Springs, CO 80909

Tennis
U.S. Professional Tennis Association
One USPTA Centre
3535 Briarpark Dr.
Houston, TX 77042

Triathlon
Triathlon Federation/USA
3595 East Fountain Blvd., Ste. F-1
Colorado Springs, CO 80910

Track-and-Field
USA Track and Field
One Hoosier Dome
Ste. 140
Indianapolis, IN 46225

Volleyball
Association of Volleyball
  Professionals (AVP)
100 Corporate Pointe, Ste. 195
Culver City, CA 90230

U.S. Volleyball Association
3595 E. Fountain Blvd.
Ste. I–2
Colorado Springs, CO 80910–1740

Water Skiing
American Water Ski Association
799 Overlook Dr.
Winter Haven, FL 33884

Wrestling
USA Wrestling
225 S. Academy Blvd.
Colorado Springs, CO 80910

World Wrestling Federation
Titan Tower
1241 E. Main St.
Stanford, CT 06905

F. SELECT SPORT HALL OF FAME MUSEUMS*

Researched by
Susan Silverman
and
James Wasson

Indianapolis Motor Speedway Hall of Fame Museum
4790 W. 16th St.
Indianapolis, IN 46222
(317) 248-6747/Fax:(317) 248-6759
Established in 1952 by members of the American Automobile Association Contest Board in cooperation with the Edison Institute of the Ford Foundation, the Indianapolis Motor Speedway Hall of Fame Museum is the official repository for anything related to the "Indy 500." Originally built in 1956. The museum was replaced by a much larger one (43,346 sq. ft.) in 1976.

Kentucky Derby Museum
704 Central Ave., PO Box 3513
Louisville, KY 40201
This three-level, 46,000-square-foot celebration of the Kentucky Derby opened at Churchill Downs in 1985, thanks to a $7.5 million grant from the J. Graham Brown Foundation. It is the largest museum in the world devoted to Thoroughbred racing. Hundreds of exhibits and artifacts from past derbies are joined with computer-animated racing and opportunities for visitors to weigh in like jockeys and bid at a yearling sale.

Green Bay Packer Hall of Fame
855 Lombardi Dr., PO Box 10567
Green Bay, WI 54307–0567
Dedicated in 1976 by President Gerald R. Ford (a Packer draftee), it is the largest museum dedicated solely to one pro team. You'll be welcomed by "The Receiver," a 25-foot-high statue of a Packer receiver atop the world's largest autographed football. A $750,000 facelift was completed in 1990. Features include the Lambeau Era and the Lombardi Era.

International Beach Volleyball Hall of Fame
Ms. Ebe MacNider, Director
40 Causeway Blvd.
Clearwater, FL 34619

---

*For additional information on Sport Halls of Fame refer to the *International Association of Sports Museums and Halls of Fame.*

Incorporated in December 1990, this organization has the support of Clearwater's Chamber of Commerce. The Gulf of Mexico area is a hotbed for beach volleyball, and the Hall of Fame will occupy 972 square feet of display space within the Chamber of Commerce Visitor Information Office in Clearwater Beach.

International Swimming Hall of Fame
1 Hall of Fame Dr.
Fort Lauderdale, FL 33316
Established in 1965, this complex re-opened its doors in 1993 following a $13 million renovation. It is recognized as the leading information center for all aquatic disciplines. This 10,000-square-foot museum honors the sport's heroes. In the Aquatic Library are hundreds of films and videotapes, displays on each of more than 200 inductees, and an art collection.

Maine Sports Hall of Fame
3 Delano Park
Cape Elizabeth, ME 04107
The Maine Sports Hall of Fame, established in 1972, has awarded scholarships totalling $26,000 in a single year. Most of its funds are raised through a "Bingo Night" series. Another big fund-raiser is a pre-season Celtic's game in Portland. The hall plans to erect permanent display cases in Portland, Bangor, and Aroostook; portable showcases take the Hall of Fame story to other sectors of the state.

National Football Foundation's College Football Hall of Fame
Century Center
1200 S. St. Joseph St.
South Bend, IN 46601
College football's shrine, established in 1978, is being moved from Kings Island, Ohio, to South Bend, Indiana. It is scheduled to reopen in the summer of 1995 in a $13 million building downtown, across from the convention complex. The new hall will be only minutes from the Notre Dame University campus.

National Rivers Hall of Fame
American House
McGregor, IA 52157
The Riverboat Museum is located at the Port of Dubuque (Iowa) Ice Harbor, where 150,000 people take steamboat cruises each year. Plans call for 40,000 square feet of new construction for the Hall of Fame in Iowa's oldest community. The hall recognizes the men and women of America's inland waters, including steamboat racers.

Oregon (State of) Sports Hall of Fame and Museum
PO Box 4381
Portland, OR 97208–4381
Oregon's dream of a Sports Hall of Fame Museum was realized in 1985 through the sponsorship of Standard Insurance Company. It is located in the firm's building in downtown Portland.

Pennsylvania Sports Hall of Fame
937 Willow St., PO Box 1140
Lebanon, PA 17042–1140
Founded in 1963 with three regions—Delaware Valley (Philadelphia), Western (Pittsburgh), Central (Lebanon-Hershey)—Pennsylvania now has a fourth region: Northeastern (Scranton–Wilkes-Barre). Some 7,400 members represent 30 chapters, which conduct their own inductions and also participate in a statewide vote. The headquarters Hall of Fame is now under construction in Harrisburg.

Pro Football Hall of Fame
2121 George Halas Dr., NW
Canton, OH 44708
More than five million fans have visited the Pro Hall since its opening in 1963. Included in the four-building complex are four large exhibition areas, a 350-seat movie theater, a library, and a museum store. A fifth building that features a centerpiece theater will open in 1994. A seven-foot bronze statue of Jim Thorpe, who played his first pro football game with the Canton Bulldogs, greets the 210,000 yearly visitors. "Football's Greatest Weekend" in August includes a parade, banquet, and a Hall of Fame/NFL benefit game.

United States Slo-Pitch Softball Association Hall of Fame Museum
PO Box 2047, South Crater Rd.
Petersburg, VA 23804
The 13,000-square-foot structure also serves as USSPSA national headquarters. The museum, costing over $1 million, opened in 1984 and draws 8,000 fans annually. There are three main areas: Hall of Champions, which contains a 200-seat theater; Hall Inductees; and Hall of Accomplishments.

Virginia Sports Hall of Fame
420 High St.
Portsmouth, VA 23704
Lew Worsham, Sam Snead, Bobby Dodd, and Shelly Mann are among Virginia Sports Hall of Fame inductees dating back to 1972. Each inductee has an individual memorabilia case, and each year up to five persons are honored for their contributions to sports in a "Wall of Fame." The City of Portsmouth donated the building and doubled the exhibit space in the 50,000-square-foot structure in 1986.

Women's Basketball Hall of Fame
PO Box 1331
Jackson, TN 38302–1331
The City of Jackson, recognized as the capitol of women's basketball because it has been host for many years to the National Intercollegiate Athletic Association Championships, now will be the site of the sport's shrine. Ground was broken in late 1993 on land provided by the city after its offer to build a Hall of Fame was accepted by the Atlanta-based Women's Basketball Coaches Association.

Other Halls of Fame by Sport

Auto Racing
**International Motor Sports Hall
    of Fame**
3198 Speedway Blvd.
Talledega, AL 35160

Baseball
**National Baseball Hall of Fame &
    Museum, Inc.**
PO Box 590
Cooperstown, NY 13326

Little League Baseball Museum, Inc.
PO Box 3485
Williamsport, PA 17701

Basketball
**Naismith Memorial Basketball Hall
    of Fame**
1150 W. Columbus Ave.
Springfield, MA 01101

Bowling
**National Bowling Hall of Fame and
    Museum**
111 Stadium Plaza
St. Louis, MO 63102

Boxing
International Boxing Hall of Fame
PO Box 425
Canastota, NY 13032

Equestrian Events
Museum of Polo and Hall of Fame
4639 Hunting Trail
Lake Worth, FL 33487

**National Museum of Racing Hall
    of Fame**
Union Ave.
Saratoga, NY 12666

**Trotting Horse Museum, Inc.,
    Hall of Fame of The Trotter**
PO Box 590, 240 Main St.
Goshen, NY 10924

Fishing
**International Bass Fishing Hall
    of Fame**
290 S. Main St.
PO Box 295
Lakeport, CA 95453

Football
**National Football Foundation and
    Hall of Fame**
1865 Palmer Ave.
Larchmont, NY 10538

Golf
PGA World Golf Hall of Fame
PGA Boulevard
Pinehurst, NC 28379

**Professional Golfers' Association
    Hall of Fame**
100 Ave. of the Americas
Palm Beach Gardens, FL 33410

Gymnastics
**International Gymnastics Hall
    of Fame & Museum**
227 Brooks St.
Oceanside, CA 92054

Hockey
**International Hockey Hall of Fame
    and Museum**
York and Alfred Sts., Box 82
Kingston, Ont., K7L 4V6
Canada

Figure Skating
**The World Figure Skating Hall
    of Fame and Museum**
20 First St.
Colorado Springs, CO 80906–3697

Lacrosse
Lacrosse Hall of Fame Museum
113 W. University Pkwy.
Baltimore, MD 21210

Shooting
**Trapshooting Hall of Fame
  and Museum**
601 W. Vandalia Rd.
Vandalia, OH 45337

Skiing
U.S. National Ski Hall of Fame
PO Box 191
Ishpeming, MI 49849

Snowmobiling
**International Snowmobile Racing
  Hall of Fame and Museum**
34355 Rue Chantilly
Dousman, WI 53118

Softball
**National Softball Hall of Fame and
  Museum & Stadium Complex**
2801 N.E. 50th St.
Oklahoma City, OK 73111

Surfing
International Surfing Hall of Fame
5580 La Jolla Blvd.
Ste. 373
La Jolla, CA 92036

Swimming
**International Swimming Hall
  of Fame**
1 Hall of Fame Drive
Ft. Lauderdale, FL 33316

Tennis
**International Tennis Hall of Fame
  and Museum**
194 Bellevue Ave.
Newport, RI 02840

Track-and-Field
**National Track and Field Hall
  of Fame**
One Hoosier Dome
Indianapolis, IN 46225

Volleyball
Volleyball Hall of Fame, Inc.
444 Dwight St.
Holyoke, MA 01040

Water Ski
**American Water Ski Educational
  Foundation/Water Ski Hall
  of Fame**
799 Overlook Dr.
Winter Haven, FL 33884

Wrestling
National Wrestling Hall of Fame
405 W. Hall of Fame Ave.
Stillwater, OK 74075

G. SPORT AWARDS BANQUET: SAMPLE SCRIPT

Note: This script may be adapted for individual team sports by using decor, music, and analogous sport stories in the text to match the sport being showcased.

[ ] = Stage directions and cues

6:00 P.M.   Registration area. Guests receive name badges and place cards.

6:25 P.M.   Preset salad placed at each place setting.

6:30 P.M.   Doors open to banquet. [*Prerecorded march music is playing*]

6:45 P.M.   Guests are seated.

6:46 P.M.   *Announcer/emcee:* Ladies and gentlemen, please rise for the presentation of colors and our national anthem.

(Note: When many international athletes are present you may wish to display flags of each country and substitute the United Nations prayer for peace in place of the anthems.)

[*Guests rise for patriotic opening. Color guard enters from rear and marches to front of head table. Colors are presented and placed. Pledge is recited. Guard exits right. Audiotape of "Star Spangled Banner" is played and audience sings. Vocalist may lead.*]

6:50 P.M.   *Announcer/emcee:* Please remain standing for our invocation. (Note: delete this activity when event is sponsored by a public school system.) (Reverend, Rabbi, Mr. or Ms.) _____ will lead us in prayer.

6:51 P.M.   *Invocation* [*Minister or private individual walks to lectern and speaks. Dim lights to 50 percent.*]

Let us pray. We are grateful for this opportunity to gather together and celebrate the achievement of these athletes and enjoy this fellowship. Please grant them and all of us the strength to compete as best we can and the humility to accept our victories with grace as well as to understand that our defeats are only temporary and with courage may be overcome. Thank you for this unique opportunity to recognize and reward achievement and grant peace to all who are assembled here. Amen. Please enjoy your dinner. Our program will continue in a few moments.

6:53 P.M.   Minister is seated. [*Raise lights to 100 percent*]

7:00 P.M.   Clearing of salads begins.

7:15 P.M.   Entree is served.

7:45 P.M.   Clearing of entree begins.

7:46 P.M.   *Emcee:*
In honor of our athletes and coaches, we have prepared a spectacular dessert. Please welcome your servers with a taste of victory!

7:47 P.M.   [*Play audiotape of football march. Cheerleaders lead in servers who parade the dessert to the head table. Music fades.*]

7:50 P.M.   Coffee is served.

8:00 P.M.   Servers leave the room. [*Dim lights to 50 percent.*]

8:01 P.M.   *Emcee*: I hope you enjoyed your dinner. [*Lead applause*] Let's thank those who organized this fine event [*List names*]. Join me in giving all of them a well-deserved round of applause! [*Lead applause*]

It is time to recognize our heroes and heroines of sport. During both practice and actual play, these individuals have distinguished themselves as outstanding competitors and team mates. As I call their names and present their awards, please join in enthusiastically recognizing their achievements. [*Name individuals in either alphabetical order by team or by sport. Each recipient walks to the head table, receives award, poses for pictures and remains standing in a straight line behind emcee. Once all are assembled emcee speaks.*]

Emcee:

Here they are. The best and the brightest. Now, once again join me in saluting them! [*Lead applause. Those assembled behind emcee exit left and right and return to their seats.*]

8:30 P.M.   In honor of these individuals we have invited coach_____ from _____ to speak to us tonight. [*Read introduction of coach*] Please join me in welcoming coach _____.

Note: An alternative to a speaker is to show slides or a video of the season's highlights. Some organizations prefer to first show a bloopers program, which is a humorous look back at the season followed by an inspirational review of the season's triumphs. The blooper tape is particularly useful when staging a golf awards banquet for corporate executives. Some resorts such as Innisbrook Hilton Resort in Tarpon Springs, Florida, feature a bloopers videotape as part of the golf package offered to individual groups. Bonus: Mail a copy of the videotape to each corporate executive. [*Raise house lights to 100 percent*]

8:33 P.M.   Coach speaks or video/slide program is shown.

8:58 P.M.   [Conclusion of coach's speech or video slide program.]

8:59 P.M.   *Emcee*:

Thank you coach for that inspiring and motivational program. Let's thank coach _____ once more. [*Lead applause*]

9:00 P.M.   *Emcee*:

Thank you for joining us this evening. We look forward to your continued support and an even more successful season next year. Thanks and good night! [(*Audiotape of marching music plays as guests depart*]

H. PRODUCTION SCHEDULE DESIGNED BY ROBERT W. HULSMEYER AND ADAPTED FOR BASKETBALL BY DYLAN ARAMIAN

Basketball Game Halftime Show on November 9

Time	Activity	Location	Responsibility
November 8			
3:00 P.M.	Site inspection of facility	Arena	Venue manager, event manager
4:00 P.M.	Meet with venue manager. Discuss needs and limitations including loading dock, door width, parking information, electrical and sound limitations, and necessary licenses and insurance certificates.	Arena	Venue manager, event manager
4:30 P.M.	Find storage area accessible to center court. Oversee loading in of equipment to storage area. Make sure all equipment has arrived: stage, microphone, podium, signs, table, chair, and gobos	Arena	Venue manager, event manager
5:00 P.M.	Meet with lighting, sound, and moving crew supervisors. Discuss needs and time availability. Require crew to be on hand for entire performance, not just setup and breakdown. Determine responsibility for feeding the crew.	Arena	Crew supervisors, venue manager, event manager
6:00 P.M.	Meet with dancers/cheerleaders, choreographer. Discuss expectations and needs.	Arena	Choreographer, event manager, sound manager
7:00 P.M.	Meet with celebrity/agent. Discuss needs and speech, including time and equipment.	Arena	Celebrity, agent, event manager
November 9			
8:00 A.M.	Meet with venue manager and crew supervisors to discuss risk management and start setup	Arena	Venue manager, crew, crew managers, event manager
8:30 A.M.	Check equipment. Decide on best lighting and sound support. Use gobos of stars for the dance section.	Arena	Sound and lighting crew, event manager

Time	Activity	Location	Responsibility
	Decide where the celebrity will sit during the game—preferably in the front row with easy access to center court.	Stands	Venue manager, event manager
9:00 A.M.	Rehearse the setup and breakdown time of stage and equipment. Make sure all cables are taped down and secure, and that signs are posted.	Arena	Crew, event manager
10:00 A.M.	Take pictures of risk management areas.	Arena	Assistant
10:20 A.M.	Rehearse performance with stand-ins and time each segment.	Arena	Event manager, assistants, crew
11:00 A.M.	Dress rehearsal. Make sure everyone has arrived, including client.	Arena	Event manager, celebrity, cheerleaders, choreographer
11:10 A.M.	Lights dim. Set up temporary stage, podium, and microphone.	Center court	Sound and light crew
	Announcer introduces celebrity.	Arena	Sound crew, announcer
	Cue celebrity.	Arena	Event manager
11:12 A.M.	Celebrity enters stage right, walks to podium.	Center court	Celebrity
11:15 A.M.	Celebrity gives speech.	Center court	Celebrity
11:25 A.M.	Celebrity exits stage left.	Center court	Celebrity
	Lights dim, stage is removed.	Center court	Crew
	Cheerleaders move to center court.	Center court	Cheerleaders
	Announcer introduces cheerleaders.	Arena	Announcer
11:28 A.M.	Music starts, lights up, gobos of stars projected on audience.	Stands	Lighting crew
	Cheerleaders start performance.	Center court	Choreographer, cheerleaders
11:35 A.M.	Cheerleaders end performance.	Center court	Cheerleaders
	Lights up full. Performance ends.	Arena	Lighting crew
11:36 A.M.	Announcement thanking cheerleaders.	Arena	Announcer
12:00 P.M.	Lunch	Breakout room	Caterer

Time	Activity	Location	Responsibility
1:00 P.M.	Extra rehearsal time. Final changes.	Arena	As appropriate
2:00 P.M.	Clean up area. Allow for venue crew to prepare for game.	Arena	Venue crew
2:30 P.M.	Announcer introduces players.	Arena	Announcer
2:40 P.M.	Game begins.	Arena	Players

All times hereafter depend on the game. Times are approximate. Time frame is needed for each segment.

Time	Activity	Location	Responsibility
3:30 P.M. (5 min.)	Halftime starts. Players clear the field.	Arena	Players
3:35 P.M. (3 min.)	Lights dim. Temporary stage, podium, and microphone is setup.	Center stage	Venue crew, lighting and sound crew
	Cue celebrity.	Stands	Event manager
	Announcer introduces celebrity.	Arena	Announcer
3:38 P.M. (1 min.)	Celebrity walks to stage.	Center court	Celebrity
3:39 P.M. (10 min.)	Celebrity gives speech.	Center court	Celebrity
3:49 P.M. (1 min.)	Celebrity walks off stage.	Court	Celebrity
3:50 P.M. (3 min.)	Lights dim, stage is removed.	Arena	Lighting and sound crew
	Cheerleaders move into position on center court	Center court	Cheerleaders
	Announcer introduces cheerleaders.	Arena	Announcer
3:53 P.M. (5 min.)	Music starts, lights up, gobos of stars projected on audience. Performance starts.	Arena/ stands	Lighting crew
	Cheerleaders end performance.	Center court	Cheerleaders
	Lights up full.	Arena	Lighting crew
	Announcement thanking cheerleaders.	Arena	Announcer
	Performance ends. Cheerleaders exit center court.	Court	Cheerleaders
3:58 P.M. (2 min.)	Players return to the court.	Arena	Players
4:00 P.M.	Game restarts.	Arena	Players
4:30 P.M.	Table is set up outside exit area. Signs posted to show where autographs will be signed.	Outside arena	Venue crew

Time	Activity	Location	Responsibility
5:15 P.M.	5 minutes before end of game, celebrity is taken by security to sign autographs. Security is stationed around the celebrity.	Arena	Security/celebrity
5:20 P.M.	Game ends. Announcement made that celebrity will sign autographs.	Arena	Announcer
	Celebrity signs autographs.	Outside arena	Celebrity/security
6:00 P.M.	Event ends, celebrity stops signing.	Arena	Celebrity/ security/event manager
	Provide for signs and gobos to be shipped back to office.	Storage area	Event manager
	Make sure storage area is clean and inspected. Make sure podium, stage and microphone are ready to be shipped back to the rental company.	Storage area	Venue crew, event manager
	Thank and release crew and security.	Arena	Event manager
	Take celebrity out to dinner.	Arena	Celebrity, event manager

Logistics

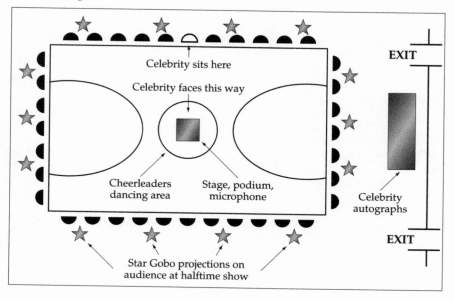

Celebrity sits here

Celebrity faces this way

Cheerleaders dancing area

Stage, podium, microphone

Celebrity autographs

EXIT

EXIT

Star Gobo projections on audience at halftime show

I. OLYMPIC GAMES OFFICIAL OPENING/ CLOSING CEREMONIES

The opening and closing ceremonies shall be held in accordance with the protocol decided by the International Olympic Committee (IOC). The detailed program of such ceremonies shall be put forward by the Organizing Committee of the Olympic Games (OCOG) and submitted to the approval of the IOC Executive Board.

The Opening Ceremony shall take place not earlier than one day before the competitions of the Games of the Olympiad and of the Olympic Winter Games. The Closing Ceremony shall take place on the last day of the competitions of the Games of the Olympiad and of the Olylmpic Winter Games.

1. Opening Ceremony
   1.1   The Olympic Games shall be proclaimed open by the head of state of the host country.
   1.2   The head of state is received at the entrance of the stadium by the president of the IOC and by the president of the OCOG. The two presidents then show the head of state into his or her box in the official stand.
   1.3   The parade of the participants then follows. Each delegation, dressed in its official uniform, must be preceded by a nameboard bearing its name and must be accompanied by its flag, to be carried by a member of the delegation. The flags of the participating delegations, as well as the nameboards, shall be provided by the OCOG and shall all be of equal size. The nameboard bearers shall be designated by the OCOG.
   1.4   No participant in the parade is permitted to carry flags, banners, banderoles, cameras, or other visible accessories or objects that are not part of his or her uniform.
   1.5   The delegations parade in alphabetical order according to the language of the host country, except for Greece, which leads the parade, and for the host country, which brings up the rear. Only those athletes participating in the Olympic Games with the right to accommodation in the Olympic Village may take part in the parade, led by a maximum of six officials per delegation.
   1.6   The delegations salute the head of state and the president of the IOC as they walk past their box. Each delegation, after completing its march, proceeds to the seats which have been reserved for it in order to watch the ceremony, with the exception of its flag bearer who remains in the field.
   1.7   The president of the IOC, accompanied by the president of the OCOG, proceeds to the rostrum positioned on the field in front of the official stand. The president of the OCOG gives an address lasting a maximum of three minutes, then adds these words: "I have the honor of inviting

_____, president of the International Olympic Committee, to speak."

1.8 The president of the IOC then gives a speech, adding: "I have the honor of inviting _____, (the head of state) to proclaim open the Games of the ____ Olympiad of the modern era (or the ____ Olympic Winter Games)."

1.9 The head of state proclaims the Games open by saying: "I declare open the Games of _____ (name of City) celebrating the ____ Olympiad of the modern era (or the ____ Olympic Winter Games)."

1.10 While the Olympic anthem is being played, the Olympic flag, unfurled horizontally, is brought into the stadium and hoisted on the flagpole erected in the area.

1.11 The Olympic torch is brought into the stadium by runners relaying each other. The last runner circles the track before lighting the Olympic flame, which shall not be extinguished until the closing of the Olympic Games. The lighting of the Olympic flame shall be followed by a symbolic release of pigeons.

1.12 The flag bearers of all the delegations form a semicircle around the rostrum. A competitor of the host country mounts the rostrum. Holding a corner of the Olympic flag in his or her left hand, and raising the right hand, the competing athlete takes the following solemn oath: "In the name of all the competitors I promise that we shall take part in these Olympic Games, respecting and abiding by the rules which govern them, in the true spirit of sportsmanship, for the glory of sport and the honor of our teams."

1.13 Immediately afterward, a judge from the host country mounts the rostrum and, in the same manner, takes the following oath: "In the name of all the judges and officials, I promise that we shall officiate in these Olympic Games with complete impartiality, respecting and abiding by the rules which govern them, in the true spirit of sportsmanship.

1.14 The national anthem of the host country is then played or sung. The flag bearers then proceed to the seats that have been reserved to enable them to attend the artistic program.

1.15 In the event that the IOC authorizes a secondary opening ceremony to take place at another Olympic venue, the IOC Executive Board shall determine its protocol, upon the proposal of the OCOG.

2. Closing Ceremony
   2.1 The closing ceremony must take place in the stadium after the end of all the events. The participants in the Olympic Games having the right to accommodation in the Olympic Village take the seats reserved for them in the stands. The flag bearers of the participating delegations and the nameboard bearers enter the stadium in single file in the same order and take up the same positions as they did at the opening ceremony of the Olympic Games. Behind them march the athletes, without distinction of nationality.

2.2   The flag bearers then form a semicircle behind the rostrum.

2.3   The president of the IOC and the president of the OCOG mount the rostrum. At the sounds of the Greek national anthem, the Greek flag is hoisted on the flagpole that stands to the right of the central flagpole used for the winners' flags. The flag of the host country is then hoisted on the central flagpole, while the host country's anthem is played. Finally, the flag of the host country of the next Olympic Games is hoisted on the left-hand flagpole to the strains of its anthem.

2.4   The mayor of the host city joins the president of the IOC on the rostrum and hands the president, for the Games of the Olympiad, the flag donated in 1920 by the Belgian Olympic Committee, and for the Olympic Winter Games, the flag donated in 1952 by the city of Oslo. The president of the IOC hands it on to the mayor of the host city of the following Olympic Games. This flag must be displayed until the following Olympic Games in the latter city's main municipal building.

2.5   After an address by the president of the OCOG, the president of the IOC gives the closing speech of the Olympic Games, which ends with these words: "I declare the Games of the ____ Olympiad (or the ____ Olympic Winter Games) closed and, in accordance with tradition, I call upon the youth of the world to assemble four years from now at ____ (in case the city has not yet been chosen, the name of the city is replaced by the words: "the place to be chosen"), to celebrate with us there the Games of the ____ Olympiad (or the ____ Olympic Winter Games)."

2.6   A fanfare then sounds, the Olympic flame is extinguished, and while the Olympic anthem is being played, the Olympic flag is slowly lowered from the flagpole and, unfurled horizontally, carried out of the arena, followed by the flag bearers. A farewell song resounds.

Source: International Olympic Charter, International Olympic Committee.

J. RULES FOR ESTABLISHING PRECEDENCE (PROTOCOL) FOR YOUR SPORT EVENT

Edited by Hugh Wakeham
Protocol by the Book

Ceremony Script Development

- Preshow
- Arrival of VIPs
- Flag raising/national anthem
- VIP introductions
- Speeches
- Performance
- Official announcement
- Performance/grand finale

Script: Energy/Time

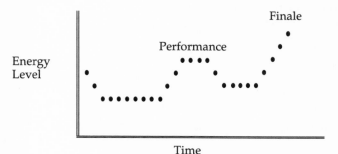

Precedence of Political Order in the United States

- President of the United States
- Vice President of the United States
  Governor of a state (when in his or her own state)
- Speaker of the House of Representatives
  Chief Justice of the U.S. Supreme Court
  Former presidents of the United States
  American ambassadors (when at post)
- Secretary of State
- Ambassadors of foreign powers accredited to the United States (in order of presentation of their credentials)
- Widows of former presidents of the United States

- Ministers and envoys of foreign powers accredited to the United States (in order of presentation of their credentials)
- Associate justices of the Supreme Court
  Retired chief justices
  Retired associate justices (associate justices who resign and have no rank)
- Cabinet officers, (other than secretary of state, ranked according to the date of establishment of department)
- President of the Senate
  Senators (according to length of continuous service; if the same, arrange alphabetically)
- Governors of states (when outside their own state). Precedence in this case is determined by the state's date of admission into the Union (see state precedence) or alphabetically by state
  Acting heads of executive departments (e.g., acting secretary of defence)
- Former vice presidents of the United States
- Members of the House of Representatives (according to length of continuous service; if the same, arrange by their state's date of admission into the Union or alphabetically by state)
  Delegates from the District of Columbia, Guam, Virgin Islands, American Samoa, and resident commissioner from Puerto Rico to the House of Representatives (nonvoting members)
- Charge d'affaires of foreign powers
- Former secretaries of state
- Other federal officials
- State officials
- Local officials

Precedence of the Order of States

(Determined by date of admission into the Union)

1.	Delaware	December 7, 1787
2.	Pennsylvania	December 12, 1787
3.	New Jersey	December 18, 1787
4.	Georgia	January 2, 1788
5.	Connecticut	January 9, 1788
6.	Massachusetts	February 6, 1788
7.	Maryland	April 28, 1788
8.	South Carolina	May 23, 1788
9.	New Hampshire	June 21, 1788
10.	Virginia	June 26, 1788
11.	New York	July 26, 1788

12.	North Carolina	November 21, 1789
13.	Rhode Island	May 29, 1790
14.	Vermont	March 4, 1791
15.	Kentucky	June 1, 1792
16.	Tennessee	June 1, 1796
17.	Ohio	March 1, 1803
18.	Louisiana	April 30, 1812
19.	Indiana	December 11, 1816
20.	Mississippi	December 10, 1817
21.	Illinois	December 3, 1818
22.	Alabama	December 14, 1819
23.	Maine	March 15, 1820
24.	Missouri	August 10, 1821
25.	Arkansas	June 15, 1836
26.	Michigan	January 26, 1837
27.	Florida	March 3, 1845
28.	Texas	December 29, 1845
29.	Iowa	December 28, 1846
30.	Wisconsin	May 29, 1848
31.	California	September 9, 1850
32.	Minnesota	May 11, 1858
33.	Oregon	February 14, 1859
34.	Kansas	January 29, 1861
35.	West Virginia	June 20, 1863
36.	Nevada	October 31, 1864
37.	Nebraska	March 1, 1867
38.	Colorado	August 1, 1876
39.	North Dakota	November 2, 1889
40.	South Dakota	November 2, 1889
41.	Montana	November 8, 1889
42.	Washington	November 11, 1889
43.	Idaho	July 3, 1890
44.	Wyoming	July 10, 1890
45.	Utah	January 4, 1896
46.	Oklahoma	November 16, 1907
47.	New Mexico	January 6, 1912
48.	Arizona	February 14, 1912
49.	Alaska	January 3, 1959
50.	Hawaii	August 21, 1959

Precedence Positions

Arriving:
1. Host
2. 8th most important person
3. 7th most important person
4. 6th most important person
5. 5th most important person
6. 4th most important person
7. 3rd most important person
8. 2nd most important person
9. Most important person

Entering a room:
1. Host
2. Most important person
3. 2nd most important person
4. 3rd most important person
5. 4th most important person
6. 5th most important person
7. 6th most important person
8. 7th most important person
9. 8th most important person

Entering a theater and seating position:
1. 8th most important person
2. 6th most important person
3. 4th most important person
4. 2nd most important person
5. Host
6. Most important person
7. 3rd most important person
8. 5th most important person
9. 7th most important person

Speaking:
Most Common Speaking Arrangement
1. Host
2. Most important person
3. 2nd most important person
4. 3rd most important person
5. 4th most important person
6. 5th most important person
7. 6th most important person
8. 7th most important person
9. 8th most important person

When a president is the most important person
1. Most important person
2. Host
3. 2nd most important person
4. 3rd most important person
5. 4th most important person
6. 5th most important person
7. 6th most important person
8. 7th most important person
9. 8th most important person

Saving the best for last
1. 8th most important person
2. 7th most important person
3. 6th most important person
4. 5th most important person
5. 4th most important person
6. 3rd most important person
7. 2nd most important person
8. Host
9. Most important person

Departing:
For pictures:
1. Host
2. Most important person
3. 2nd most important person
4. 3rd most important person
5. 4th most important person
6. 5th most important person
7. 6th most important person
8. 7th most important person
9. 8th most important person

No pictures
1. Most important person
2. 2nd most important person
3. 3rd most important person
4. 4th most important person
5. 5th most important person
6. 6th most important person
7. 7th most important person
8. 8th most important person
9. Host

K. EXAMPLES OF INVITATIONS AND PASSES TO SPORT EVENTS

THE S⚽CCER BALL

TO BENEFIT CHILDREN'S HOSPITAL,
MAYOR KELLY'S INNER CITY SOCCER PROGRAM
AND WORLD CUP WASHINGTON
HOST COMMITTEE

Sports MEMORABILIA AUCTION

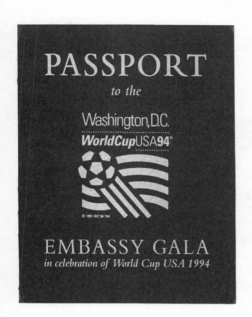

ASSOCIATION INTERNATIONALE DE LA PRESSE SPORTIVE · ATHLETICS COMMISSION

PERKINS PARK - STRESEMANNSTRASSE, 39 STUTTGART   WEDNESDAY, AUGUST 18th, 1993 9.00 PM

SGMA
INDUSTRY
BREAKFAST
AT THE
SUPER SHOW / 93
SATURDAY
FEBRUARY 6, 1993
8:30 AM
OMNI HOTEL
BALLROOM

BARCELONA '92
CENTER

Appendix Three

Bibliography of Sport Event Management and Marketing

BOOKS

Anson, Elizabeth, *Lady Elizabeth Anson's Party Planners Book*. London: Weidenfeld and Nicholson, 1986.

Bergin, Ron, *Sponsorship Principles and Practices*. Nashville, TN: Amusement Business, 1989.

Berlonghi, Alexander, *Special Events Risk Management Manual, The Definitive Text in Safety, Security and Risk Management for Events*. P.O. Box 3454, Dara Point, CA 92629, Tel: (714) 493-0529, 1990.

Blumenthal, H, and Goodenough, O., *This Business of Television*. New York: Billboard, 1991.

Brooks, Christine M., *Sports Marketing: Competitive Business Strategies for Sports*. Englewood Cliffs, NJ: Prentice Hall, 1994.

Burrus, Daniel, *Techno Trends*. New York: Harper Business, 1993.

Chase's Annual Events. Chicago: Contemporary Books, annual.

Catherwood, D. and Van Kirk, R., Ernst and Young, *The Complete Guide to Special Event Management*. New York: John Wiley & Sons, 1992.

Champion, W., *Fundamentals of Sports Law*. Deerfield, IL: Clark Boardman Callaghan, 1994.

Davis, Kathleen A., *Sport Management: Successful Private Sector Business Strategies*. Madison, WI: WCB Brown & Benchmark Publishers, 1994.

Devney, Darcy Champion, *Organizing Special Events and Conferences*. Sarasota, FL: Pineapple Press, 1990.

Getz, Donald, *Festivals, Special Events and Tourism*. New York: Van Nostrand Reinhold, 1992.

Goldblatt, Joe Jeff, *Special Events: The Art and Science of Celebration*. New York: Van Nostrand Reinhold, 1990.

Gorman, J. and Calhoun, K, *The Name of the Game.* New York: John Wiley & Sons, 1994.

Greenbaum, Edna Fine, *Protocol, The International Directory of International Entertaining/Special Events.* New York: Greenbaum Publishing, 1992.

Harris, April L., *Special Events: Planning for Success.* Washington, DC: Council for the Advancement and Support of Education, 1988.

Heitzmann, William Ray, *Opportunities in Sports and Athletics.* Lincolnwood, IL: VGM Career Horizons, 1990.

Helitzer, Melvin, *The Dream Job: Sports, Publicity, Promotion, and Public Relations.* Athens, OH: University Sports Press, 1992.

Hoffman, Dale, and Martin J. Greenberg, *SPORT$BIZ: An Irreverent Look at Big Business in Pro Sports.* Champaign, IL: Leisure Press, 1989.

IEG Directory of Sponsorship Marketing, 6 Ed. 1994. Chicago, IL: International Events Group, 1991.

IEG Legal Guide to Sponsorship, Chicago, IL: International Events Group, 1991.

ISES GOLD: An Anthology of Expertise from Members of the International Special Events Society. Indianapolis, IN: International Special Events Society, 1994.

Schmader and Jackson, *Special Events: Inside & Out.* Champaign, IL: Sagamore Publishing, 1990.

Kardong, D. (Ed.), *The Road Runners Club of America Handbook: A Guide to Club and Race Administration,* Alexandria, VA: Road Runners Club of America, 1991.

Kawasaki, Guy, *Selling the Dream.* New York: HarperCollins, 1991.

Kayser, Thomas A., *Mining Group Gold.* El Segundo, CA: Serif Publishing, 1990.

King, Frank W., *It's How You Play the Game.* Calgary: Writer's Group, 1991.

Kinkel, Coleman Lee, *Powerhouse Conferences.* East Lansing, MI: Educational Institute-American Hotel & Motel Association, 1991.

Kotler, P, and Andreasen, A., *Strategic Marketing for Nonprofit Organizations.* Englewood Cliffs, NJ: Prentice Hall, 1991.

Lewis, Guy, and Herb Appenzeller, *Successful Sport Management.* Charlottesville, VA: Michie, 1985.

Lucas, John A., *Future of the Olympic Games.* Champaign, IL: Penn State University and Human Kinetics Books, 1992.

Mack and Connell, *Naval Ceremonies, Customs, and Traditions.* Annapolis, MD: Naval Institute Press, 1980.

McCormack, M., *What They Don't Teach You at Harvard Business School.* New York: Bantam, 1985.

Mackenzie, John K., *It's Show Time!* Homewood, IL: Dow Jones Irwin, 1989.

Manning, Frank E., *The Celebration of Society, Perspectives on Contemporary Cultural Performance.* Bowling Green, OH: Bowling Green University Popular Press, 1983.

Michener, James A., *Sports in America*. New York: Random House, 1976.

Mullin, Bernard J.; Stephen Harday, and William A. Sutton, *Sport Marketing*. Champaign, IL: Human Kinetics Books, 1993.

Naisbitt, John, and Patricia Aburdene, *Megatrends 2000*. New York: William Morrow, 1990.

NCAA Legislative Staff, *NCAA Manual*. Overland Park, KS: National Collegiate Athletic Association, 1993-1994.

Noll, Roger G., *Government and the Sports Business*. Washington, DC: Brookings Institution, 1974.

Parkhouse, Bonnie L., *The Management of Sport: Its Foundation and Application*. St. Louis: Temple University and Mosby Yearbook, 1991.

Popcorn, Faith, *The Popcorn Report*. New York: Harper Business, 1991.

Price, Catherine H., *The AMA Guide for Meeting and Event Planners*. New York: Amacom (American Management Association), 1989.

Rader, Benjamin G., *American Sports: From the Age of Folk Games to the Age of Televised Sports*. 2d ed. Englewood Cliffs, NJ: University of Nebraska, Prentice Hall, 1990.

Railey, Jim H., and Peggy A. Railey, *Managing Physical Education, Fitness, and Sports Programs*. Mountainview, CO: California Polytechnic State University, and Mayfield Publishing, 1988.

Revoyr, J., A Primer on Licensing. Stamford, CT: GB Press, 1994.

Shock, Patti J., and John M. Stefanelli, *Hotel Catering, A Handbook for Sales and Operations*. New York: John Wiley, 1992.

Spalding, Betsy, and Elizabeth A. Spalding, *Creative Event Development*. Indianapolis, IN: 1991.

Stier, William Jr., *Fundraising for Sport and Recreation*. Champaign, IL: Human Kinetics, 1994.

Sport Market Place, Princeton, NJ: Sportsguide, 1994 (distributed by Sports Careers, Phoenix, AZ, tel # 800/776-7877).

The Sports Sponsor Factbook, Team Marketing Report. Chicago, IL: 1994.

Stotlar, David K., *Successful Sport Marketing*. Madison, WI: WCB Brown and Benchmark Publishers, 1993.

Sun Tzu, *The Art of War*. Transl. James Clavell. New York: Delta, 1988.

Surbeck, Linda, *Creating Special Events*. Louisville, KY: Master Publications, 1991.

Swartz, Oretha D., *Service Etiquette*. Annapolis, MD: Naval Institute Press, 1988.

Ueberroth, Peter, *Made in America*. New York: William Morrow, 1985.

Vander Zwaag, Harold J., *Policy Development in Sport Management*. Amherst, MD: University of Massachusetts and Benchmark Press, 1988.

Von Oech, R., *A Kick in the Seat of the Pants*. New York: Harper & Row, 1986.

Voy, Robert, *Drugs, Sport and Politics: The Inside Story about Drug Use in Sport and Its Political Cover-Up, with A Prescription for Reform*. Champaign, IL: Leisure Press, 1991.

Wascovich, T., *The Sports Marketing Guide*. Cleveland, OH: Points Ahead Inc, 1994.

Wilkinson, D., *Event Management and Marketing Institute Manual*. Sunnydale, CA: The Wilkinson Group, 1988.

_____. *Sponsorship Marketing: A Practical Reference Guide for Corporations in the 1990's*. Sunnydale, CA: The Wilkinson Group, 1993.

_____. *Sport Marketing Institute Resource Manual*. Sunnydale, CA: The Wilkinson Group, 1984.

PERIODICALS

Advertising Age, Crain Communications, Inc, 740 Rush St. Chicago, IL 60611-2590.

Amusement Business, 49 Music Square West, Nashville, TN 37203.

The American Spectator, PO Box 549, Arlington, VA 22216-0549.

Festival Management and Event Tourism, Elmsford, NY: Cognizant Communications, Corporation.

Hula Report, P.O. Box 440755, Kennesaw, GA 30144-9513, Tel: (404) 422-2543, Fax: (404) 799-5107.

Journal of Sport Management, 1607 North Market St. P.O. Box 5076, Champaign, IL 61825-5076: Human Kinetics Books.

The Licensing Journal, Kent Communications, LTD., P.O. Box 1169, Stamford, CT 06904-1169.

Marquette Sports Law Journal, National Sports Law Institute of Marquette University Law School, 1103 W. Wisconsin Ave, Milwaukee, WI 53233.

Special Events Report, International Events Group, 213 West Institute Place, Suite 303, Chicago, IL 60610 (312) 244-1727.

Sponsorship Opportunities Newsletter, Sponsorship Opportunities, Inc., 150 Nassau St, Suite 2030, New York, NY 10038.

The Sport Marketing Letter, 1771 Post Road East, Suite 180, Westport, CT 06880, Tel: (203) 255-1787.

Sport Marketing Quarterly, Fitness Information Technology, Inc., P.O. Box 4425T, University Avenue, Morgantown, WV 26504.

Team Market Report, 1147 West Ohio, Suite 506, Chicago, IL 60622-5874, Tel: (312) 829-7060.

Index

Goodwill Games, 18, 19, 39, 103, 337
Graham, Stedman, 15–16, 19, 145, 170, 223,
    225, 285, 301
Greater Nashville Convention and Visitors
    Bureau, 274
Green, Chris, 268
Green, Joe, 149
Groundskeeping facilities, 241
Guests, determining needs of, 84–85
Gumble, Greg, 161

H

Halas, George, 150
Hall, Bill, 66, 244–45
Hallmark events, 69, 75
Halls of Fame, 338
Hancock, David, 239
Harding, Tonya, 214
Harlem Globetrotters, 283–84
Hats, 223–24
Health department, regulations for food
    and beverages, 61
High-level consulting, 337–38
High-risk events and emergency
    precautions, 66–69
Hilton, Tom, 133, 252–53
Hilton Hotels, 203
Hiring policies, 130–32
Hitchcock, Denise, 37
Hockey, 256–57
Hogan, Ben, 297
Holtz, Lou, 121, 149
Home Box Office, 164
Homecoming game, 247–49
Home Depot, 107
Home pay-per-view (PPV), 164–65
"Hoop-it-Up" basketball tournaments, 183,
    191, 254
Hope, Bob, Classic, 238
Hospitality, 99
    contract for, 112
    typical packages, 80
Hospitality specialists, responsibilities of,
    80, 81
Hovencamp, Diane, 268
Howard, Tanisha, 298–99
Hula, Ed, 94
Hula Report, 94
Hulsmeyer, Robert, 72
Hunt Club, 82

I

IEG Directory of Sponsorship Marketing, 16
IEG Legal Guide to Sponsorship, 210

IEG Sponsorship Report, 194
Impressions, first and final, for hospitality
    planning, 90
Independent contractor agreement, 317–22
Independent or freelance consulting
    opportunities, 337
Individual sponsors, 193–94
Indoor sport events, 251–52
    basketball, 252–54
    hockey, 256–57
    tennis, 254–56
Inkamp, Klaus, 79
Innisbrook Hilton Resort, 197
Integrated marketing, 170–71, 178, 183
Intellibeam spotlights, 258, 264
Interactive media, 163
International and hallmark events, 337
International Association of Auditorium
    Managers (IAAM), 123
International Events Group (IEG), 5, 198,
    210
International Festivals Association's (IFA)
    Official Guide to Sponsorship, 207
International Olympic Committee (IOC),
    270
International Special Event Society (ISES)
    Conference for Professional
    Development, 123
    liability insurance requirement for
    membership in, 136
Inventory, of food and beverages, 62
Invitation, 99
    components of, 90
    delivering, 89–90
    key ingredients of, 87
    types of, 88

J

Jackson, Bo, 147
Jensen, Dave, 267
Jingle Bell Jog, 201
Johnson, Magic, 252
Jordan, Jennifer, 5, 19–20
Jordan, Michael, 238, 252
Junior Achievement Golf Classic, 238

K

Kalish, Susan, 233–34
Kawasaki, Guy, 219
Kelly, Jack, 39
Kemper Open, 82
Kentucky Fried Chicken, and ambush
    marketing, 105